The Archaeology of
New Netherland

A World Built on Trade

EDITED BY

CRAIG LUKEZIC AND JOHN P. MCCARTHY

University Press of Florida

Gainesville · Tallahassee · Tampa · Boca Raton

Pensacola · Orlando · Miami · Jacksonville · Ft. Myers · Sarasota

26 25 24 23 22 21   6 5 4 3 2 1

A record of cataloging-in-publication information is available from the Library of
Congress.
ISBN 978-0-8130-6688-2

The University Press of Florida is the scholarly publishing agency for the State University System
of Florida, comprising Florida A&M University, Florida Atlantic University, Florida Gulf Coast
University, Florida International University, Florida State University, New College of Florida,
University of Central Florida, University of Florida, University of North Florida, University of
South Florida, and University of West Florida.

University Press of Florida
2046 NE Waldo Road
Suite 2100
Gainesville, FL 32609
http://upress.ufl.edu

CONTENTS

FIGURES

TABLES

Introduction

JOHN P. MCCARTHY AND CRAIG LUKEZIC

In 1609 Henry Hudson, an Englishman employed by the Dutch East India Company, sailed his ship *Half Moon* into a river estuary that would later come to bear his name. He and his crew sailed up the river about as far north as where the city of Troy stands today. During this voyage, Hudson met and traded with several groups of Natives, likely Algonquian-speaking Mahicans (Mohicans) and Lenape, obtaining furs before returning to Europe (Butts 2009). Based on his explorations, Hudson's employers subsequently laid claim to the region, establishing a trading post, Fort Nassau (at modern Albany), in 1614 and establishing New Amsterdam on Manhattan island as the capital of the colony of New Netherland in 1625. Dutch control of the region was intermittent through conflicts with the English over the course of the seventeenth century, only to come to a complete conclusion with the Treaty of Westminster in 1674 (Jacobs 2005; Klooster 2016). While centered on the Hudson, or North River, and extending north into the Mohawk River valley, the Dutch colonial enterprise also extended south to the Delaware, or South River, and east to the Connecticut, or Fresh River (Figure 0.1).

This volume focuses a spotlight on the archaeology of New Netherland. Historical scholarship on the Dutch in North America blossomed over the last half-century and advanced exponentially with Gehring's (1977, 1980, 1981, 1983, 1991, 1995, 2000, 2003; Gehring and Starna 2008) many translations of colonial documents. Beginning in 1974 with the New Netherland Project, and subsequently from 1986 with founding of the New Netherland Institute, there has been organized intuitional support for these and related efforts. Many scholarly conferences and impressive publications resulted including the Beautiful and Fruitful Place series of conference papers

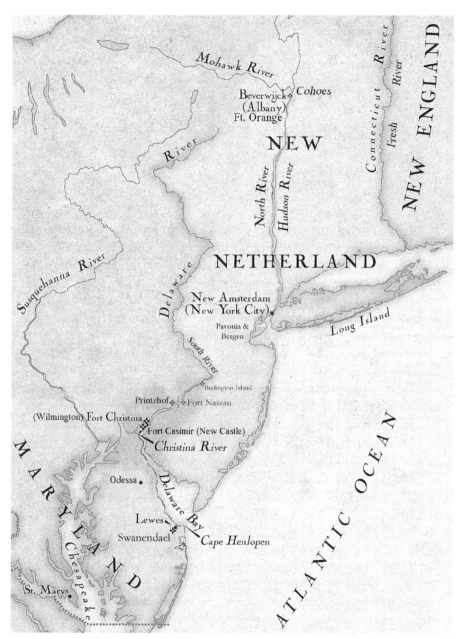

Figure 0.1. Seventeenth-century geography in the footprint of New Netherland.

(Zeller 1991; Funk and Shattuck 2011; Lacy 2013). The institute also recognized that archaeology could be an important aid in researching the story of New Netherland, including archaeological presentations as part of its conferences (e.g., Huey 1991; Pipes 2006; Lukezic and Catts 2016), including archaeological publications in its online New Netherland Bibliography, and publishing Paul R. Huey and Hartgen Archeological Associates, Inc.'s (2018) *Annotated Bibliography of New Netherland Archaeology: Rensselaer and Albany Counties, New York.*

However, most of the archaeological literature on New Netherland has remained buried in limited-distribution "gray literature" and conference papers that were difficult to access, even if one was aware of them. With the research and analysis of Fort Orange, a transportation salvage project that resulted in Huey's 1988 dissertation, the New York State Museum informally served a center for the study of Dutch colonial archaeology for a time. However, there is no ongoing research institute project or university program in the United States specializing in the archaeology of New Netherland.

We, the editors of this volume, feel that the archaeological study of New Netherland is at a turning point, with Anne-Marie Cantwell and Diana diZerega Wall (contributors to this volume) currently engaged in a synthesis of the archaeology of New Netherland and the recent publication of the exhaustive annotated bibliography cited above (Huey and Hartgen Archeological Associates, Inc. 2018). The moment seems ripe for the publication and wider distribution of papers that express the breadth and depth of the archaeological contribution to the emerging, richer understanding of New Netherland.

Of the 15 chapters herein, at least eight have benefited from legally mandated compliance archaeology, and the collection of much of that data has been funded by federal agencies and their proxies. We are that fortunate these authors are willing to go to the not-inconsiderable extra effort of ensuring that their findings are not buried in limited-distribution reports but circulate in academic and public realms.

We have approached this volume with the assumption that many readers will not necessarily be completely familiar with the story of the Dutch in North America or their cultural milieu. Accordingly, the first two chapters set the stage for those that follow. The first of these presents an overview of New Netherland history in broader context by Charles Gehring, one of the towering figures of the field. This is followed by Marijn Stolk's chapter exploring urban ceramic consumption and worldwide trade networks in

Amsterdam, the central port of the Netherland home county, to serve as a basis of comparison with North American finds that others report in subsequent chapters.

The remaining chapters are divided into three sections. The first two, North and South River, group chapters based on locality in the two main centers of Dutch activity and settlement. The final section focuses on particular artifact types or categories. Finally, we have summarized key findings and directions for further research in a concluding chapter.

The archaeology of the North River, or Hudson Valley, region differs from the rest of New Netherland in that the colony's administrative center was located there and much more of the documentary record survives, enabling stronger and deeper interpretations of archaeological results. However, the region has also been the seat of much of America's industry and commerce in the following centuries, resulting in deleterious effects to the archaeological record.

The North River section opens with Ian Burrow's chapter, which frames the problems associated with locating Dutch colonial sites in the highly developed nature of the centers of Dutch settlement and considers why, consequently, relatively little work on this period has been published. Adam Luscier and Matthew Kirk then discuss their research on European-Mahican trade at Van Schaick Island, where recovered artifacts suggest that Dutch trade was shaped by the demands of Native clients. Taverns and drinking, especially at Fort Orange, are the subject of Michael T. Lucas and Kristina S. Traudt's paper. Beer, drunk from delicate glass roemers and façon de Venise beakers, was the main beverage, in contrast to rum and cider consumed in the Chesapeake colonies. Marie-Lorraine Pipes provides a synthetic analysis of faunal (food bone) remains from Dutch sites in the Albany area, where a wide variety of wild species were consumed, suggesting that meat was a significant aspect of trade with Native people. Completing this section, Anne-Marie Cantwell and Diana diZerega Wall consider how female Natives acted independently as traders in their own right and may have been motivated by more than material gain in their trading activities.

The South River, or Delaware Valley, differed from the Hudson perhaps most significantly as the locus of rivalry with Swedish traders and settlers, the eventual incorporation of the colony of New Sweden, and the ongoing presence of Swedes and Finns in that portion of New Netherland. This begs the question of how this multiethnic population might be reflected in material culture. Additionally, this region was at the periphery of Dutch authority in the New World. As recently argued by George and colleagues (2019), the material world can reflect the psychosocial dissonance of changes in physical and sociocultural environments. Colonists in the South River faced not only a new physical world but one that was culturally diverse and subject to shifting imperial influences.

Lu Ann De Cunzo opens this section with her study of New Castle, as the English renamed the principle center of Dutch settlement on the Delaware River, examining settlement patterns, landscape design and land use, property ownership and transfer practices, architecture, and material life generally. Wade P. Catts and the senior editor of the volume, Craig Lukezic, focus on another aspect of New Castle, the site of Fort Casimir. Fieldwork has recently confirmed the projected location of the surviving elements of the fortifications. William B. Liebeknecht solved the mystery of an unusual archaeological feature in his study of wolf trapping practices and the colonist's attitudes toward this animal. The multiethnic makeup of the South River region is reflected in Marshall Joseph Becker's report on excavations at Fort New Gothenburg and the Printzhof (36DE3). Although the site was a center of Swedish colonial government, aspects of the results reflect the region's multiethnicity and the lack of clear material distinctions among the various groups present there.

The three artifact studies included herein focus on classes of objects that are distinctive, but not exclusive, to New Netherland. The papers consider how these items defined a part of the lives of people living here while reflecting trade practices as well. Meta F. Janowitz and Richard G. Schaefer discuss the distribution and use of the distinctive three-legged ceramic cooking vessels commonly found on Dutch colonial sites. Marbles are the subject of Paul R. Huey's contribution. Part of a much larger work, Huey examines their occurrence and use, not always by children. Finally, David A. Furlow reviews the archaeology of Edward Bird's clay tobacco pipes, providing insights into smoking behavior and trade.

We would like to thank Charly Gehring for his patient support of this endeavor and his essay that sets the stage for the archaeology that follows. We thank Meredith Babb at the University Press of Florida for her encouragement of this project. We are grateful for the patience and perseverance of our contributing authors. Finally, we thank Jaap Jacobs, Oscar Hefting, and Hans Van Westing for their support and insightful guidance and Charles E. Orser Jr. and Mary Beaudry for their helpful comments.

I

Setting the Stage

1

Why the Dutch?

The Historical Context of New Netherland

CHARLES T. GEHRING

The past is elusive. No matter how hard we try to imagine what the world was like centuries ago, the attempt conjures up only blurry images, which slip away like a dream. However, we do have tools available to sharpen these images of the past: primary source materials and archaeological evidence. With both we can attempt to construct a world in which we never lived. If we have any advantage at all, it's only that we know what that past world's future will be like.

The goal of this book is to provide the latest archaeology of the area that the Dutch once called Nieuw Nederlandt. As an increasing number of translations of the records of this West India Company (WIC) endeavor become available to researchers, it is hoped that this collection of articles will enhance the words that the Dutch left behind. It's fitting that we review why the Dutch were here in the first place.

Most of the narrative facts of the Dutch story are well known and accepted among historians who specialize in the history of the Dutch Republic and its colonial undertakings. Accordingly, I use citations here sparingly; however, the reader wishing a deeper understanding should consult the sources cited at the end of this chapter.

In the seventeenth century, the Dutch possessions lay between the New England colonies to the northeast and the tobacco colonies of Maryland and Virginia to the southwest. In 1614 the region appeared in a document of the States General of the United Provinces of the Netherlands as New Netherland. Its boundaries were defined by three river systems: the Fresh (Connecticut), North (Hudson), and South (Delaware). The central river system opened access to the interior of the country through its connection with the Mohawk River. Until the discovery of the Cumberland Gap in 1751, it would be the only passage westward to the Great Lakes and the interior of the country below the Saint Lawrence River. How did a country with a population of a little more than one million gain control of an area that would become the center of the fur trade in the New World?

During the late Middle Ages many nations, such as Sweden, France, Spain, and Russia, expanded their territories and commercial interests through war. However, the Netherlands' rise to a global commercial powerhouse began by virtue of a marriage.

In the fifteenth century, a large part of Western Europe came under the control of the House of Habsburg, when Frederick III was crowned emperor of the Holy Roman Empire. The marriage of his son Crown Prince Maximilian to Princess Mary of the House of Burgundy brought the 17 provinces of the Low Countries into the empire. Overnight, this northwestern corner of Europe, which had been serving mainly as a delta to three major river systems, had been added to a commercial network that spanned the globe.

The Low Countries' location fit in perfectly with the worldwide ambitions of the Habsburgs. Halfway between the Baltic and the Mediterranean, they were positioned ideally to serve as a warehouse, processing center, and distribution facility for ships loaded with goods from abroad. From this location, England, France, and the Baltic and Scandinavian countries were all accessible by water. The provinces, especially Holland and Zeeland, were flourishing from this water-related commercial activity. What could possibly go wrong?

To a certain extent, it all began with the Reformation. John Calvin's rendering of Luther's reform of the Catholic church struck a responsive chord in the Low Countries. The Counter-Reformation, led by the Habsburgs, attempted to stamp out this "heretical" movement. Although Emperor Charles V, grandson of Maximilian and Mary, was a devout Catholic, it was his son Philip who forced the issue when he succeeded his father as king of Spain. Coupled with this was Philip's attempt to consolidate the collection of taxes in the Low Countries. Philip's wars with France and the Ottoman Turks required a more consistent income flow. However, this more efficient way of squeezing money out of the "fatted cow" violated privileges, which had been granted to the provinces over the centuries. Religion and politics, the two taboo subjects of conversation at a cocktail party, were now on everyone's lips.

Armed combat broke out in 1568. This struggle against the empire would not end until 1648. Cities were besieged, atrocities committed, and thousands of people displaced. If that wasn't enough, in 1618 a war broke out between Protestants and Catholics in central Europe which lasted for 30 years. The massive disruption caused by this war sent thousands of refugees into the Low Countries. The only respite from this turmoil was a truce in 1609 between the Dutch and Spanish combatants. During this period of 12 years, the Dutch East India Company took advantage of the suspension of hostilities by hiring Henry Hudson, an experienced English navigator, to find a northern route to the Far East. Many attempts had been undertaken by both the Dutch and English to find shorter trade routes and less hostile waters to sail in, but all had failed. Although Hudson's attempt was also a failure, his explorations along the northeastern coast of America defined an area that the Dutch would claim by right of discovery.

For the Dutch, the establishment of trade routes was now a matter of survival. When the Dutch severed political ties with the empire, it also severed all economic ties. Ships that had been adding to its wealth were now enemy combatants. It was now up to a population of only one and half million people to create a commercial trade network that could compete with England, France, Spain, and Portugal. Everything depended on water. To supply grain from the Baltic to feed the population, ships had to be built. Ships required large supplies of wood which all had to be transported in from Scandinavia. It was do or die. Not only did the Dutch succeed in maintaining its break with the empire, they exceeded all expectations. Noted English historian Jonathan Israel (1989:12) states: "Except for Britain around 1780 no one power ever achieved so great a preponderance over the processes of world trade as did the Dutch for a century and a half."

However, it was not just their ability to build ships and to exercise the navigational skills learned while part of the empire. It was the creation of the Bank of Amsterdam in 1609. As Barbara Tuchman (1988:28) states: "It was the heart that pumped the bloodstream of Dutch commerce. By introducing new methods of regulating the exchange of foreign currencies it allowed checks to be drawn on the bank, providing credit and loans and assuring the reliability of deposit. Dutch guilders soon became the most desired currency."

At the end of the truce in 1621, the West India Company was founded on the model of the East India Company. Its primary mission was to resume the war with the empire; secondary was the establishment of a trade network from the west coast of Africa westward across the Atlantic and Pacific to the easternmost reaches of the Indonesian archipelago. The region called New Netherland, which had been an area of interest since 1614, was of special interest to merchants in the Netherlands because of the abundance of furs available through the Mohawk-Hudson corridor.

In spite of the WIC's early preoccupation with Africa and Brazil, it managed to take possession of New Netherland. The initial plan was to take control of the three river systems that served as conduits for the fur trade. In 1624 the first group of colonists were settled at the mouth of the Connecticut, on High Island (present-day Burlington Island) in the Delaware, and at the newly constructed Fort Orange on the upper Hudson. In the same year, colonists also settled on Governors Island, just south of the island of Manhattan, where a fort and windmill were constructed.

However, this large expanse of land, which would eventually become parts of Connecticut, New York, New Jersey, Pennsylvania, and Delaware, was not devoid of people. The indigenous peoples of the area were divided linguistically into two distinct language families: Algonquian and Iroquoian. Algonquian speakers occupied roughly the eastern half of New Netherland and Iroquoian speakers the western half.

Shortly after Hudson's explorations in the area, Adriaen Block was sent out to find the source of Hudson's reference to "a beautiful and fruitful land." What must have caught the eye of Dutch merchants during the height of the Little Ice Age was mention of the abundance of fur-bearing animals. Fur garments and castor hats were the fashion in Europe. During several centuries of exceptionally cold winters caused by increased volcanic activity and the paucity of sunspots, fur-bearing animals were sacrificed for the sake of comfort and fashion. It wasn't long before new sources of furs were being sought.

Block was hired by Lutheran merchants in Amsterdam to find the fur-rich river Hudson had described. He sailed along the coast of Connecticut, entering every river from the Thames to the Housatonic, and finally into the Hudson. Along the coast of Connecticut, he encountered Indians who were eager to trade for European goods. Among the items he received in return was *sewant*, or wampum. This decorative device was prized by Indians from other regions. It not only required a certain type of shell to produce but also the hole bored through the cylinder was labor intensive. When Block reached the upper Hudson around present-day Albany, the Indians there must have spotted the sewant aboard his ship. It soon became evident that furs could be traded for this device. It was so sought after that it was referred to as the "source and mother of the whole beaver trade"

(O'Callaghan 1868, 2:543). Dutch traders could exchange Dutch goods for sewant along the coast of Connecticut and Long Island, then take the sewant up the Hudson to trade for furs. Block played a role not only in setting up this profitable trade but also in establishing the trading post, Fort Nassau, on Castle Island (present-day Port of Albany) in 1614.

It was in this context that the Dutch established a fur-trading operation that became the envy of their European rivals, the English and the French. Although trading posts were located on the three river systems, it was Fort Orange on the upper Hudson that would prove the most productive. It was this post's access to the interior of the country via the Mohawk Valley that made it irreplaceable.

Relations with the various Indian bands depended mostly on location and politics. Allen W. Trelease uses the terms "expendables" and "valuables" to describe whether such relations were positive or negative for the Dutch and English. For example, in 1626 the commander at Fort Orange made the mistake of supporting the Mahicans in an attack on the Mohawks. This was contrary to instructions to remain neutral in Indian political affairs. Things didn't go well. The Mohawks ambushed the Mahican war party, killing the Dutch commander and several of his soldiers. Mahican losses are unknown. Only after all settlers were withdrawn from the area did the Mohawks agreed to resume normal trade relations (Jameson 1909:84). Thus, the Mahicans became "expendables," as the Dutch needed them on land for agricultural expansion, while the Mohawks became "valuables" as the major supplier of furs to Fort Orange.

During the period of WIC administration of the region called New Netherland, the shape of the actual ground under its control varied. In the early years, the Dutch "right of discovery" extended from Cape Cod (called Cape Malabar by the Dutch) to Cape Hinlopen at the mouth of Delaware Bay. However, over time the borders shifted according to political pressures from exterior forces.

Exclusive control of the Delaware was temporarily lost when Sweden established the trading colony of New Sweden in 1638. However, 17 years later aggressive action by Governor Petrus Stuyvesant brought the river back under Dutch control. As payment for the city of Amsterdam's loan of a warship for the "Swedish expedition," a section of the river was brought under the city's direct administrative control.

In the Northeast, aggressive pressure was coming from New England. The Dutch had initially established a trading post at the mouth of the Connecticut River. However, they soon moved the operation farther upriver to establish a permanent trade post deeper in Indian country. The trading post, called 't Huys van Hoop (the House of Hope), was serviced by a small agricultural community. But it wasn't long before the growing English population to the east invaded. Pressure became so relentless that the Dutch sought a secure border. The Treaty of Hartford in 1650 formed a provisional border that was never ratified but at least brought about temporary stability with New England.

The final reshaping of New Netherland's area of settlement came in 1661, when Arent van Curler was granted land along the Mohawk River. This agricultural community was named Schenectady. Altogether, there were 17 communities when the English gained control of the Dutch possession in 1664. The Dutch regained control of New Netherland in 1673 during the third Anglo-Dutch war. However, 14 months later, it was ceded permanently to the English under terms of the Treaty of Westminster.

Evidence of the existence of New Netherland didn't vanish with the arrival of the English. Most of the inhabitants didn't just pack up and return to Europe. They had large families and were for the most part firmly rooted in the New World. Their language and customs survived for generations. The Dutch left a significant footprint, which would contribute to the characteristics we call *American*.

Certain prominent traits of Dutch culture transmitted to New Netherland included social mobility, tolerance, and free trade. It wasn't necessary to be born to an upper level of society to become a respected participant in commerce and politics or society in general. You only needed to be ambitious and talented to rise to the top (but it also helped to marry well). Religious tolerance was guaranteed in article 13 of the Union of Utrecht, the de facto constitution of the United Provinces, which stated that no one would be prosecuted or persecuted because of their religion. Everyone was guaranteed "freedom of conscience." No one was ever hanged in New Netherland because of their religious convictions. And the Dutch were proponents of open trade everywhere. Free trade, also known as *mare liberum* (freedom of the seas) was valued as essential in the "carrying trade," as opposed to *mare clausum* (restricted waters), as exhibited by the English Navigation Acts. Not a trait but rather a consequence of history is multiethnicity. In contrast to the English and French, the "Dutch" population of New Netherland reflected the multiethnic makeup of its home country. Displaced persons from all over Europe had found refuge in the Netherlands. Many were fleeing the various wars in Europe, others natural disasters. In many ways, the Netherlands had become a kind of halfway house for desperate people rolling the dice for a better life. The United East India Company offered opportunities in the Far East, while the WIC offered the prospects of Hudson's "beautiful and fruitful land" in North America. New Netherland became the crucible that produced the beginning of the American "melting pot." It can be argued that the New York City of today is a reflection of the city of Amsterdam in the seventeenth century.

In addition to these somewhat intangible and subjective characteristics, the Dutch also left behind layers of material culture as witness to their presence here at the beginning of European settlement of North America. In the articles that follow in this volume, various aspects of what was left below the surface of New Netherland are explored and analyzed to provide new insights into that time and place.

SELECT WORKS SUGGESTED FOR FURTHER READING

Bradley, James W. 2007. *Before Albany: An Archaeology of Native-Dutch Relations in the Capital Region 1600–1664*. Albany: New York State Museum.

Gehring, Charles T., and William A. Starna (translators and editors). 2013. *A Journey into Mohawk and Oneida Country, 1634–1635: The Journal of Harmen Meyndertsz van den Bogaert*. Syracuse: Syracuse University Press.

Jacobs, Jaap. 2005. *New Netherland: A Dutch Colony in Seventeenth-Century America*. Leiden: Brill.

Klooster, Wim. 2016. *The Dutch Moment: War, Trade, and Settlement in the Seventeenth-Century Atlantic World*. Ithaca: Cornell University Press.

Parker, Geoffrey. 2013. *Global Crisis: War, Climate Change and Catastrophe in the Seventeenth Century*. New Haven: Yale University Press.

2

Between Trade and Tradition

Household Ceramic Assemblages from Amsterdam in the Age of Early Modern Globalization

MARIJN STOLK

The study of early modern material culture in the Netherlands and northern Europe is a relatively young sub-field within archaeology. Generally speaking, the early modern period in Europe spans from the late Middle Ages through as late as the end of the eighteenth century. While systematic excavations and analysis of sites within the city centers of the Netherlands started in the mid-twentieth century, archaeological consideration of the early modern period remained rare. However, with the extensive publication of archaeological finds from the city of Amsterdam, Jan Baart (1977) established the legitimacy of this field of study. Over the following decades, the archaeological study of urban centers through the late medieval and early modern periods developed, focusing on the excavation and analysis of cesspits and other urban waste deposits (e.g., Baart 1989; Bartels 1999a, 1999b; Bitter et al. 2002; Ostkamp et al. 2001).

CESSPIT ASSEMBLAGES

It should be noted that the features discussed here as *cesspits* are similar to the features North American archaeologists call *privy pits* or *vaults*, but since this paper is concerned with data from sites in the Netherlands, we will use Dutch terminology. In the end, many processes influence the compositions of cesspit assemblages. We must take into account that the "life assemblages" between different households varied, but also different households or generations could have made use of the same cesspit, and that there could have been some differences in waste management practices. Indeed, cesspits were used as latrines and as waste pits at the same time and had to be emptied every couple of years. Sometimes they were emptied completely, but sometimes only part of the fill from a cesspit was removed, so such post-depositional processes could quite easily mix up these assemblages.

The first large scale excavations of a neighborhood with house plots and their corresponding cesspits was that of the Vlooienburg neighborhood in Amsterdam. These excavations revealed the remains of more than 100 households dating roughly from 1600 and 1800, resulting in an enormous number of assemblages and containing comprehensive sets of artifacts as well as well-preserved organic remains (Baart 1987, 2001; Gawronski et al. 2016). Recently, these rich and numerous finds became the focus of the ongoing interdisciplinary Diaspora and Identity research project, directed by James Symonds (2019) of the University of Amsterdam in collaboration with the archaeological department of the City of Amsterdam and the Jewish Historical Museum. Most of the examples discussed in this paper are from Vlooienburg assemblages and are identified by their find code numbers, starting with "WLO," followed by a several numerals.

This chapter seeks to provide a review of prevailing ceramics used in Amsterdam households during the early modern period, focusing on the seventeenth century. Current research on seventeenth-century Dutch household complexes indicates that such goods cannot be simply defined as Dutch material culture; from the start of the seventeenth century, ordinary households, especially within cities and their surrounding areas, were able to acquire a variety of imported goods, resulting in eclectic collections of objects. This chapter presents and discusses some examples of household ceramic assemblages from Amsterdam.

Following this introduction, a brief historical overview focuses on economic and trade-related developments that shaped the cross-border connections and interactions from the end of the sixteenth and seventeenth century. Case studies of household waste assemblages from seventeenth-century Amsterdam are then discussed within a broader historical and theoretical framework, considering themes of trade, tradition, and identity from an archaeological perspective. The chapter concludes with a discussion of "Dutch" material culture and to what extend we should incorporate European or global trends to understand to the meaning and value of objects within household contexts.

HISTORICAL BACKGROUND

The early modern period in the Netherlands is regarded as transitional phase in terms of both political and economic development. During the sixteenth century, trade with ports along the Baltic Sea formed the foundation for the Dutch trading networks, providing grains, wood, hemp, flax, pitch, and tar. By the end of the century, however, Dutch merchants had developed a flourishing trade with the Mediterranean region as well, from which wine, fruits, oil, and alum were the most significant import products. However, probably the most crucial economic advancement at the beginning of the seventeenth century was the expansion of the maritime trading network outside of European waters into markets much more distant, with the founding of the United East India Company (VOC) in 1602 and the establishment of the West India Company in 1621 (Van Houtte 1979:163–178). By this time ceramics shipping extended from local potters in Bergen op Zoom and along the coast from the German Weser area to trade of exotic goods and porcelain via the colony Batavia in the Dutch East Indies (Bartels, personal communication, 2019).

Among the investors in the VOC were the cities of Amsterdam, Middelburg, Hoorn, Enkhuizen, Delft, and Rotterdam, with Amsterdam being the shareholder with the largest interest in the company (Gawronski 2012:56–67; Van Houtte 1979:163–178). Under the influence of war and while struggling with European competition and indigenous peoples, the VOC aimed to claim monopoly positions in specific areas to safeguard trade in exotic spices, such as nutmeg, mace, cloves, pepper, and cinnamon. From the seventeenth century, other essential trading products for the VOC included tea, coffee, porcelain, metals, and silk (Van Houtte 1979:227–241). In contrast, the trading network of the WIC included salt, sugar, tobacco, gold, and ivory. Within a few decades, the goods these trading companies made available drove the development of Dutch patterns of consumption, especially in the larger cities. In Amsterdam there were approximately 40 new sugar refineries in 1650, and by 1692 there were 24 coffee houses serving the city. By the end of the seventeenth century, tea, coffee, sugar, and tobacco had become common commodities in most ordinary Amsterdam households (Gawronski 2012:71).

In the archaeological record, this change in consumption is evidenced by increased diversity of ceramic forms, increase in the number of clay tobacco pipes, and the introduction of spices and other exotic products, the remains of which are found among the botanical remains recovered.

For example, botanical samples from a cesspit associated with an Amsterdam tavern and dating between circa 1600 and 1750 contained residues from figs, citrus fruits, black pepper, Spanish pepper, cloves, and "grains of paradise." These findings demonstrate trade with the Mediterranean, parts of Africa, Southeast Asia, and the West Indies (Van Haaster 2002). The flow of such commodities changed from rare and costly luxury products to exotic goods that were traded in bulk and became affordable to the mass of consumers. Thus it was that global goods, originally the province of elites, became available to common people and worked their way into daily life in Amsterdam (Gerritsen and Riello 2015:1–28).

Obviously, it has to be noted here that it was not only goods that were moving around the globe in at the time. Migrants from diverse backgrounds found their way into Amsterdam and other Dutch cities, leaving some traces within ceramic assemblages (Kuijpers 2005; Stolk 2018). Many Scandinavians, for example, traveled to the western Netherlands looking for work (Municipal Archives of Amsterdam: Index Burgher Books, 1531–1652). The Netherlands tolerated migrations of Sephardim from the Iberian Peninsula and of Ashkenazim fleeing religious persecution in Eastern Europe, of whom many came to live in the Vlooienburg neighborhood in Amsterdam (Levie 1987:7–17; Wallet 2007). Historical accounts describe a cosmopolitan mix of people at the Amsterdam Stock Exchange. One could encounter people from a wide variety of European countries, ranging from Russia to Italy and from Poland to France, but there were also people coming from as distant as Persia, Turkey, or even South Asia (Bodian 1997). Additionally, there was even a small community of Afro-Atlantic people living in Amsterdam during the seventeenth century (Ponte 2019:33–62). Thus, we may conclude that immigration, along with trade, developed the cosmopolitan character of this city.

DUTCH CERAMIC HOUSEHOLD ASSEMBLAGES IN THE SEVENTEENTH CENTURY

When studying seventeenth-century ceramic assemblages recovered from household refuse deposits on sites in the Netherlands, there are generally a couple of usual suspects among the various ceramic wares. The most common of these from the fourteenth century onwards are locally made redwares. Next, there is a strong presence of Dutch majolica and faience and Asian porcelain in sixteenth- and seventeenth-century assemblages. Less well represented but frequently found are slipwares and whitewares of

Dutch or German origin. The slipwares are characterized by a red surface decorated with motives in clay-slip. The so-called whitewares are recognizable by a pale cream-colored ceramic fabric and are often glazed in a flat yellow or green color. In addition to the wares mentioned above, there were also stonewares from Germany, which are characterized by their brownish or grayish color and denser, waterproof, stone-like, ceramic quality. Seen in smaller numbers are wares imported from other countries, such as finely tin-glazed and beautifully decorated table wares from France, Italy, or Portugal, or redwares from the Mediterranean area, which were often used as storage jars to transport specific goods such as olive oil (Gawronski 2012). The Dutch and German whitewares were essentially used for cooking, food preparation, and as tablewares, whereas the stonewares consisted principally of different kinds of jugs. In the following sections, some common ware types and forms found in Amsterdam household assemblages are briefly discussed, along with changes in consumption patterns and shifts in ceramic preferences.

DUTCH REDWARES

The dominant element in almost every household is formed by redwares, which were for the larger part of Dutch origin, cheap to purchase, and used for daily activities. The ceramics consist of relatively low-fired earthenware bodies covered with lead-based glaze on the interior and a partly or completely glazed exterior. Forms used for cooking, food preparation, food consumption, storage, sanitary purposes and lighting and heating in the house are recovered. Of course, variation in these forms was influenced by local or regional differences, but they shared a more or less similar shape and function throughout the Netherlands. An example of the diversity of shapes and functions in redwares can be seen in Figures 2.1 and 2.2. The redwares generally comprise 30% to 60% of ceramic assemblages from Vlooienburg. This general pattern occurs at other sites in Amsterdam as well (Gawronski et al. 2002:47–48; Ostkamp 2017:37).

A more specific and slightly more expensive type of Dutch redware are the so-called slipwares, which were found in many households throughout the seventeenth century both inside and outside of Amsterdam. This ceramic type was produced in the North Holland area and the Nederrijn area of the Netherlands and has a typical and easy recognizable decoration of yellowish slip motifs, sometimes combined with green glaze, on a red surface (Figure 2.3). For the larger part, these slip wares were used for

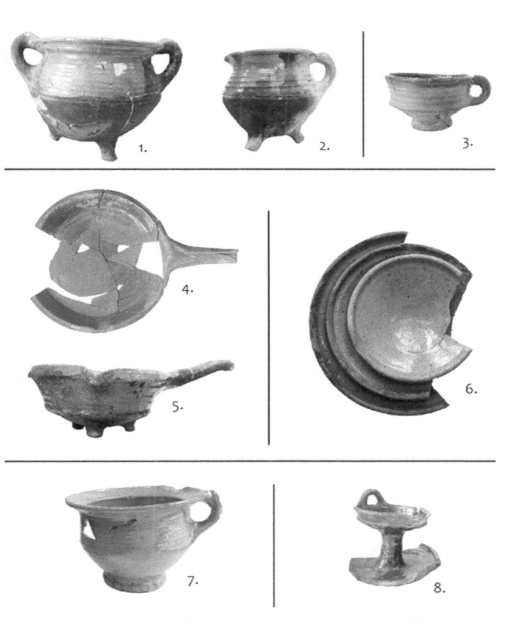

Figure 2.1. Dutch redwares derived from the Vlooienburg site in Amsterdam: 1) cauldron (WLO-114-29), 2) tripod pipkin (WLO-139-61), 3) cup (WLO-283-59), 4) frying pan (WLO-283-68), 5) skillet (WLO-139-66), 6) dishes (WLO-235-#41/#36/#38), 7) chamber pot (WLO-250-51), 8) oil lamp (WLO-139-44). Photographs by M. Stolk.

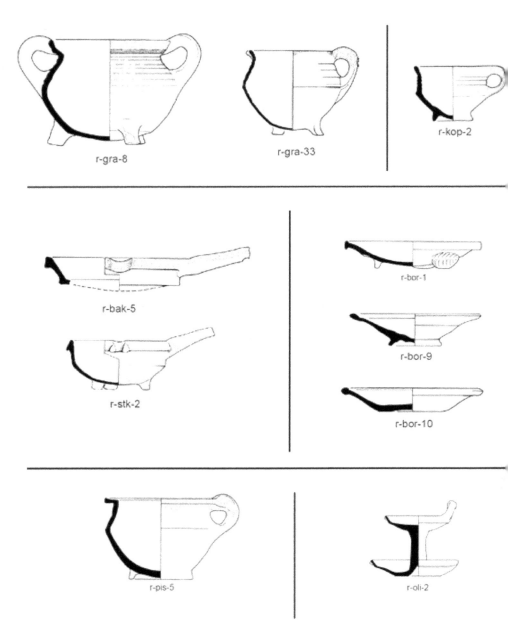

Figure 2.2. An overview of drawings of shapes that are comparable with those shown in Figure 2.1. The drawings and typological references are based on the so-called Deventer System, which is the primarily used typological system in the Netherlands. The Deventer System works with a threefold code: the first part is an abbreviation for the ware, the second part stands for the sort of shape, and the third part is the type number. Image by M. Stolk.

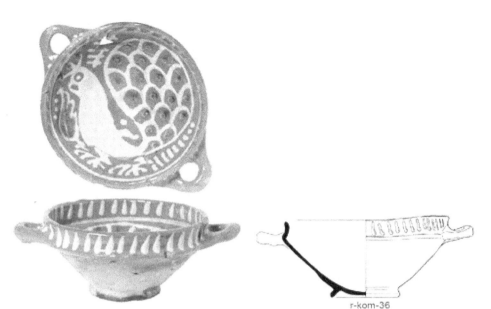

Figure 2.3. A porringer (WLO-138-53) in Dutch slip ware from the North Holland area with the slip decoration of a peacock in the center. Photographs and drawings by M. Stolk.

dishes and bowls, though sometimes one can find cooking pots, small jugs, or some other shapes with slip decoration as well. Next to the typical Dutch slip wares, German slipwares, mainly coming from the Werra and Weser regions, are found among the assemblages quite often as well (Figure 2.4).

DUTCH MAJOLICA AND FAIENCE

Inspired by the decorative tin-glazed wares that were imported from Italy and Portugal and the small amount of porcelain goods that had already made their way to the Netherlands by the end of the sixteenth century, Dutch potters started mimicking these colorfully decorated wares, resulting in the Dutch production of majolica and Delftware, also known as faience (Ostkamp 2014). We distinguish Dutch faience from majolica, as the former exhibits a solid white subsurface, a thinner sherd thickness, and the use of kiln furniture that prevented minor damage to the glaze on the topside of the product (Ostkamp 2014:14). Both majolica and faience were primarily used as tableware, in forms such as plates, bowls, and porringers

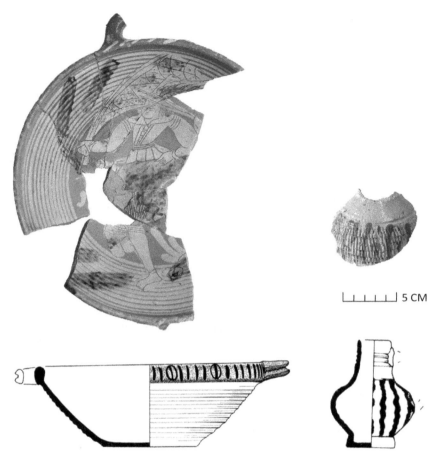

5 CM

Figure 2.4. *Left:* a slip-decorated bowl in typical Werra style (WLO-283-35), ca. 1590–1625. *Right:* fragment of a small slip-decorated jug from the German Weser region, ca. 1590–1625. Photographs and drawings by M. Stolk.

(Figure 2.5). Majolica was mostly produced in the first half of the seventeenth century, after which production dropped off. Initially, faience was made alongside or within the same potteries as majolica. As it became more fashionable, it was produced in larger quantities from the mid-seventeenth century (Ostkamp 2014). As the VOC and WIC introduced coffee, tea, and chocolate, consumers embraced the new fashionable forms of faience associated with these products. Faience was shaped into various cup forms (Figure 2.6). The developments in faience production were not limited to new shapes, but new sorts of decorations came into fashion too, inspired by Asian symbols, landscapes, figures and layout (Figure 2.7).

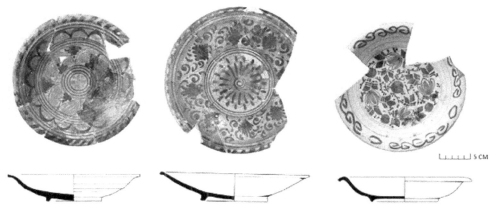

Figure 2.5. The two left dishes are Dutch majolica (WLO-283-54, WLO-283-55), dating circa 1600–1650, the right dish is Dutch faience (WLO-301-43), most likely produced in Delft, dating circa 1675–700. Photographs and drawings by M. Stolk.

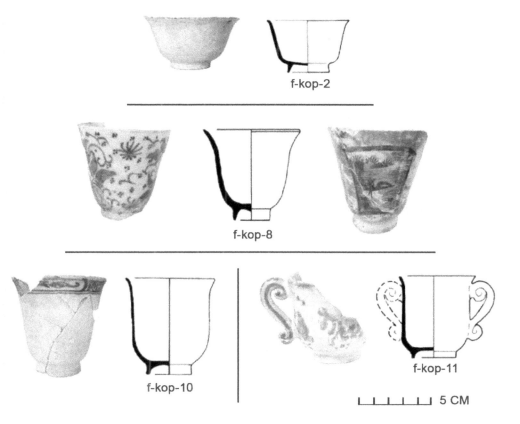

f-kop-2

f-kop-8

f-kop-10

f-kop-11

5 CM

Figure 2.6. Types of Dutch faience cups (WLO-301-46, WLO-301-49, WLO-301-51, WLO-301-50, and WLO-138-46), dating between ca. 1650 and 1725. Interesting is the decoration of the chocolate cup (*bottom right*), which features a depiction of a black person. Photographs and drawings by M. Stolk.

Figure 2.7. Dutch faience dish (WLO-138-9), with Asian and European influenced decoration, dating between ca. 1625 and 1675. Photograph by M. Stolk.

CHINESE PORCELAIN

One of the famous new products introduced into seventeenth-century households was Chinese porcelain. In the sixteenth century, porcelain was a rare luxury that mainly reached the Dutch Republic through gift exchange, indirect trade, or plunder from Spanish and Portuguese merchants. Later, the systematic importation of porcelain by the VOC made this product available for the middle class. As a result, ceramic assemblages from cesspits in the larger cities of the western coastal area of the Netherlands start to include porcelain sets, occasionally containing up to dozens of porcelain pieces. These finds consist of drinking and table wares such as drinking cups, saucers, bowls, and plates (Figure 2.8). Some porcelain items appear to have been used not only for food consumption but were also used as items of domestic display. Aesthetically, most of the seventeenth-century porcelain in the Dutch Republic depicts Asian subjects such as exotic landscapes, animals, figures settings, or geometric patterns (Gawronski 2012; Llorens Planella 2015:282–307; Ostkamp 2014).

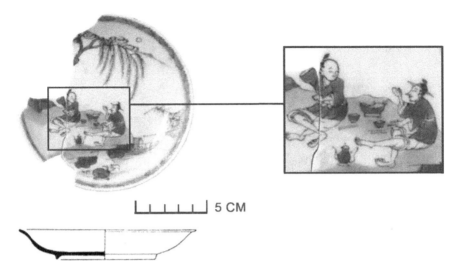

Figure 2.8. Example of a porcelain saucer (WLO-98-103) from a cesspit layer from Vlooienburg, dating between ca. 1675 and 1750. The image shows an Asian setting of two people, who seemingly share pot of tea and are consuming a dinner with the use of traditional eating sticks.

Interestingly, a few European forms found their way to Asia. In Taoyuan, a coastal region of northern Taiwan that was colonized under Dutch rule from 1624 to 1662, pottery workshops produced unusual porcelain forms such as beer mugs, saltcellars, candlesticks, wine jugs, and bowls or dishes for Dutch merchants. Although the Dutch did not request porcelain decorated with family coats of arms or emblems, as was done by Portuguese and Spanish traders, VOC representatives did request items decorated with more European motives for the Dutch market (Llorens Planella 2015:282–307). A reason for this could be that some of the porcelain depicted animals, such as crickets or toads, that in the Buddhist-Taoist culture were seen as positive symbols but that in Dutch culture were seen as vermin or related to negative connotations (Ostkamp 2014:55). The export items that were specifically shaped and made for the Dutch market were limited in number compared to the overall production of porcelain, which mainly displayed Chinese decorative motifs and scenes; nevertheless, their production indicates mutual exchange of ceramic shapes and decorations, depending on the shapes' function and the wishes of potential consumers. One must keep in mind, though, that the ceramic forms that found their way from the Netherlands to China were determined by Dutch merchants concerned with potential sales to consumers in the Netherlands, and were not meant for the Asian market.

CONCLUSION: BETWEEN TRADE AND TRADITION?

All in all, we can ask ourselves what makes a ceramic assemblage typical of seventeenth-century Amsterdam or what can be described as typical Dutch material culture. I think that the foregoing demonstrates how complex the answer to such questions is, since, especially in the period of early modern globalization, there was a serious level of cultural interconnectedness, resulting in a mutual exchange of ideas and products. There were, of course, traditional Dutch ceramics, such as the redwares, that did not undergo a lot of change in shape, decoration, and function. But when we look at the faience and porcelain from ceramic assemblages in Amsterdam, it is clear how pervasive intercontinental-trade-dominated consumption patterns were, as reflected in ceramic wares and forms used as everyday goods in Dutch households. Although characteristically Dutch cooking wares might not have changed much over time, diet did, as is indicated by the varied and exotic nature of botanical remains found at Amsterdam and other places in the Netherlands. This, by the way, underlines the importance of a combined research approach combining different archaeological subfields and datasets.

Rather than drawing a hard line between trade- or tradition-related artifacts, we should approach seventeenth-century Dutch material culture as gradually evolving, where different cultural elements, expressions, and habits came together, creating new traditions within everyday life experience. Based on the composition of the ceramic assemblages and the function of specific ceramic wares, one could say that the trade-related items seem to represent the social role of the household as they were used for display and for eating and drinking. This could mean that members of the emergent middle class at least to some extent felt the urge to demonstrate that they could afford international products and were interested in other cultural elements, copying the elite's fashion of collecting and displaying rare and luxurious objects. A clear example of this is the phenomenon of "curiosity cabinets" or "cabinets of wonders," in which members of the elite displayed collections of imported exotic or finely crafted goods. On the other hand, more traditional ceramics were to be found in the private areas of the household, related to cooking, food preparation, and sanitary activities. For local Dutch households this would mainly include local ceramics, whereas for example in migrant households cooking wares from their home country are present (Stolk 2018). Perhaps this is what defines typical Dutch material culture of the seventeenth century: the diversity of international materials, shapes, decorations, and behaviors directly related to products of not only international but also intercultural exchange.

II

The North River

3

Finding New Netherland in New Jersey

Retrospect and Prospect

IAN BURROW

Finding archaeological evidence for the Dutch colony of New Netherland in modern New Jersey is like searching for two very small needles in two separate and very messy haystacks. The smaller of the two needles lies on the east bank of the Delaware River, downstream of the Falls at Trenton. This needle is the smaller because the documentary sources demonstrate that permanent and extensive settlement of this portion of New Netherland was not seriously contemplated by the Dutch and carried out on only a very small scale by the Swedes. The second needle, on Bergen Neck across the Hudson River from Manhattan Island and New Amsterdam, is a little bigger but lies deeply buried in an enormously complex metropolitan urban haystack. Tenacious myths of a third needle in the extreme northwest of New Jersey appear to have little basis in fact, as we shall see.

There is, of course, no such thing as a Dutch colonial New Jersey. To the Dutch, what is now New Jersey was an unhelpful landmass separating their colonial enterprises on the North (Hudson) and South (Delaware) Rivers. This landmass could be indeed crossed "in three short days' journey from Sankikan (the Falls of the Delaware at Trenton) to New Amsterdam" (Federal Writers Project 1938:40), and the route was sufficiently well defined for a force of 120 armed men to march across it easily in 1655 (Weslager and Dunlap 1961:152). It is, however, only on the shores of those rivers that we can expect to encounter archaeological evidence of attempts at permanent control and settlement. In addition, on both rivers, the New Jersey shores were of much less importance to New Netherland than were the opposite banks. On the Hudson, New Amsterdam on Manhattan Island completely dwarfed the attempts at settlement on the opposite (Jersey) side, and on the Delaware River, Dutch (and Swedish) efforts were considerably more intense on the western shore, in what are now Delaware and Pennsylvania.

This chapter is an attempt to evaluate both the actual and the potential archaeological signature of the New Netherland Colony within the limits of modern New Jersey. It is not a rich haul, but there are a few locations where dogged research can reasonably be expected to produce significant information on the Dutch colonial enterprise.

The portions of New Netherland that lie within the modern states of New York, Pennsylvania, and Delaware have been subjected to rather more research than those in New Jersey. New York State especially has seen both extensive archaeological research and effective synthesis, most notably by Paul Huey (1987, 1988a and b, 2005). With the lone exception of the report of the discovery of a wooden Dutch shoe in the Hudson near Weehawken in 1911, New Jersey is however noticeably absent from reviews of both the archaeology and history of colonial New Netherland on the North River.

What Are We Looking For?

The excavations at the site of Fort Orange in Albany, New York, in 1970–1971, together with subsequent investigations in the adjacent settlement of Beverwijck (later Albany) and elsewhere provide a tantalizing glimpse of what could be recovered from New Netherland colonial sites in New Jersey (Huey 1987, 1988a, 1988b, 2005).

There is now a considerable body of literature and resources on Dutch colonial material culture. In addition to Huey's research and syntheses there is the important collection of essays edited by Roderic H. Blackburn and Nancy A. Kelley (1987), an overview of the evidence for household artifacts (Wilcoxen 1985), research on foodways in seventeenth-century New Amsterdam and New York (Janowitz 1993), and a number of major cultural resource management studies from sites along the Hudson (Huey 2005).

The richness of Dutch material culture and the restrictive trading practices of the seventeenth century combine to make the archaeological signature of the colonial Dutch into an almost textbook case of pattern recognition. Roemer glasses with prunts (decorative blobs) are characteristically Dutch in a New World context. For ceramics, research on the Fort Orange material highlighted the importance of Dutch majolica as a ceramic indicator of sites of the early 1600s up to about 1660, and the need to differentiate it from faience, or Delft, which appears in about 1630 (Wilcoxen 1987).

Reexamination of existing New Jersey collections containing Delft might identify previously unnoticed majolica pieces.

Thanks to meticulous documentary research in the Netherlands (De Roever 1987), we can be confident that clay tobacco pipes with "EB" on the heel are from Amsterdam. They are probably good markers for Dutch sites within the geographical limits of New Netherland, even though they are also found elsewhere (Huey 1988a:572). The pipes were made by Edward or Evert Bird, an immigrant to Amsterdam from Surrey (immediately south of London). Bird was already plying his trade in the city in 1630 and continued to do so until his death in 1665. At that time his inventory listed more than 376,000 finished pipes! His son, also called Evert, continued the pipe business, possibly into the 1680s.

Distinctively Dutch *sith* and *mathook* iron reaping tools are recorded in New Netherland documents from before 1664 (Cohen 1987:195–196 and Figure 2). These artifacts remained in use for many generations as signature Dutch cultural characteristics.

There is both archaeological and documentary evidence relating to houses in New Netherland. A 1649 contract for two somewhere on the Delaware specifies framed buildings of pine 32 ft long by 18 ft wide, apparently two stories high and with planks for roof covering (the Dutch *voet* [foot] was similar in size to its English equivalent). These are modest in comparison to the only known description of a pre-1664 house definitely in New Jersey. The contract for Joannes Winckelman's 1642 *bouwhuys* at Achter Col describes a Dutch-framed aisled building 90 ft long and a total of 43 ft wide, combining a dwelling and barn under one roof. It is known that the building was actually constructed and that it had a thatched roof (McMahon 1971:226–229). We may expect some if not all houses to have had distinctive wooden cellars of the type observed in New York State (Huey 1987). Cohen (1992) discusses the wider characteristics of colonial Dutch farmsteads. Clifford Zink's (1985, 1987) studies of Dutch framing provide essential information for understanding the spatial logic used in colonial Dutch buildings.

THE SOUTH RIVER: IS ANYBODY THERE?

Although there are indications that the South River was initially seen as the prime focus of New Netherland efforts, it was quickly eclipsed by the North River activity focused on New Amsterdam. This situation in New Jersey is further complicated by the superimposition of the New Sweden colony from 1638 to 1655 and by repeated English efforts to establish colonies at Salem and elsewhere (Federal Writers Project 1938; Weslager and Dunlap 1961). While there certainly was some specifically Dutch settlement (for example on Burlington Island and adjacent to Fort Nassau), it appears to have been on a limited and short-term basis. Archaeology may alter this perception, but the absence of detailed property-related records makes detailed documentary research difficult.

1. Falls of the Delaware and Adjacent Islands

The falls (*fal*) at what is now Trenton marked the effective upstream limit of Dutch (and Swedish) aspirations on the South River. Claims for a stone Dutch fort located in the Lamberton area of south Trenton have been firmly refuted (Kalb et al. 1982), but the possibility of a seasonally used trading post structure cannot be ruled out. Early seventeenth-century contact period sites close to the river have produced trade items and evidence for wheat residue in Native American ceramics (Hunter and Burrow 2014:336–337). One of the islands between the falls and Burlington (Verhulsten or Mekekanchkon Island) may also have seen some activity. This was either Biles Island (Pennsylvania) or possibly Houten Eylandt (Wooded Island), the modern Newbold Island west of Fieldsboro, New Jersey. The latter has received relatively little attention archaeologically.

2. Burlington Island

Charles Conrad Abbott's work on Burlington Island in the 1890s provided what remains by far the clearest archaeological evidence for pre-1664 Dutch activity on the New Jersey side of the South River (Dillian et al. 2014).

The island features prominently in Dutch colonial records under several different names: High Island, Matinakonk Island, and Beautiful Island. C. A. Weslager and A. R. Dunlap (1961:Chapter 3) demonstrated not only that these three names refer to the same island, later called Burlington, but also that this was the site of the first Dutch settlement in New Netherland. In 1624 three or four Walloon families were settled on the island in "two or three houses," according to a 1681 account (Weslager and Dunlap 1961:80). A trading post was also established, and the first governor, Willem Verhulst, was instructed to make the island his usual residence on the South River. These apparent plans to make the South River the major focus of New Netherland were abandoned when the advantages of Manhattan became obvious. In 1626 the Walloon settlers were withdrawn and resettled in New Amsterdam.

While it is possible that intermittent trading activities may have continued on the island after 1626, trading from yachts was evidently the preferred and less expensive option (Weslager and Dunlap 1961:75). A permanent settlement was established on the island in 1659 by Governor Alexander d'Hinijossa, who retained it until the English conquest of 1664. The island, however, remained in a sense Dutch until 1678, when it was confiscated from Dutchman Peter Alricks and leased to English Quaker Robert Stacey.

Some of the material Charles Conrad Abbott recovered (evidently only a portion of his original collection) remains in the collections of the Peabody Museum at Harvard University. The 196 items are discussed in detail by Dillian and colleagues (2014:57–61). Of the 56 European clay tobacco pipes, 15 could definitely be identified as of Dutch manufacture and include the ubiquitous EB pipes of Edward Bird. Trade items comprise glass trade beads and tinklers, but the researchers conclude that, overall, the collection has the appearance of a domestic site. It seems probable that most of what Abbott encountered relates to the d'Hinijossa/Alrichs occupation of 1659–1678. The location of the earlier Walloon settlement is not known, but this same well-drained high ground at the southern end of the island is a logical site, since it would be a good vantage point for observing ships approaching from downriver. Perhaps coincidentally, this situation is very similar to that of New Amsterdam.

Although Burlington Island has been greatly modified by gravel mining and dumping of dredge spoil in the twentieth century, Dillian's (et al. 2014) field reconnaissance suggested that a zone along the southeastern shore of the gravel quarry lake retains archaeological integrity and also seems likely to be the location of Abbott's discoveries (on the basis of his written descriptions).

These conclusions are supported by the U.S. Coast and Geodetic Survey of 1843 (Figure 3.1), which shows the island as largely cultivated. A building and adjacent orchard are reached by a road from the southwestern shore, and a group of buildings also lies near the northern shore close to the eastern tip of the island. Much of the southeastern side of the island is occupied by drained and embanked meadows, which later reverted to marshland. The extent of the 1950s gravel quarry lake has been added to the 1843 image to show the extent of its impact on the original topography.

3. Fort Nassau and Associated Settlement

The site of Fort Nassau, which was built in 1626 and abandoned in 1651, remains to be firmly established. In 1919 a historical marker for the fort

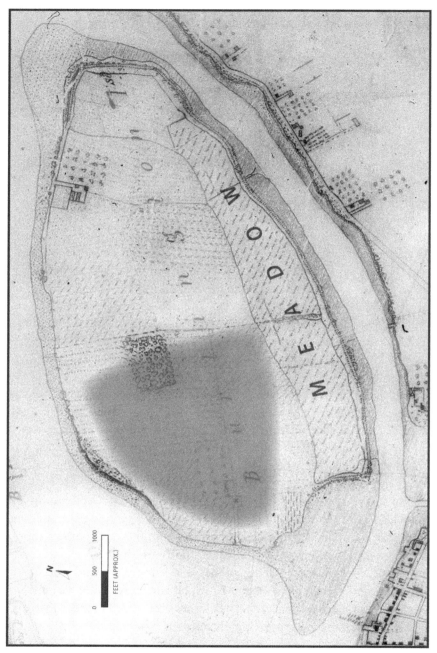

Figure 3.1. Burlington Island in 1843 as depicted on the U.S. Coast and Geodetic Survey (1843). Note the zone of embanked meadow along the southeastern side of the island. The approximate location of the gravel quarry lake created in the late 1950s is indicated.

was placed in the center of Gloucester City just west of Broad Street, and Weslager and Dunlap (1961:125) also argue that the fort was on Gloucester Point within the present city. Their hypothesis depends on the identification of Timmer Kill with Newton Creek (which delimits the north side of the point), rather than with Timber Creek to the south (the conventional identification). Timber Creek was, they suggest, actually called Verkeerde Kill. The placement of the fort south of the Timmer Kill on maps of 1630 and 1643 therefore puts it on Gloucester Point. Other researchers have accepted that Timmer Kill is the modern Timber Creek and therefore place the fort in the Westville area. (Brown n.d.). Of the two options, the Gloucester Point location makes the greater sense, both as an area of fast land and as a vantage point for viewing activity for some distance both up and downriver.

Like the better-documented Fort Casimir at New Castle, Delaware, Nassau was essentially a fortified storehouse or trading house with cannons mounted on the corner bastions of a small surrounding palisaded enclosure (Weslager and Dunlap 1961:124). In 1631 it housed 10–12 company employees. In 1638–1639 soldiers were garrisoned there and the storehouse was apparently rebuilt on a larger scale (Weslager and Dunlap 1961:121, 122, 134). Fort Nassau is also one of the few locations where there was actual Dutch settlement. An unknown number of settlers were withdrawn from the fort vicinity in 1651 and resettled in the area of Fort Casimir (Weslager and Dunlap 1961:191).

THE NORTH RIVER: PAVONIA AND BEYOND

The North River saw much more concerted settlement attempts, though these remained small in scale and were repeatedly subject to Indian attacks, usually prompted by inflammatory behavior on the part of the Dutch. There are indications that trading posts were established at Communipaw, Paulus Hook, and Hoboken before 1620, although these were probably only used seasonally and were not permanent settlements. In 1630 Michael Pauw took up a patroonship from the Dutch West India Company on Bergen Neck. This patroonship of Pavonia extended 8 mi north from Bergen Point as far as Weehawken (Figure 3.2). Pauw had to relinquish his rights a couple of years later, but the name stuck, and the company began granting lands for boweries and plantations. Many of these were destroyed by the Indians in 1643, and the area was apparently evacuated, although settlement resumed and expanded in the late 1640s and early 1650s. After the disruption of the

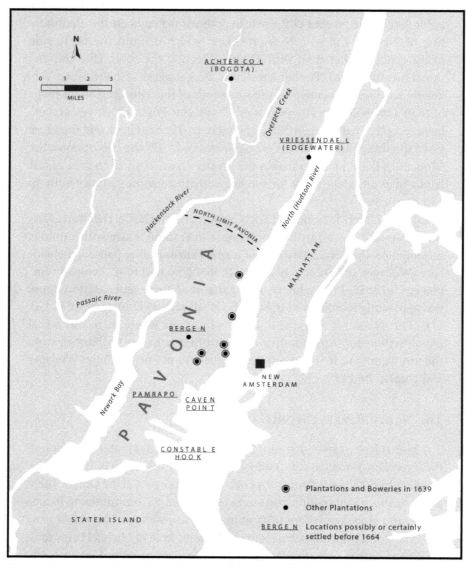

Figure 3.2. Pavonia and outlying settlements of New Netherland in northeast New Jersey.

Figure 3.3. Bergen Neck as shown on Joan Vinckeboons's 1639 "Manatvs gelegen op de Noot [sic] Riuier." Probable locations of the numbered boweries and plantations are indicated. Also shown are other documented settlement locations, the approximate northern boundary of the patroonship of Pavonia and of Stuyvesant's repurchase, and the site of Bergen village of 1660. North is to the right. Same orientation as Figures 3.5 and 3.6 (Library of Congress, Geography and Map Division, https://www.loc.gov/re-source/g3804n.ct000050/, with additions and identifications).

Peach Tree War in 1655, Governor Petrus Stuyvesant formalized the reacquisition of Pavonia from the Indians, and in 1660 the fortified village of Bergen was established on the top of the ridge inland from Paulus Hook and Communipaw (Rink 1986; Wacker 1974:239).

The Pavonia Plantations

The 1639 Vinckeboons map of Manhattan on the North River (Figure 3.3) provides a starting point for locating the Pavonia boweries and plantations. By comparing this map (with its informative key) with later maps (particularly the 1844 "Map of New-York Bay and Harbor and the Environs" and the series of informative fill maps produced by the New Jersey Geological Survey), it is possible to pin down the probable locations of these sites.

There are six mapped locations on the eastern side of the Bergen Ridge, numbered 27 to 32 on the 1639 map. Three (27, 28, 29) are identified as "boweries" and are shown with tower-like structures that are almost certainly hay barracks. The other three are described as "plantations" and do not have hay barracks, perhaps implying that these are less developed or less important. Of these plantations, only the northernmost (32) is ascribed to an individual, in this case one Maerytensen. At Paulus Hook, the most readily identifiable location, there are *dry* (three) plantations listed and shown. The southernmost plantation (30) is described as being "on Lachers Hook."

31. Paulus Hook Plantations

Paulus Hook remained a prominent landmark on the lower Hudson until the mid-nineteenth century, when its distinctive topography was overwhelmed by surrounding fill and the expansion of Jersey City. Three or four buildings are shown close to the ferry landing on late eighteenth-century maps, and these may be successors to the three "plantations" on the 1639 map. Hunter Research, Inc. (2013b) presents the historical development of the Hook in detail, including reproductions of the key maps.

27. Van Vorst Bowery at Harsimus

Working from the known location of Paulus Hook, it is fairly clear that the Van Vorst Bowery was in the area of Harsimus Cove, perhaps half a mile northwest of Paulus Hook. Harsimus is the name given to an area of well-drained or fast land separated from the Bergen Ridge to the west by the Harsimus and Mill Creeks.

28. Van Vorst Bowery at Hoboken

Like Harsimus, Hoboken was an island-like feature somewhat isolated from the Bergen Ridge. Its most prominent feature is the headland of Castle Point, but early settlement was to the south of this in the area west of the present Hoboken Ferry, and this is the likely location of the bowery here.

32. Maerytensen Plantation at Weehawken

Based on comparisons between the 1639 map and modern topography, this plantation probably lay on the north side of Weehawken Cove but south of the point at which the Bergen Ridge reaches the Hudson shore as a high cliff: "the great rock above Wiehacken," which formed the northern boundary of Pavonia as r-acquired by Stuyvesant in 1658. This, unfortunately, places the site in the heavily developed Lincoln Harbor area and the approaches to the Lincoln Tunnel! A 1647 grant to Maryn Andriaensen for land at Weehawken may reflect the reoccupation of this location after Kieft's War (Doherty 1986:11).

29 and 30. Communipaw and Lachter Hook

The 1639 map is less helpful in pinning down the modern location of these two sites. Site 30 is identified as "Plantation on Lachter Hook," and 29 as the "Bowery of Jan Everts." Lachter Hook appears to be specifically the name given to a prominent hill on the south side of Mill Creek where the latter entered the Hudson River. This location now lies at the extreme western end of the Morris Canal Basin and is largely underneath Interstate 78 and the adjacent railroad. It appears likely that the 1639 cartographer mislocated both sites. "The Plantation on Lachter Hook" is what later came to be called Communipaw and lies much closer to Paulus Hook than is shown. Site 29, the bowery of the prominent Dutch settler Jan Everts Bout, is depicted somewhat west of Paulus Hook and north of the plantation. The location of Communipaw is well known, and the most obvious location for the bowery is on the hill on Mill Creek immediately to the north. This places the two sites in close proximity, not widely separated as they are shown in 1639.

The first detailed map of the area where these two sites lay (Figure 3.4) probably gives a good impression of the earlier Dutch colonial landscape, even though 200 years separates them. The settlement of Communipaw extends along the shoreline south of Mill Creek. This nucleated settlement may be the result of a 1658 ordinance by Governor Stuyvesant requiring Pavonia settlers to create villages rather than living in more vulnerable dispersed farmsteads (McKinley 1900). Like Bergen, Communipaw evidently had a defensive palisade (Doherty 1986:13). At the mouth of the creek was the then-prominent hill which is very likely the site of the bowery. The adverse effect of the construction of I-78 and of adjacent earlier railroads is self-evident. The site of Communipaw is blessed with at least two contaminated sites with ongoing remediation programs.

Figure 3.5 places all these six sites within the present-day topographic setting of northern Hudson County, using the 1844 map and a combination of the New Jersey Geological Society fill and U.S. Geological Society topographic maps. This shows these early settlements all placed on pieces of dry terrain on the low-lying ground close to the Hudson and directly opposite New Amsterdam. Figure 3.6 shows the modern reality of this setting as revealed by Google Earth. Archaeologically, it is somewhat discouraging.

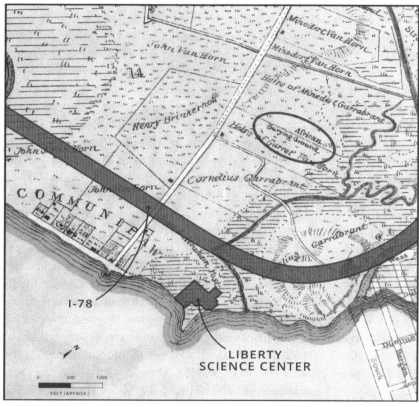

Figure 3.4. Communipaw and Lachter Hook in 1841. Communipaw is shown as a linear settlement along the shoreline (defined by modern Phillip Street), connected to Bergen Ridge (at the top of the view) by a road (modern Communipaw Avenue). This runs westward across fast land divided into larger lots associated with Dutch names. The hill occupied by Cornelius Garrabrant, with a substantial house and attached grounds by Mill Creek, is probably the original Lachter Hook. The locations of the Liberty Science Center and Interstate 78 are added for reference. The latter passes right across the probable site of Cornelius Garrabrant's house (and therefore probably of Jan Everstens's Bowery). Note also the "African Burial Ground" on the Van Horn/Garrabrant boundary north of the road (Douglass 1841).

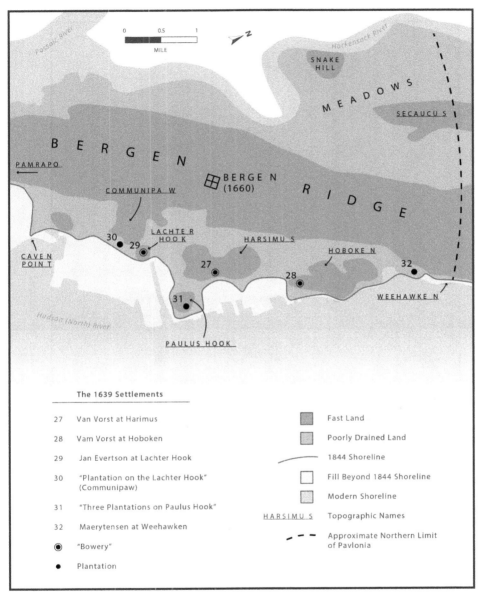

Figure 3.5. Pavonia: Locations of boweries and plantations in 1639, as deduced from historic maps, topographic analysis, previous research and historic fill distribution. Same orientation as Figures 3.4 and 3.6.

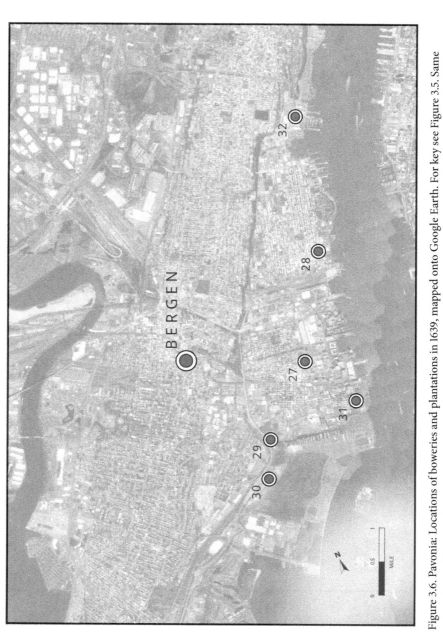

Figure 3.6. Pavonia: Locations of boweries and plantations in 1639, mapped onto Google Earth. For key see Figure 3.5. Same orientation as Figures 3.4 and 3.5.

Other Settlements in Pavonia

An uncertain number of additional boweries and plantations were established within the limits of Pavonia before 1664 (Pavonia 2018). Among these locations were Constable Hook; Pamrapo, Minkakwa, and Caven Point (three adjoining areas south of Communipaw); and the farmstead of Aert van Putten (reputedly with a brewery), north of Castle Point at Hoboken. There may have been others.

Two Settlements beyond Pavonia

Achter Col

The 1642–43 patroonship of Achter Col is of interest in a couple of respects. It was located much further inland than the other documented boweries and plantations. Although "further" is a relative term, since it was "only a short hour's walk" from David Pietersen de Vries's plantation at Vriessendael (Edgewater) on the North River (De Vries quoted in McMahon 1971:233), its placement on the east bank of the Hackensack marks a departure from its close dependence on the North River and New Amsterdam seen in the Pavonia settlements. It is also the only site in New Jersey where the dimensions, structure, and materials of the main house are known. Tellingly, the contract for the house specified that the main timbers were to be cut and squared on Manhattan and then hauled to the site. This indicates that it was considered quite feasible to transport bulky materials to this location, presumably by bringing them through the Kill Van Kull and up Newark Bay into the Hackensack.

Where exactly was Achter Col? The historic marker lies in a small park on the west side of River Road and south of Fort Lee Road in Bogota, Bergen County (Figure 3.7). This area has been a park since at least 1908 (Sanborn Insurance Maps 1908) and is shown as open ground in 1876 and apparently also in 1861 (Hopkins 1861; Walker 1876). This intersection of two routes, one running along the east bank of the river and the other running east across Overpeck Creek to the Hudson, has with good reason been traditionally regarded as a likely location for Winckelman's settlement.

Topographically this setting makes sense. The park area is set on a terrace that slopes down gradually to the west and that lies immediately adjacent to the Hackensack, from which it is now separated by the 1872 railroad alignment. Fort Lee Road, having descended a moderate hill to the east of River Road, curves northwestwards across the floodplain west of River

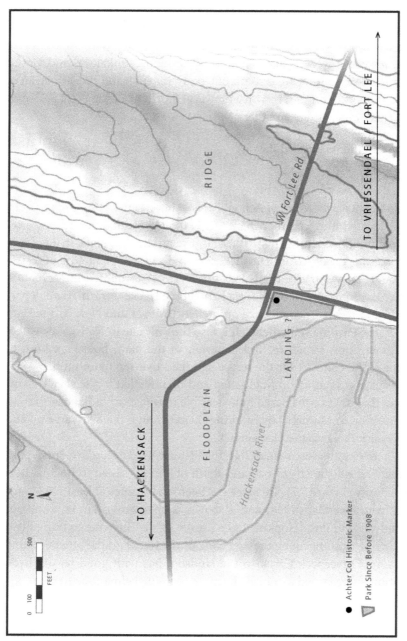

Figure 3.7. The topography and setting of the probable location of Achter Col at Bogota (USGS Hoboken Quadrangle 2016).

Road to reach the Hackensack about half a mile away. This alignment has been in place since at least 1839, but it may be wondered if the road originally ended at a landing immediately northwest of the present park. On this hypothesis the road was only later extended to cross the river closer to the village of Hackensack, perhaps once the latter had become the Bergen county seat in the early 1700s.

Of the known Dutch pre-1664 sites in northern New Jersey, Achter Col has perhaps the best chance of surviving as a coherent archaeological site. The park area appears never to have been developed, and there are good reasons for placing Winckelman's *bouwhys* here. The remarkable documentary record and the tight chronology of the settlement would make the identification of physical remains of this site of particular interest. An archaeological evaluation of the park is an obvious next research step. Are the cannons thrown into the Hackensack by the Indians in 1643 (McMahon 1971:237) still in the riverbed?

Vriessendael (Edgewater)

The Bergen County Historical Society's marker for the Vriessendael site sits somewhat forlornly on the east side of River Road at the northwest corner of Veteran's Park in Edgewater. In common with so much of the Hudson River waterfront, this area has been massively redeveloped and reworked in the last few decades. Consequently, it is hard to be optimistic about the chances of archaeological survival of David Pietersen de Vries's plantation of 1640–1643 (McMahon 1969). Detailed research would be required to confirm the validity of the choice of location for the marker, although its placement near the former dock seems reasonable.

Bergen Fortified Village

The foundation of Bergen was one of the last major acts of the government of New Netherland and shows a renewed interest in the planned settlement of Pavonia and the Bergen Ridge after the disastrous Indian wars of the 1640s and 1650s. The consensus is that these conflicts had led to the virtual abandonment of the New Jersey portion of New Netherland. The assertive leadership of Petrus Stuyvesant laid a secure foundation for the reoccupation of the peninsula with his 1658 renegotiation of the earlier Pavonia land purchase.

Key to the strategy for the new enterprise was the establishment of a 15-acre fortified settlement on the ridge, placed among former Indian fields at the intersection of a preexisting north-south route (present Bergen Avenue) with the road leading eastward down to the shore at Paulus Hook. Settlers were to take up lots within the village, and each would provide one man for the defense of its palisade. By 1662 the settlement had a church (just outside the defenses), a school, and a public well.

The importance of the remarkable survival of the street pattern, central square, and palisade line of the 1660 planned and fortified village of Bergen was first recognized by Peter Wacker (1975:123, 239). Since 2004 a series of archaeological studies have been undertaken at the Van Wagenen or Apple Tree House, the only pre–Revolutionary War structure surviving in the village area (Hunter Research, Inc. 2004, 2012, 2015, 2017). These built on the historical research and historic structural analysis completed in 2005 (Newman 2005). Contextual study of the settlement (Burrow 2011) showed that 18 of the present-day lot lines in the village are on their original mid-seventeenth-century alignments. Despite extensive redevelopment in the early twentieth century, it was additionally demonstrated that seventeenth-century archaeological deposits could still survive at five locations (Burrow 2011:Figure 6). Analysis of historical maps suggested that large houses may have been intentionally placed in semidefensive configurations at the four entrances.

Although most of the 32 original lots had already been taken up by 1661, it is unclear how many of these were actually occupied. Recent archaeo-logical and historical research on the Van Wagenen property (Hunter Re-search, Inc. 2017) suggests that no structures were erected on this lot (113) before the end of the seventeenth century. If maps of the Revolutionary War period and later are a reliable guide, it appears that many lots may have remained similarly undeveloped (see the high-quality reproductions of maps from 1778 to 1844 in Hunter Research, Inc. 2017:Figures 2.4–2.7).

Archaeologically, the Van Wagenen property has yielded only one ar-tifact that might date to the brief pre-English phase. This is a fragment of an early Westerwald vessel that probably dates to before 1700 (Hunter Research, Inc. 2017:Photograph 4.1). Some of the other ceramics could also be this early. Despite the presence of soils containing eighteenth-century materials, the integrity of the site is not as good as might have been hoped. The identification, along the street frontage, of the cellar of a house primary in the site sequence (and perhaps dating to the late seventeenth century) does however show that important information on the development of the village remains in the ground. The archaeological capital of Bergen is, how-ever, close to expended at this point.

DUTCH MINERS IN NORTHWESTERN NEW JERSEY

The effective inland reach of New Netherland in New Jersey was limited. On the South River, control was only claimed as far upstream as the Falls at Trenton, and on the North River, settlement extended only a few miles inland.

Nevertheless, there is an enduring story of pioneering Dutch copper miners working at Pahaquarry north of the Delaware Water Gap in Sussex County, at least 50 mi in a direct line from any permanent Dutch settlement. Before 1664, it is claimed, ore or copper was being hauled from Pahaquarry more than 100 mi northeastward to the Hudson at Esopus (Kingston), New York, along the Old Mine Road.

Attractive though this story is, the careful research of Herbert Kraft (1996) has shown it to be without any reliable foundation. A key element is the intractability and low yield of the Pahaquarry copper ore deposits, which, combined with the distances involved and the limited technology available, would have made such a project impracticable. The Old Mine Road itself is a composite route not shown on early maps, and in any case did not connect the Pahaquarry area with Esopus until after 1790. European settlement of the area north of the Water Gap did not begin until about 1700, delayed before then both by poor communications and the considerable Native American presence in the Minisink Valley until that time.

Kraft convincingly shows how confusion, misunderstanding of early sources, unwarranted assumptions and wishful thinking all combined to create what is essentially a modern myth. The tenacity of the idea is however shown by its appearance as late as 2004 in the *Encyclopedia of New Jersey* (Hordon 2004).

PROSPECT

New Netherland in New Jersey was a small-scale enterprise. In 1665 the population of Bergen (roughly the present Hudson County east of the Hackensack) is estimated to have been only 132 (Wacker 1975:129–130), but earlier numbers were higher. There appear to have been at least 250 settlers on Bergen Neck in 1655 and even more before 1643. Among these settlers were enslaved Africans, as many as 50 being present in the 1630s (Hodges 1999: 9). Such is the sophistication of modern historical archaeology that we can now hope to identify these "invisible" people from the observable patterns they created in the earth. The full-scale archaeological and historical study of just one of the sites discussed in this paper would enrich history of both New Jersey and of the Dutch colonial enterprise.

All is not lost. Despite more than 350 years of mutilation it remains possible to obtain some sense of the extent and nature of colonial Dutch New Jersey. Although the task of identifying archaeological evidence for this colony seems daunting, experience in New Jersey and beyond has shown repeatedly that archaeological sites are remarkably hardy, surviving in areas where common sense would predict their complete erasure from the landscape. For example, despite considerable nearby disturbance, there appears to be some archaeological integrity remaining in the key location on Burlington Island. Newbold Island could benefit from a modern evaluation and survey. While Fort Nassau may appear to be a lost cause, probably lying beneath Gloucester City, careful evaluation of the archaeological sensitivity of the urban area could at least point to places to look.

The archaeology of Pavonia and Bergen Neck is also not without hope. It seems safe to say that Jan Everts Bout's hilltop bowery near Communipaw is a lost cause, and much of Communipaw itself is inaccessible. Paulus Hook, however, may well retain some of its colonial archaeology, although here the Revolutionary War fortifications may have taken a toll on the colonial Dutch features. It is also difficult to feel optimistic about the Harsimus Cove, Hoboken, Weehawken, and Edgewater sites, although intensive documentary work and archaeological sensitivity evaluation may help to both pin these sites down to within an urban block and better assess the likelihood of their survival.

The Achter Col site at Bogota holds out the best hope for the survival of a 1640s bowery, and here we have the extraordinarily useful addition of a detailed documentary record of the building erected here. It is fortunate that at least part of the area most likely to be the site of the bowery is and has been a public park. An archaeological survey of this park should be able to establish its integrity and potential. If justified, the site could then be afforded a degree of protection by being entered on the State Register of Historic Places.

This leaves Bergen. Although excavations so far undertaken have not encountered archaeological resources earlier than the late seventeenth century and the village was not fully developed in the colonial period, the area within the palisade must be regarded as archaeologically significant. Despite scholarly recognition of the significance of the surviving street pattern and of the general importance of the Bergen settlement, the only historic designation is the inclusion of the Van Wagenen House property on the state and national registers. Bergen village is not a historic district, and the city zoning makes no recognition of the historic nature of the place. The handful of lots where seventeenth-century archaeology may survive have no protection and could be lost to development at any time.

This is a sad fate for the earliest nucleated settlement in the state. There are two available options, both requiring resources and political vision and will. One is for the city to adopt an overlay zoning map that would identify both the street pattern and the areas of archaeological sensitivity and to develop planning policies under the Municipal Land Use Law that would encourage archaeological assessment of sensitive lots and require the preservation of the street pattern and routine monitoring of utility work and repaving. A second option would be to create a local, state, and national historic district in which all development would be subject to review and recommendation by the City Historic Preservation Commission. Judicious use of the powers provided by these measures could ensure that a little more of colonial New Netherland is recorded for posterity.

ACKNOWLEDGMENTS

Thanks to:

Colleagues at Hunter Research, Inc. for providing information, observations, and the results of recent work at the Van Wagenen House in Bergen.

Elizabeth Cottrell for preparation of the graphics.

Staff of the Jerseyana Collection of the New Jersey State Library for the diligent and successful pursuit of obscure references.

Colleagues at the New Jersey Historic Preservation Office for assistance and insights.

4

Quamhemesicos (Van Schaick) Island

Archaeological and Historical Evidence of European-Mahican Interactions at the Twilight of Dutch Colonialism in New York

ADAM LUSCIER AND MATTHEW KIRK

Mahican inhabitants called the towering waterfall Chahoes (Gehring and Starna 2008:9). Here the waters of the Mohawk River, draining a large part of north-central New York, meet the Hudson River, which on its way south toward Manhattan and the Atlantic Ocean drains the southern portion of the Adirondack Mountains region. These two river systems were important transportation routes in pre-contact times, and the mouth of the Mohawk served as a critical intersection. The modern-day Van Schaick Island is the largest of a cluster of islands where the sprouts of the Mohawk (or rivulets of water) carved through shallow bedrock, eventually falling into the deeper channel of the Hudson. The Mahicans called the island Quamhemesicos (Dunn 1994:211) and the area around the sprouts Mathahenaach (Masten 1877:17) or Nachtenack (O'Callaghan 1845:437).

Recent archaeological excavations on the east side of Van Schaick Island by the authors have revealed a circa-1650 Dutch trading outpost with perhaps contemporaneous, related Mahican occupation, a wide range of Dutch trade items, and apparent decline of Mahican artifacts and proliferation of European goods through the remainder of the seventeenth and first part of the eighteenth century. This chapter reviews the documentation of settlement and associated land transactions and the results of the excavations on east side of Van Schaick Island to provide important insights into Dutch-Mahican relationships in the mid-seventeenth century.

Mahican Settlement and Ownership

Janny Venema (2010:40–41) has extensively documented the complexity of Native land sales to Europeans over the 1650s and 1660s. To the Mahicans, the signing of deeds was the culmination of a series of ceremonial celebrations that included feasts and gift giving. According to patroon's agent Barent van Slichtenhorst, the full cost of land transfers, which often included large sums of food, gifts, and alcohol, were not reflected in deeds (Venema 2010:40). Further complicating matters, the Mahicans viewed unsettled lands as unclaimed, despite previous sales. As a result, numerous parcels were the subject of repeated or overlapping claims through time (Van Laer 1928:267). European owners, when visiting or using unsettled land they had been deeded but which was occupied by Mahicans, were required to bring gifts in each instance. Thus, many Dutch refrained from purchasing land until necessary, or as Van Slichtenhorst noted, "the daily cost will exceed the buying price" (Venema 2010:41).

The Van Scheyndel (1632) *Map of Rensselaerswyck* indicates that there were two Mahican settlements in the area, including Monemin's and Unawat's "casteel" or castles, likely small fortified farmsteads with extensive associated farm fields. The Vinckeboons map of 1639 also depicts two Mahican settlements in the vicinity labeled as "vasticheyt," a term Shirley Dunn (1992:37) has interpreted as meaning a palisaded settlement or stronghold (Starna 2013:42).

Monemin died, possibly was killed, during the Mohawk and Dutch Mahican War in 1626 (Dunn 1994:103). But the castle remained an important geographic landmark over time, as Kiliaen van Rensselaer understood the northern extent of his patroonship as lying to just south of Monemin's settlement (Van Rensselaer et al. 1908:167).

Most of the Native inhabitants in the area during the 1650s and 1660s were led by the Mahican sachem Schiwias, also known by a Dutch nickname of Aepjen (Dunn 1994:112, 166; Starna 2013:114–118; Venema 2010:40). Apparently born around 1600, Schiwias was a hereditary leader of a local group of Mahicans. As evidenced in the historical Dutch records, however, his political influence reached far up and down the Hudson River valley (Dunn 1994:167). He rose to prominence from about 1637 and remained an influential person, especially with respect to Mahican-Dutch relations, until his death in 1665. Schiwias resided to the south of Fort Orange, perhaps on Schodack Island, yet he commonly acted as a broker between the Dutch and local Mahican residents affected by the sale of land. As a result, his name appears on many land records from the mid-seventeenth century (Starna 2013:16).

Around 1650 Itamonet, Ahemhameth, and Kishocama appear to have occupied or used Quamhemesicos Island for farming and hunting. Little is known of Kishocama or Itamonet, perhaps suggesting they were women. Ahemhameth, however, is named in deeds and court records concerning the land at the mouth of the Mohawk between 1665 and 1686. His brother, Machanakack, also appears to have lived on the islands of the sprouts at some point (Dunn 1994:312).

Dutch Settlement

Dutch trading in this area appears to have begun by at least 1636. Arent van Curler, an agent of the patroon, purchased land north of Fort Orange in what is today Menands, New York, by 1640. Within the next few years he also retained a local trader to stay on the property, effectively opening a trading outpost for himself on the patroon's land (Dunn 2009:23; Huey 1974). He reportedly reinvigorated the trade by introducing more and better quality merchandise (Baart 2005; Bradley 2007).

On the east side of the river, Jan Barentsen Wemp purchased a large tract of land in 1659 in the area of modern Troy (Weisse 1889:11) in an effort to increase his success in trading with Natives traveling south along the Hudson to Fort Orange. When New England speculators tried to purchase the islands in the Hudson, Albany traders moved quickly to seek legal title from their Mahican counterparts. In 1665 Aepjen, and likely his son Sauwachquanent, offered Quamhemsicos Island to Philip Pieterse Schuyler and Goosen Gerritsz van Schaick (Dunn 1994:211). This occurred during the English conquest of New Netherlands, and the arrangement was recorded in various legal instruments over the next several years. As late as 1670, Van Rensselaer's agents were challenging the patents to Schuyler and Van Schaick and had even persuaded Ahemhameth to contradict the claims of the two men, despite his participation in the earlier deed (Dunn 1994:57). These protests were largely in vain, as Schuyler and Van Schaick had already begun settlement. Further, islands in the Hudson were not clearly part of the patroonship, as the West India Company had claimed privilege over them as early as 1659 (Van Rensselaer 1935:172).

Goosen van Schaick arrived in New Netherland in 1630, as a brewer in the employ of the patroon Kiliaen van Rensselaer. He quickly assimilated, married in 1637, and never returned to his native Utrecht (O'Callaghan

1845:437; Venema 2010:17). Like many of the tenants who worked the patroon's land, Goosen's annual salary was supplemented with illicit trading for furs and goods with Native Americans drawn to Fort Orange (later Beverwijck, Williamstadt, and finally Albany). Trade with Native Americans was legally the sole prerogative of the Dutch West India Company, who built and maintained Fort Orange. Such policies, however, were unenforceable and the monopoly was dissolved by 1638. As a small consolation, the company was still given the exclusive rights to convey goods between the colony and Europe (O'Callaghan 1845:202). After the death of his first wife, Goosen married the daughter of the local magistrate and sent for other family members to join him from Utrecht, reflecting his rising prominence and growing wealth. By the time the English wrested control of the colony from the Dutch, he owned five village lots and farms north and south of Fort Orange and was starting to invest heavily in lands north of the Mohawk in the modern town of Half Moon (Venema 2010:17).

Philip Pieterse Schuyler immigrated to the Dutch outpost in 1650. As a gunstock maker, Schuyler practiced an art that was in great demand among both colonists and Native Americans in the area. Like others, however, the lucrative beaver trade captured much of his attention. Schuyler was an adept entrepreneur, and by 1656 he was appointed vice director of Fort Orange by Governor Petrus Stuyvesant. Even after the English takeover in 1664, Schuyler remained an important and well-respected civil servant.

The two men appear to have been working in concert since 1660 and were actively looking to purchase land around Fort Orange (Van Rensselaer 1935:237–238). After working for several years to confirm his and Van Schaick's patent in the Half Moon, Schuyler purchased the old Van Curler lot in 1672 (Bradley 2007:102–103; Grumet 1995:170; Van Rensselaer 1935:7), in a strategic location (known as the Flatts) to manage his growing land holdings in both Albany and Half Moon. His sons Pieter, Johannes, and Arent likely aided him in his daily trading efforts. Schuyler eventually sold his interest in Quamhemesicos back to Van Schaick, at about the time he purchased the Flatts. Van Schaick passed away in 1676, and his holdings transferred to his wife Annetje Lievns (Van Laer 1928:72–73). Shortly afterward, she sold the island to her son Anthony (Pearson and Van Laer 1916:108, 165–166). He may have already developed his own farm and trading outpost on the island by this time, with the recorded land transfer formalizing a long-established family arrangement.

In summary, by the time of the Dutch arrived, several Mahican families were living on and around Quamhemesicos Island. Philip Schuyler and

Goosen van Schaick, along with the patroon and his agents, aggressively courted Mahican residents to purchase the islands and lands near the falls. Through establishing a trading outpost on the island, Van Schaick, Schuyler, and their agents entered into complex social negotiations built on long-term relationships. After working and trading closely with Itamonet, Ahemhameth, Kishocama, and Schiwias (among others), Schuyler and Van Schaick formalized an understanding of community building with the land patent. The Mahicans likely viewed the agreement as part of ongoing social contract, while the Europeans thought the deed transfer would lead to exclusive (and permanent) land use on the island. Both were also keenly aware that the deed also entailed formalizing a trading partnership that each expected and hoped to endure.

ARCHAEOLOGICAL INVESTIGATION

In April 2012 Hartgen Archeological Associates, Inc. undertook an archaeological study of a 1.4-acre parcel near the circa-1740s Van Schaick Mansion. The potential for deeply buried archaeological deposits was considered high as the island is prone to flooding and has been filled with river dredge over the years. A testing program based on the excavation of backhoe trenches was considered the most effective method and was used to identify archaeological remains.

Starting at the southern edge of the parcel, nine trenches were excavated. It was soon recognized that the original ground surface was intact below the historic fill. The fill used to flatten and broaden the shoreline had also preserved the integrity of the original ground surface and the potential for intact archaeological sites. After trench 1, the rest of the trenches were excavated by removing the fill to the depth of the original ground surface, then sampling it with hand-excavated tests where possible. Backhoe excavations then continued to search for deeper deposits. The original ground surface was encountered at various depths ranging from 55 to 105 cm (21 to 41 in) below existing grade.

The site was discovered in the northeast corner of the parcel in trenches 3, 7, and 9, and what was found in trench 3 alluded to its significance. This trench identified two features, ±4 m (13 ft) apart, that included a Native American hearth/roasting pit and the southwest corner of a European-style palisade. Stratigraphically, both features occurred in the subsoil below the original ground surface and in the east wall of trench 3. The absence of the

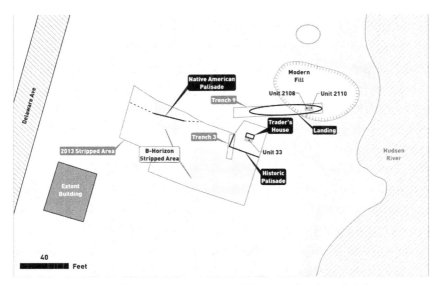

Figure 4.1. Overview of the recent excavations of the Van Schaick trader's house, historic palisade, and presumed Native American palisade on Van Schaick Island, Cohoes, New York.

palisade feature in the west wall of the backhoe trench suggested that the trench revealed its southeast corner.

The historic fill was subsequently removed to the depth of the original ground surface over a ±617 m² (6,644 ft²) area surrounding the trench. This was followed by the hand-excavation of tests at 2.5 and 5 m (8 and 16 ft) intervals. Two discrete distribution patterns around the archaeological features could be discerned from the tests. The first included a cluster of historic artifacts immediately north of the palisade feature, likely indicating the interior of the palisade (Figure 4.1). The second concentration included Native American fire-cracked rocks and chert debitage west of the palisade. Subsequent unit excavations revealed evidence of additional structures that included a Dutch trader's house within the palisade and a Native American structure west of the palisade.

Palisade

This feature is the remains of a European-styled palisade wall that was made from wood posts. In profile it appeared as a ±20-cm (8-in) postmold in a back-filled trench. The palisade trench was 40 cm (15 in) wide and all

Figure 4.2. Plan view of the seventeenth-century palisade trench and the post molds. The inset at top left is preserved portion of the 1750s Albany stockade (Hartgen Archeological Associates, Inc. 2002). The diameters of the preserved timbers are the similar to the post molds of the Van Schaick Island palisade.

together extended 85 cm (2.9 ft) below the original ground surface. The base of the palisade wall was set about 3 ft below the historic grade. In plan, about 1.6 m (5.2 ft) of the south wall was exposed, revealing 5 to 6 post-molds side by side, 20 to 25 cm (8 to 9.8 in) in diameter. The archaeological plan view and profile suggest that the palisade wall was constructed with large vertical wooden posts set into a .9-m (3-ft) deep trench with a plank board at the bottom (Figure 4.2).

TRADER'S HOUSE

Dutch-style red and yellow bricks recovered on the north (interior) side of the palisade suggests the presence of a structure. Excavation uncovered the southwest corner of a cellar hole filled with red and yellow Dutch brick. The bricks were similar in size, composition, and appearance to those excavated at the patroon's brickyard just outside of Beverwijck in the mid-1600s (Hartgen Archeological Associates, Inc. 2005). The feature is likely the collapsed remains of a wall and/or chimney of a seventeenth-century

Dutch-styled structure. Brick samples, pantile, nails, window glass, and a number of domestic artifacts were recovered; however, excavation did not extend below the brick demolition layer. Elements of the foundation, footings, and perhaps a wood-lined cellar and occupation-related deposits are likely sealed below this layer.

As a whole the artifact assemblage (discussed in more detail below) and the archaeological features suggest that this site contains the buried remains of a seventeenth-century trading outpost. Archaeological evidence suggests that it was situated on the eastern side of the island, above the original Hudson River shoreline for about 70 years, from the 1650s until the first quarter of the 1700s. As such, it appears to predate the Schuyler and Van Schaick patents and indicates the partners established themselves on the island well before they applied for purchase.

NATIVE AMERICAN STRUCTURE

Evidence of a second structure, believed to be Native American, was found immediately west of the Dutch trade outpost. Excavation exposed about 6.6 m (21 ft) linear feet of a feature that appeared to the base of a wall. In the subsoil below the original ground surface this feature appeared as a shallow trench, 20 to 35 cm (8 to 14 in) wide, with postmolds on alternating sides (Figure 4.3). Its shape suggested a wall that was constructed with logs laid horizontally, the first course laid below grade, and the upper portions held in place with vertical posts (likely smaller saplings) staggered on opposite sides every 0.57 to 1 m (2.1 to 3.2 ft).

A 1-m (3.2-ft) section of the trench feature and one postmold were excavated, yielding fire-cracked rock, chert debitage, and a chert knife, supporting the interpretation that this structure is Native American.

Exact dating of the structures is not possible at this point, and the precise relationship between the two sets of features is speculative. However, since the European features and Native American features do not overlap, it suggests they may have been contemporaneous or near contemporaneous, with the Dutch building in an area previously cleared but no longer inhabited by Natives.

If, as we have hypothesized, the feature west of the Dutch trading outpost is a Native American palisade, it would be an important archaeological find (Starna 2013:40–41). The Mahicans are thought to have "fortified" their settlements in the early to mid-seventeenth century, but to date no clear archaeological evidence of such features have been found (e.g. Largy et

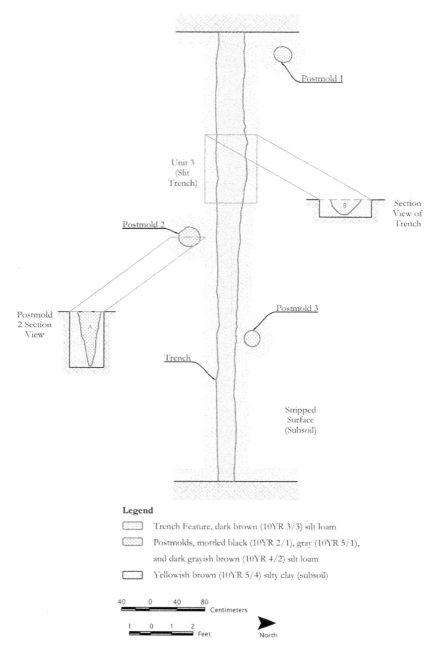

Figure 4.3. Plan of the 6.6-m (21-ft) section of a feature that is the remains of a Native American structure. The feature is composed of narrow trench with alternating postmolds. This is possibly the imprint left by a wall constructed with saplings laid horizontally and held in place with vertical saplings as posts.

al. 1999:69–70). As mentioned, early mapping of the area appears to show several nearby "fortified" Mahican settlements, but none were found on this island.

LANDING

The landing represents the area east of the palisade and trader's house, where the original landform slopes toward the Hudson River. A trench excavated away from the archaeological features, toward the river, revealed the slope of original ground surface. Starting at the original ground surface (0.60 m [2 ft] below surface), the trench revealed that the historic surface dipped sharply and at its deepest point was more than 2.6 m (8.5 ft) below the existing surface. A single unit excavated on the landing produced some of the most important artifacts recovered from this site.

This landscape feature was likely a key element in the early development of the site. It would have allowed easy access to the river. Yet this location was also high enough above typical flood waters to remain dry most of the year.

Today the water level of the Hudson is higher at this location than it was in the 1600s and 1700s, due to the Troy Dam, built in the early 1900s about a mile down river from Van Schaick Island. The artificial height of the river was likely the reason the low spot along the shoreline and the rest of the parcel was filled up and leveled out. This action not only raised the height of the land for flood prevention; it sealed and preserved an important archaeological site.

ARTIFACTS

A review of the artifact assemblage, which includes a significant number of trade goods, suggests that the trading outpost was active between the 1650s and early 1700s. We highlight some of the earlier and more interesting items from the collection. This includes a lead cloth seal dated 1662, Dutch tobacco pipes, a Native tobacco pipe, red trade bead, and wampum fragment, as well as sherds of Westerwald with an Amsterdam coat of arms and parts of a Dutch grapen (earthenware cooking pot).

Lead Cloth Seal

The lower portion of a lead cloth seal was found along the landing area. It appears to have been intentionally halved, perhaps to increase its potential

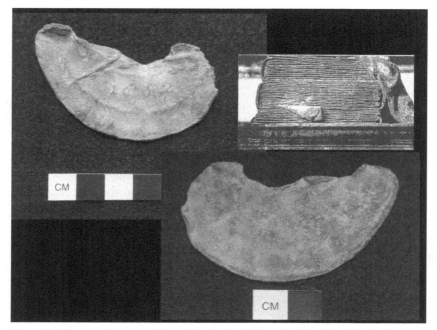

Figure 4.4. Front and reverse sides of the cloth seal from the Van Schaick Island site, along with an illustration (*top right*) of how the seal was likely affixed to a shipment of wool duffels (Baart 2005).

trade value. The impressed design features a coat of arms and two standing lions. Our interpretation is that the seal represents the Amsterdam coat of arms with the date 1662. There is no discernable stamp on the reverse side, but there do seem to be fabric impressions (Figure 4.4).

As early as the thirteenth century, lead disks impressed with a seal were commonly used to mark goods of all kinds, especially textiles, as proof that the item met the standard set by the guild or manufacturer that controlled the material. They were a reliable guarantee of quality and authenticity. They were also used to show that tax or custom duties had been paid. These are extensively recovered from post-medieval sites in northern Europe (Egan 1985). Cloth, being one of the most valuable and highly regulated and controlled materials in the seventeenth century was often so labeled with two to four disks joined by a wire attached to cloth, often a different stamp was used on each side of the seal (Endrei and Egan 1982).

Duffel, a coarse wool cloth, was produced in large quantities in the seventeenth century. Leiden was the primary center of production, with much of this material shipped through Amsterdam. Bolts could be sealed with the manufacturer's or, if let out on credit, a seller's seal. In the beaver trade, even the lead bale seal itself had some value and were often separated from the bundle.

As might be expected, Schuyler and Van Schaick appear to have carefully cultivated long-distance business relationships. Philip Schuyler was back in the Netherlands as early as 1658, apparently coordinating with suppliers associated with the patroon's family (Van Rensselaer 1935:319). In 1664 Goosen traveled to the Netherlands to obtain trade goods for his ventures in and around the Half Moon (Van Laer 1928:72). The Van Schaicks continued to visit potential homeland suppliers until at least 1678, well after English takeover of the colony (Van Rensselaer 1935:24).

On seventeenth-century Iroquois sites, lead cloth seals predominately originate in Kampen in Overijssel, with fewer originating from Leiden, and even fewer from Amsterdam. There is some suggestion that since the Amsterdam dyeing process was regarded as superior and thus was more expensive, Amsterdam cloth was less likely to be used in trade (Baart 2005:86). The seal is the most powerful evidence of trade activity on Van Schaick Island before a patent for the land had been issued.

Dutch and Native Tobacco Pipes

More than 35 tobacco pipe fragments from the seventeenth century were recovered from the trader's house and landing area. The majority were stems with bores between 6/64 to 8/64 in. Among the finds were several bowl fragments with markings: "EB," "ID," and a chalice stamp. The forms included both the bulbous variety and funnel-shaped variety. In general, the bulbous form of Dutch pipes was produced before the 1650 and funnel or elbow-shaped forms more typical after 1650 (Bradley 2007:119).

In 1658 Jeremias van Rensselaer noted the discerning nature of Native traders, who were seeking both the bulbous and funnel-shaped forms at the time and were not content to choose a single type (Huey 1988:456). These forms support the idea that the trading outpost was established in the 1650s.

The heel marks of "EB" for Edward Bird (Huey 1988a:455) with a funnel shape were common on the nearby Schuyler Flatts site (Bradley 2007:170). Similarly, 12 pipes with the "ID" heel mark of John Draper were found at that site. Finally, the chalice mark has been associated with pipe markers in Gouda, who started production of this type as early as the 1660s. But in the context of New Netherland, they typically date to the last quarter of the

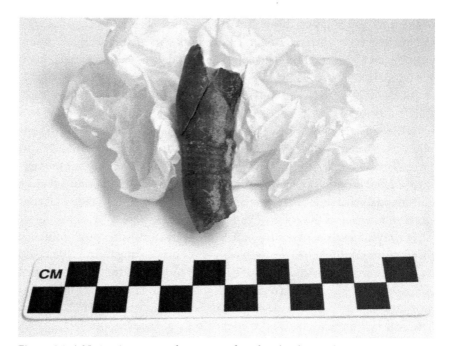

Figure 4.5. A Native American tobacco pipe, found with other trade items at the land-ing portion of the site. The pipe features aspects of both bulbous and funnel-shaped forms and suggest the dynamic and fluid nature of Native pipe forms in the mid-seven-teenth century.

seventeenth century and have been found on Iroquois sites that fall within the 1674 to 1683 date range (Bradley 2007:186).

There is some speculation that Edward Bird derived the funnel-shaped variety from Native forms that were brought to him in 1648 by Arent van Curler. This hypothesis is partially supported by the recovery of a Native American tobacco pipe that appears to include forms of both bulbous and funnel-shaped Dutch pipes (Figure. 4.5). This pipe fragment was found among the other trade items at the landing. The pipe featured a bore of 14/64 in and was smoothed, except for six rings between the stem and bowl. Additional rings appear to have been impressed along the rim of the bowl, although only a small section was recovered. The pipe's form is very different from trumpet-style Iroquoian pipes and suggests stylistic influences from Dutch imports. Or conversely, Dutch traders such as Van Curler, Schuyler, Van Schaick, and others took Native forms back to the Netherlands and thus influenced pipes produced there for the fur trade.

Regardless, the pipe fragments further support that trading had begun at

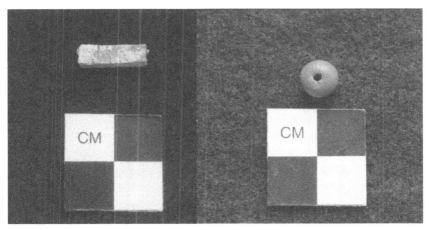

Figure 4.6. *Left:* fragment of a clipped clam, a rejected part of the wampum-making process. This indicates that Dutch traders had started to make their own wampum by about 1650. *Right:* a round red trade bead (IIA1) found in the Native American deposits on the west part of the site, these have been dated from about 1675 to 1690.

the site by the mid-1650s and continued on into the 1680s, when Anthony van Schaick became the sole resident of the island.

Trade Bead and Shell

A singe trade bead was found associated with the Native American features on the western portion of the site (Figure. 4.6). The round red bead did not feature a green core (Kidd IIA1) as some other common varieties from the seventeenth century do. Quantities of trade beads have been found on many seventeenth-century Iroquois sites. As a result, a fairly reliable chronology based on bead typologies has been generated for the period. Bradley (2007) has suggested that the red bead was most common in the beaver trade between about 1675 and 1690.

A "clipped" clam shell fragment, an unfinished wampum bead, cut to size, roughly shaped, and partially drilled was also part of the assemblage at the landing area. However, it is unknown of this object is the result of Native or European effort (Figure 4.6).

Coastal Native groups appear to have made wampum from quahog shell as late as the 1650s. A period source notes, "It is also traded in quantity, often by the thousands, because it is made in the coastal districts only and is mostly drawn for spending in the parts where the pelts come from" (Van der Donck, in Gehring and Starna 2008:95). Wampum produced by Dutch makers begins to be found from 1650, and such fragments are common on later seventeenth-century sites and occur into the eighteenth century in Albany (Bradley 2007:76, 121; Pena 1990). At Van Schaick Island, there was at least an initial effort at wampum-making reflected in the oldest deposits at the site that dates to the 1650s.

Ceramics

Hundreds of the ceramic vessel sherds were recovered. The traders who lived at the site certainly used the ceramics for cooking and eating; however, there were also fragments of vessels that were likely trade goods. Three types of ceramics are highlighted here: Dutch yellowware, Pipkins, and Westerwald stonewares with medallions and prunts (Figures 4.7 and 4.8).

Eight sherds of Dutch yellowware were recovered, likely from at least three different vessels. The fragments are likely from a three-legged pot made for open-fire cooking, and called variously a *kookpotten, grapen,* or a *pipkin* (Janowitz and Schaefer herein; Schaefer 1994:77–78). The sherds found at Van Schaick Island were lead glazed only on the interior, the glazing helping to make the pots water-tight. The burned leg bottoms suggest that the pots were used at the site and suggest that the Van Schaicks or their agents occupied the trading outpost at least semipermanently.

Several varies of stoneware were recovered, including a sherds of Rhenish Bellermines and two styles of gray Westerwald tankards. Altogether the fragments suggest there were three to four vessels present. One style of Westerwald was decorated in blue with raised prunt-like medallions all over the exterior of the body; similar to examples recovered at Fort Orange and from the fort well at Martins Hundred (Huey 1988:365; Noël Hume 1988:170). The other style of Westerwald tankard had a molded medallion of the Amsterdam coat of arms on the body. One of the larger fragments recovered has three vertical "X"s down the center of the shield, flanked by two lions. Another smaller fragment is the edge of the same medallion, with the number 30, likely part of the date 1630 as found on examples recovered at Fort Orange and multiple Native sites throughout the Northeast (Huey 1988a:365). A nearly intact example of this vessel type was recovered from the Lipe Site, a seventeenth-century Mohawk Village (c. 1670s to 1690s) in Palatine New York (Bradley 2007). It is believed that this particular Westerwald tankard, with the relief-molded medallion of the Amsterdam coat of arms, was a popular trade item (personal communication, Joe McEvoy 2014).

Figure 4.7. *Left*: two fragments of the medallion from two separate Westerwald vessels recovered from the Van Schaick Island site. *Right*: a whole example that was recovered from the excavation of a Mohawk Village (c. 1670s to 1690s) known as the Lipe Site in Palatine, New York (Bradley 2007).

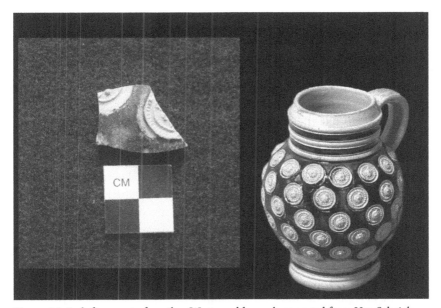

Figure 4.8. *Left*: fragment of another Westerwald vessel recovered from Van Schaick Island that likely had a prunt motif (c. 1680s) similar to the example displayed at right.

SUMMARY AND CONCLUSIONS

The archaeology at Quamhemsicos or Van Schaick Island suggests that the Mahicans occupied the island from about the mid-1600s to perhaps as late as the 1670s. At the same time, Philip Schuyler and Goosen van Schaick may have started a trading outpost on the northeast side of the island along a natural landing in the relatively calm waters of the Hudson River. The historical record indicates that the Dutch partners did not seek formal title to the island and surrounding mainland, just north of the patroonship, until 1664. At this time, just before the English takeover, the Mahicans reported that English traders from Connecticut had approach them to purchase the land. While this seems unlikely, the Mahicans recognized the potential value of the island for the Dutch and their need for the continued use of the island. As a result, they likely sought to initiate the long social and ceremonial process of patent negotiations. Both the Dutch buyers and Native "sellers" had likely hoped to solidify their trading relationships with each other.

Regardless of the participants' intent, the unsettled political future of New Netherland under the English meant that formalizing the patent was not quickly accomplished. In the meanwhile, it appears the Mahican and Dutch continued their interactions on the island. After Schuyler purchased the valuable nearby Flatts farm, he sold his share of Quamhemsicos Island back to Goosen van Schaick, and his son came to own the island by 1681, when it appears he also constructed a farmstead in addition to the trading outpost. Later site deposits, not described here, suggest that trading activities continued at the landing portion of the island until at least the first quarter of the eighteenth century.

We believe that the foregoing provide three important insights into Dutch-Mahican relationships in the mid-seventeenth century. First, land transfers were results of relationships built on cohabitation and close economic ties. Thus, such transfers were not transactional in the sense of modern exchanges but long-term investments that widened social networks and strengthened interpersonal ties. Second, successful Dutch trade networks in the New World were intimately tied to patria and were shaped by the desires and demands of Native trade partners. As a result, recovered cultural materials were carefully chosen for trade to Native traders, who themselves were sophisticated traders. Despite English control after 1664, many local traders retained cultural and economic ties to the Netherlands (Fisher 2006). Third, these relationships appear to have broken down by the 1680s. Disease and increasing European presence (Bradley 2007:86) and a disastrous conflict with the Mohawks (Brasser 1978:204) forced the remaining resident Mahicans to move from the Fort Orange/Albany area. Many removed to the area of an early "reservation" in Schaghticoke established by English governor Edmund Andros in 1676 (Dunn 1994:111).

The historical record also supports this final thesis, as by 1680 Anthony van Schaick was likely the sole resident on the island, and he had by this time broadened his economic pursuits to including farming and leasing land to other European settlers in addition to trade. He would eventually build a wooden house on the southern part of the island (Masten 1877:24), and his descendants would build the brick and gambrel-roofed Van Schaick Mansion sometime between 1735 and 1755.

At the twilight of Dutch New Netherland, European settlers were still building and sustaining relationships with Native residents. Although the excavations on the island have been limited at this point, they suggest that a large deposit of artifacts related to the fur trade, evidence of a Native structure and perhaps fortification, and trading outpost are present. Any one of these alone would be important archaeological find; together they form a unique resource that is likely to shed new light on the Mahican-Dutch relations in the seventeenth century in northern New Netherland and later colonial New York.

5

A Mid-Seventeenth-Century Drinking House in New Netherland

MICHAEL T. LUCAS AND KRISTINA S. TRAUDT

Public drinking houses, variously termed inns, public houses, taverns, ordinaries, or alehouses, have been a compelling subject of study for both historians and archaeologists interested in the social and economic dimensions of everyday life from the seventeenth through nineteenth centuries (e.g. Baum 1973a, 1973b; Bragdon 1988; Cheever 2015; Chenoweth 2006; Cofield 2009; Cofield and Holly-Robbins 2009; Coleman et al. 1990; Conroy 1991, 1995; King 1988; Li 1992; Lucas 2016; McDaid 2013; Meacham 2009; Rice 1983; Rockman and Rothschild 1984; Salinger 2002; Thompson 1999; Wholey 2006; Victor 2019). These lively social and entertainment spaces incorporated a variety of breakable material culture that is stable in the archaeological record. Yet historical archaeologists have at times struggled to make sense of a material record that often shares many similarities with domestic assemblages (e.g., Cofield 2009; Cofield and Holly-Robbins 2009; Coleman et. al. 1990; Lucas 2016). It was common for drinking establishments to also house the keeper and members of his or her family, as well as servants and enslaved people, further complicating the analysis of such assemblages.

This chapter considers the regional context for drinking houses in New Netherland during the 1650s by combining archaeological and historical data associated with the 1624 Dutch WIC outpost of Fort Orange, in present downtown Albany, New York. Excavations at the site of Fort Orange were completed under the direction of Paul Huey (1988a) in 1970 and 1971 ahead of the construction of I-787. The excavations identified several structures within the fort, the fort's south curtain wall, and a cobble-lined moat surrounding the fort. More than 20,000 artifacts dating to the Dutch occupation were recovered. A layer of domestic refuse dating to the early 1650s was discovered within the portion of the moat south of the curtain wall. While it is possible that this debris originated from within the fort, it is most likely associated with a structure that stood outside and south of the fort. Specifically, based on the large quantity of vessel glass, Huey (1988a) speculated that the assemblage was related to one of the drinking houses that stood in that location.

The assemblage was recovered from bluish clay sediments (Stratum 77) within the moat, that most likely formed between the time the cobblestones were laid following the 1648 flood, and 1663 (Huey 1988a:332–333). The potential for quantitative comparative analyses with other sites is limited due to the extreme level of fragmentation and small size of the assemblage (n = 500), but a better contextual understanding of the materials results from the use of primary historical documentation. The following analysis builds on Huey's initial archaeological findings and Janny Venema's (2003) more recent historical research on drinking houses near Fort Orange, to suggest a more specific attribution of the Stratum 77 artifact assemblage. We argue that the collection is a keen representation of a moment in time and space, of a particular Dutch experience on the New Netherland frontier during the mid-seventeenth century.

We proceed by considering the broader context of drinking houses in Dutch culture and the nature of drinking houses on the New Netherland frontier. We then review the history of Dutch development of the Fort Orange area and Rensselaerwijck to set the stage. We detour to review Dutch sources documenting the material culture of drinking before focusing our analysis on the Stratum 77 artifact assemblage.

DUTCH DRINKING HOUSES AND THE NEW NETHERLAND FRONTIER

When Dutch and English colonists arrived in the New World, one of the first institutions they established were public drinking houses. From initial settlement through the eighteenth century, drinking houses were the most numerous public intuitions in the colonies (Conroy 1995:2). In this, at least, the Dutch followed a pattern established at home; in 1613 Amsterdam boasted over 500 licensed alehouses, approximately 1 for every 200 people in the city (Salinger 2002:10).

While the Dutch Reformed Church, true to its Calvinist origins, condemned alcohol and tobacco as "devil's food," it did not go so far as to stigmatize their consumption as morally unclean. Their use was accepted as part of embedded culture (Salinger 2002:11). Smoking and drinking combined to loosen social inhibitions and break down class or other barriers (Kross 1997:43). These were liminal spaces where norms of otherwise expected behavior were relaxed through the effects of intoxicants (Cheever 2015:31).

Drinking houses were common in late medieval Europe, with many functional differences evolving through time. Drinking houses varied considerably and the profile of patrons depended on a range of variables including regional customs, location, type of establishment and season (Kümin 2002:62). European drinking houses generally ranged from inns that catered to the traveling public, offering sleeping accommodations and meals, to specialized facilities that served wine exclusively, to the alehouse or tippling house that served alcohol with few restrictions (Clark 1983; Everitt 1973:100–101; Jennings 2007:20; Pennington 2002:117).

In 1637 Director Willem Kieft estimated that a quarter of the houses in New Amsterdam served as beer and tobacco dispensaries (Baum 1973a:10). A decade later, Petrus Stuyvesant claimed there was roughly 1 "dramshop" for every 28 citizens of New Amsterdam, and by 1663 that figure was estimated to be 1 for every 90 citizens (Baum 1973a:10; Salinger 2002:185).

During the sixteenth and seventeenth centuries, officials in the Netherlands characterized rural inns as places where drunkenness, fighting, and a range of vices were rampant (Unger 2001:185–186). Public drinking houses were recognized as a socially necessary evil and as such were one of the most extensively regulated institutions throughout the colonies. Price gouging, drunkenness, fighting, gaming, and drinking on the Sabbath were viewed as problems requiring regulation (Rice 1983:25–28; Salinger 2002:83–120). Stuyvesant codified the requirements for keeping an alehouse, tavern, or tippling place in New Netherland in 1648 (Gehring 1991:14–16; Van Laer 1974:497–500). These regulations established licensing, defined building requirements, set hours of operation, and prohibited the sale of alcohol to Native Americans. Yet even these rules never attempted to limit the number of drinking houses, and without a mechanism for enforcement, the number of taverns and tippling houses continued to increase unabated (Salinger 2002:194–196).

A robust brewing industry and the ability to ship hops-stabled beer, aided in the expansion of the Dutch economy during the sixteenth and seventeenth centuries (Meussdoerffer 2009:20). The long history of brewing and its emergence as an important commodity ensured that beer was the most common libation served at drinking houses in New Netherland. In fact, beer was drunk by all family members at every meal, with distilled liquors more commonly reserved for medicinal purposes and wine prohibitively costly (Venema 2003:293–294). Smoking was equally common. One mid-seventeenth-century traveler declared that the inhabitants of New Netherland "all drink here, from the moment they are able to lick a spoon. The women of the neighborhood entertain each other with a pipe and a brazier; young and old, they all smoke" (Van Laer 1920:102). Drinking houses merely extended the consumption of alcohol and tobacco to the public sphere.

Drinking houses in New Netherland sometimes doubled as, or were otherwise associated with, a brewery. Jasper Danckaerts (1913) commented on the close relationship between brewhouse and tavern during his travels through New York in 1679. Danckaerts found himself coaxed into visiting a "delightful" tavern in the city where he "would be able to taste the beer of New Netherland, in as much as it was also a brewery." On arriving at the tavern, Danckaerts (1913:47) remarked on his displeasure, saying, "it was resorted to on Sundays by all sorts of revellers, and was a low pot-house." Danckaerts's last comment echoes Kieft's and Stuyvesant's earlier concerns about the great number of drinking houses offering minimal services. While catering to travelers as well as local clientele, drinking houses along the Hudson River valley often did not offer lodging, though most establishments served as the keeper's dwelling (Baum 1973a:9; Kross 1997:31).

Excessive drinking was one problem Stuyvesant attempted to address through legislation. He was careful to make a distinction between what he considered to be upstanding houses and less reputable ones. He publicly stated that "decent taverns established and licensed for the use and accommodations of travelers, strangers and inhabitants which honorably and honestly pay their taxes and excise and own or lease suitable houses, sitting under heavier expenses, are seriously injured in their licensed and lawful business by these clandestine groggeries" (Van Laer 1974:497).

At least 12 drinking houses operated legally in New Amsterdam in 1648 (Van Laer 1974:500). Certainly, many more "groggeries" and rudimentary beer and tobacco dispensaries existed without official notice, especially in more remote areas of the colony. Venema (2003:447) identified no fewer than 26 individuals who at some point between 1652 to 1664 plied the trade in the vicinity of Fort Orange. By 1657 there were as many as nine separate drinking houses operating in and around Beverwijck (Venema 2003:303).

Women operated many, if not all, of these establishments, similar to the pattern observed in the Chesapeake colonies (Lucas 2016:95–96; Meacham 2009:70–74; Venema 2003:313–314).

Venema (2003) also identified the locations of 14 drinking houses operating before 1664 (Figure 5.1). Location seems to have been dependent on the distance to four primary features: Fort Orange, Beverwjick, the main north-south road (now Broadway) near the bank of the Hudson, and one of the breweries. Drinking houses were not situated adjacent to each other but were distributed along the length of the road, with a wider gap between the boundary of Fort Orange and Beverwjick. Eight of the drinking houses were either near the entrance or within the village of Beverwjick. Locating near Fort Orange was also advantageous, and four drinking houses were located at or very near the trading post. Finally, at least four of the drinking houses were located directly adjacent to one of the breweries that supplied wholesale beer.

That drinking houses were located along the main road, is not surprising. The community that would become Beverwjick, formed as a peripatetic landscape along the north-south running road before the village was laid out, and later enclosed in a palisade. Drinking houses were merely waypoints following this linear movement, rather than destinations per se.

SETTING THE STAGE: THE DUTCH WEST INDIA COMPANY AND RENSSELAERSWIJCK

Henry Hudson's voyage up the Hudson River occurred at the beginning of the Dutch "Golden Age," the Netherlands' emergence as the dominant mercantile force in the Atlantic world. Hudson's news of the potential beaver trade with Native groups on the upper extent of the river piqued the interest of merchants in Amsterdam. Seeking to extend their commercial interests, a group of Amsterdam merchants formed the New Netherland Company in 1613 to exploit the North River fur trade. In 1614 the company constructed a small fort called Nassau, located just south of present-day Albany. Dutch traders found the Mohawk and Mahican peoples eager to exchange furs for any number of European-made goods including glass beads, copper kettles, axes, and other available objects (Bradley 2007:35). The fort was partially destroyed by flooding in 1617, though traders continued to anchor in the location until the early 1620s (Bradley 2007:36).

The New Netherland Company was dissolved in 1618, and the WIC was formed in 1621 to fill the void and establish a solid foothold for the New

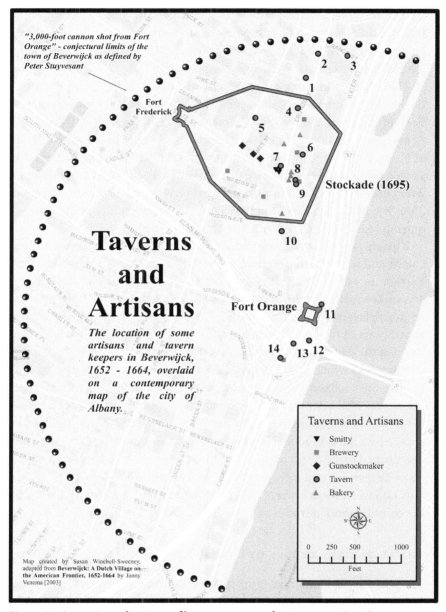

Figure 5.1. Approximate locations of known taverns and artisans near Fort Orange.
1) Ulderick Cleyn, 2) Maria Goosen, 3) Jurriaen Teunisz, 4) unknown, 5) Marcelis Janz,
6) Pieter Bronck, 7) unknown, 8) unknown, 9) Hendrick Jochimsz and Maria Dijckmans, 10) William Frederickz Bout, 11) Hendrick Jochimsz and Maria Dijckmans,
12) Gysbert Cornelis then Maria Jansz (de Vrouw Maria), 13) Adriaen Jansen van Leyden, 14) Steven and Maria Jansz.

Netherland colony. Fort Orange was constructed in 1624 just north of the ruined Fort Nassau as the first permanent Dutch settlement on the upper Hudson River. The WIC enjoyed a legally mandated trade monopoly along the Hudson River until it was dissolved in 1639.

The area around Fort Orange grew slowly during the 1620s, with few settlers willing to establish roots beyond the security of New Amsterdam. Settlement increased during the 1630s with the establishment of Kiliaen van Rensselaer's patroonship of Rensselaerswijck. As part of the 1629 Charter of Freedoms and Exemptions, patroonships, similar to feudal manors that existed in the Netherlands, were granted with perpetual title to lands along with control over the administration and jurisdiction of tenants (Venema 2010:242–243). Van Rensselaer seized on the opportunity and began acquiring Mahican lands around Fort Orange in 1630.

Kiliaen van Rensselaer envisioned Rensselaerswijck as an agricultural colony and sought fertile lands along both banks of the Hudson River with Fort Orange at its center (Folkerts 1991; Venema 2010:246). The patroon was successful in recruiting settlers, and by 1651 more than 200 people lived in Rensselaerswijck (Venema 2010:257). Though Kiliaen and successive generations of the Van Rensselaer family administered Rensselaerswijck, they left the daily operations of the colony to agents.

Rensselaerswijck was well established and the population around Fort Orange was increasing by the time Petrus Stuyvesant was appointed director of New Netherland in 1647. Soon after his appointment, Stuyvesant set his sights on stabilizing trade around Fort Orange and repairing damage caused by a flood in 1648. He found a small community, or *bijeenwoninge*, had formed to the north of the fort. In 1652 Stuyvesant renamed this settlement Beverwijck and incorporated it under the jurisdiction of the WIC at Fort Orange. Tavern keepers took advantage of the opportunity offered by the consolidation of trades and dwellings clustered in Beverwijck.

THE MATERIAL CULTURE OF DUTCH DRINKING HOUSES

Much of the substantial literature on colonial drinking houses is weighted heavily toward the English colonies and the eighteenth century. What archaeologists expect to find at drinking houses is thus biased. Archaeologists should expect significantly different material culture on seventeenth-century sites in New Netherland as compared to English colonies in North America.

The best historical evidence for the material culture of drinking houses comes from estate inventories, ledgers, store accounts, court records, and period paintings. Detailed inventories showing the contents of drinking houses are ideal, if they exist. Yet, even detailed inventories remain problematic. Namely, the few accounts that do exist, often do not exclusively represent the contents of the decedents' drinking house. Keeping a tavern was often a secondary occupation, and the whole of an estate inventory might represent elements of many separate pursuits (Bielinski 1991:127–128). Also, keeping a drinking house in New Netherland, as in the Chesapeake, was not a lifelong pursuit, and might be pursued for only a few years (Lucas 2016; Venema 2003). If an individual abandoned the business many years before their death, then the estate inventory would likely not include material culture used in the drinking house. Tavern ledgers, store accounts, and court records showing the purchases made by keepers are excellent sources, but they are also rare.

The most abundant source of information on the material culture of drinking houses comes from seventeenth-century Dutch and Flemish genre paintings. Thousands of paintings were produced during the seventeenth century depicting domestic activities in the Netherlands. The public drinking house was a central theme for many artists during the period. The material culture and activities depicted in a sample of 42 seventeenth-century Dutch and Flemish paintings were tabulated as a baseline of the types of objects that were used in taverns and might be found in the archaeological record.

Thirty-six individual types of material culture were tabulated according to their presence or absence in the painting rather than by volume (Table 5.1). Only those forms related to food, drink, and entertainment were recorded, including furniture. Forms of material culture associated with personal adornment and architecture were thus excluded. Of the 36 forms present, 19 (53%) would have a fair chance of making it into the archaeological record due to breakage or loss. Together, the eight most common object types can be classified as related to smoking (pipes and braziers), drinking (glass tableware and stoneware jugs, bottles, and tankards), and food preparation (earthen pots and three-legged vessels). Much of the same material culture would likely be found in a home as well, but what is less commonly included may be most instructive.

Fragments of earthen dishes, tin-glazed plates, ewers, drinking pots, and colanders would be considered uncommon in a tavern assemblage based on their occurrence in genre paintings. The general absence of tin-glazed plates and other table vessels suggests very little food, other than oysters,

Table 5.1. Material culture represented in seventeenth-century Dutch tavern paintings

Material Culture	Percent of Paintings Included
Tobacco Pipe	93
Chair	79
Stoneware Jug	69
Bench	69
Table	62
Earthen Brazier	52
Table Glass	50
Stoneware Bottle	40
Tobacco Paper	36
Stoneware Tankard	33
Earthen Pot/Unid	33
Barrel	26
Barrel Chair	26
Earthen Trilegged Pot	24
Fiddle	21
Cards	21
Barrel Table	19
Knife	17
Earthen Pitcher	14
Glass Bottle	12
Chamber Pot	12
Brass Kettle	12
Pewter Tankard	10
Trictrac Game	7
Earthen Dish	7
Barrel for Decanting	7
Tin-Glazed Plate	5
Earthen or Stoneware Ewer	5
Pewter Plate	5
Spoon	5
Small Trilegged Table	5
Earthen Drinking Pot	2
Colander	2
Wooden Tankard	2
Metal pot unknown	2
Pewter Ewer	2

Source: Data was compiled from a sample of 42 Dutch tavern paintings dating from ca. 1620 to ca. 1704. Percentages represent presence of the form.

was consumed in the tavern. The material culture of gaming is also represented in trictrac boards (7%), playing cards (21%), and fiddles (21%). Only trictrac, a variation of backgammon, would have produced material remains likely to survive in the archaeological record. Many New Netherland archaeological sites have produced handmade ceramic disks that were likely substitutes for lost trictrac pieces.

Dutch drinking houses are generally represented as places to drink, smoke, play games or gamble, and occasionally fight. This depiction coincides with what is known about drinking houses in New Netherland from the historical record (Venema 2003). The paintings suggest that fragments of stoneware vessels, drinking glasses, pipe stems, and earthenware braziers should be recovered in volume from drinking house sites, and the opposite should be true of bowls, plates, and serving vessels.

A Moment in Time: The Material Culture of the Cornelisz and de Vrouw Maria House

At least three drinking houses were established south of Fort Orange between 1647 and 1654. The first of these was operated by Gysbert Cornelisz, who was named as a tavern keeper in court documents by 1648 (Van Laer 1922:48). A garden owned by Carsten Carstensen appears to be the only piece of ground separating the Cornelisz house and the southern gate of the fort, and Cornelisz was granted permission to use the garden in December of 1650 (Van Laer 1922:140,157–158). Business transactions, such as land sales, were regularly conducted at the Cornelisz drinking house, and public notices were posted at the house (Van Laer 1922:102, 106, 200). Gysbert and his wife, Lysbeth, operated their drinking house until Gysbert's death in 1653.

Another drinking house was operated by Maria Goosen on land owned by her husband, Steven Jansz, located south of the Cornelisz drinking house (Venema 2003:302). This drinking house was named de Vrouw Maria, meaning "The Woman Maria" (Gehring 1989:176). It is possible that Maria operated this business under Goosen Gerritsz's 1650 tapping grant. Maria appears to have been related to Gerritsz in some way (Venema 2003:302, 417n222). Steven Jansz was listed as a carpenter in historical documents and unlike Gysbert Cornelisz was never referred to as a tavern or inn keeper, though he is cited in incidents involving drinking at his house. Maria was clearly in charge of the operation.

Lysbeth Cornelisz married Francois Boon shortly after Gysbert's death, and there is no evidence that they continued the drinking house business (Van Laer 1908:833). Boon sold the Cornelisz house and lot in August of 1654 to Steven Jansz (Gehring and Venema 2009:10–11). Maria Goosen and Steven Jansz may have operated the de Vrouw Maria between 1654 and 1655 out of the Cornelisz house, but Jansz attempted to sell the house in 1655 when the couple's marriage had failed, and Maria was banished from the retail trade for selling brandy to an "Indian woman" (Gehring 1989:194; Venema 2003:303). At the time, the lot contained a hog pen, garden, and cookhouse occupied by Peter "the Fleming," in addition to the drinking house (Gehring and Venema 2009:73).

In 1654 Petrus Stuyvesant granted Adriaen Jansen "Appel" van Leyden permission to operate a "public house" south of Fort Orange. Stuyvesant's instructions were very specific: Van Leyden was not to operate his establishment "as a tavern or tipling house, but as a house of entertainment for travelers" (Gehring 1980:78). Clearly Stuyvesant wanted Van Leyden to abide by newly instituted statues guiding drinking house management.

Huey (1988a:473–474) originally suggested that the Stratum 77 artifact assemblage recovered from the south moat might be associated with the Appel (Van Leyden) house, but Venema's reconstruction of the lot transfers places his drinking house south of Cornelisz. The Cornelisz house was the closest dwelling space to the southern entrance to the fort. This drinking house was likely operated by Lysbeth and Gysbert Cornelisz between 1647 and 1653 and by Maria Goosen between August 1654 and April 1655. Huey's (1988a:333) reconstruction of the sequence of historical events around Fort Orange suggests that Stratum 77 was formed sometime between 1654 and 1663. The post-1654 date for the assemblage, Maria's having ceased operating after May1655, and the lack of any evidence for someone else either buying the property or continuing the business suggests that the source of this material may be Maria Goosen's brief tenure at the house between August 1654 and May 1655.

Artifacts associated with alcohol, tobacco, and food consumption recovered from domestic and drinking house sites in Rensselaerswijck and Beverwijck—Fort Orange are summarized in Table 5.2. Stratum 77 is unique in that it has by far the highest percentage of drinking related artifacts along with the lowest percentages of smoking and food consumption artifacts. Since smoking was a primary activity at drinking houses, greater representation of tobacco pipe fragments would be expected. Comparing the assemblage with the historical data on the Jansz-Goosen drinking house provides a clearer understanding of the material culture of the establishment.

Table 5.2. Artifacts associated with eating, drinking, and smoking recovered from Dutch sites in Albany

Collection	Dates	Function	Food		Drinking		Smoking		Total
			#	%	#	%	#	%	
Van Doesburgh—Fort Orange	1649–1664	Dwelling	234	43	68	13	240	44	542
Staats–Van Twiller—Fort Orange	1648–1668	Dwelling	29	20	32	22	87	58	148
Stratum 77—Fort Orange	1654–1663	Drinking House	24	17	69	48	51	35	144
Hans Vos—Fort Orange	1657–1676	Dwelling	8	32	2	8	15	60	25
Brick Maker Early—Rensselaerswijck	1631–1654	Dwelling	90	19	1	13	328	68	479
Brick Maker Late—Rensselaerswijck	1654–1686	Dwelling	62	32	31	16	101	52	194
Jurrian Theunisz Lot—Rensselaerswijck	1640s	Trading House	77	42	17	9	91	49	185

The numbers in the table represent artifact counts, rather than minimum number of vessels.

Steven Jansz liquidated a portion of the goods from de Vrouw Maria in April of 1655 as Maria Goosen was being banned from selling alcohol in Beverwijck and the couple's marriage was essentially over (Gehring and Venema 2009:65–66; Pearson and Van Laer 1918:263–264). The inventory of goods includes material apparently used in the drinking house (Table 5.3). This list of goods, coupled with the archaeological data, provides a narrative of Goosen's operation as constituted in 1655.

Beer makes up 37% of the sale value of the drinking house goods. Perhaps more important is the fact that several grades of "Holland" beer were available for consumption appealing to an economically diverse clientele. Brandy is conspicuously absent from the inventory, being the beverage that Maria was found guilty of supplying to an "Indian woman" in 1655 (Gehring 1989:194). Beer glasses were provided to customers, but there is no indication of the style or quality of the six glasses in the inventory. Fortunately, the archaeological assemblage provides documentation of the types of glass used by customers.

Throughout the seventeenth century, certain forms of glassware were extremely popular among the Dutch and exported throughout their colonies. Glass bottle forms included, but are not limited to 1) large flat-sided molded bottles with rounded, sloping shoulders and pewter tops (used for transporting and holding wine from casks), 2) smaller bottles similar in

Table 5.3. Goods from de Vrouw Maria sold by Steven Jansz in April of 1655

Buyer	Goods	Price Paid in Guilders
Baeljen	a trictrac table	16.00
Rensselaer	11 axes with some odds and ends	9.10
Seger Cornelisz	36 1bs tobacco	25.00
Seger Cornelisz	6 beer glasses	6.04
Jan met de baert	3 small pictures	2.00
Henderick Jochemse	a sign	3.12
Jacob Adriaensz	a gun	13.00
Pieter Bout	a canoe	35.00
Jan Thomasz	3 gutters at 20 guilders apiece	60.00
Steven Jansz	a sow	17.00
Henderick Gerritsz	a hog	15.00
Huybert de Guyt	a cask of no. 1 Holland beer	41.00
Philip Pietersz	ditto no. 2	33.00
Willem Pietersz	a barrel of no. 8 Holland beer	30.00
Willem Pietersz	no. 9, ditto	24.00
Seger Cornelisz	some tobacco pipes	2.10
Jan Verbeeck	barrel of no. 4 Holland beer	24.00
Joan de Hulter	a chest	9.10
Huybert de Guyt	a bag of lime	2.12
Huybert	a trough with a basin	9.01
Young Kees	3 benches	8.10
Joan de Hulter	4 hogs at 14 guilders a piece	54.00
Anthony de Hooges	a barrel of Holland beer	24.00
Leendert Philipsz	a sleeping bench	4.00
Dooretge	a billy goat	16.00
Total		481.69
Jacob van de Vlacte	a dog	—
Juryan the glazier	2 hogs	3 ½ beavers

style (used for containing distilled liquors), 3) various sized flat-sided case bottles (used regularly for containing wine, distilled liquors, and other liquids), 4) round bodied wine bottles of varying forms, and 5) molded bottles with more than four flat sides (McNulty 1971:100–113). Popular tableware forms included: roemers of varying styles, beakers, goblets, *passglases*, and *stangenglases*. Dutch roemers were ubiquitous and the form contains a cup, a stem, and a foot, with variations in all three. Cups could be shaped into cones, barrels, half barrels, or brandy glasses. The stems are hollow and decorated with applied prunts drawn in the form of thorns, raspberries, or round glass drops. The roemer foot is either a wound conical glass thread or a ridged rim (Brongers and Wijnman 1968:1).

Of these many forms and styles, one would expect less expensive, simple vessel styles to be used most frequently in a tavern setting, such as case bottles, plain beakers, and *passglases*. Yet the Dutch, and those living under Dutch rule, appear to have almost universally embraced more delicately elaborate vessel forms, and many, it seems, owned at least one or two roemers or façon de Venise beakers. As Haynes (1964:91) summarizes, "the Dutch were glass-lovers, and no people in the world could surpass them in the arts of living."

Stratum 77 differed from most others on the site in the amount of glass and faunal material it contained. There were a total of 18 glass bottle fragments with a minimum vessel count of two case bottles and one rounded wine bottle. The sherds included a case bottle base made up of 4 crossmended sherds, 1 partial case bottle finish 2 cm in diameter, and 10 case bottle body sherds. Also present were wine bottle body sherds.

The assemblage included a total of 40 glass tableware sherds with a minimum vessel count of 3 drinking glasses. There were 10 fragments belonging to a façon de Venise beaker with white-spiraled *vetro a filli* string decoration dating from the early seventeenth century (Figure 5.2). The remaining 30 fragments all belonged to roemers. Stem remains consisted of 5 raspberry prunts, 1 attached to a nearly complete stem base, another attached to the section of decorative ribbed string at the base of the bowl, and 3 with little attached stem remaining. Three stem fragments with applied thorn prunts were also found, dating probably between 1630 and 1660. Roemer bases included 1 complete base with a conical spiral string foot of 11 coils (Huey 1988a:470–471), 2 crossmended remains of a stem kickup and basal foot consisting of 6 coils and measuring 5.5 cm in diameter, and 2 separate stringed foot sherds measuring roughly 5 and 5.5 cm in diameter. The remaining bowl sherds vary in thicknesses of 0.3 to 1.8 mm.

The explanation as to why the roemer and other costly drinking vessels were popular among the wealthy and poorer classes alike is most likely intertwined with the rise of nascent national identity and the desire to surround oneself with finely made material goods (Bradley 2007:30–31; McNulty 2004:1–2). Seventeenth-century glassware is also a direct reflection

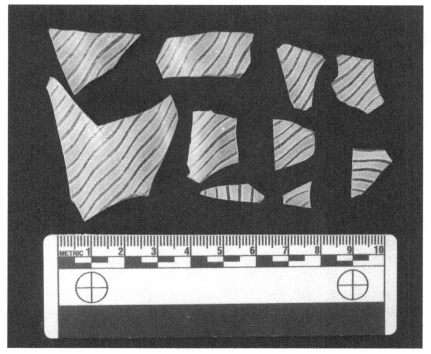

Figure 5.2. Façon de Venise glass beaker recovered from Stratum 77.

of alcohol consumption and drinking behavior, which was thoroughly wo-ven into Dutch culture.

Smoking was also clearly popular at Dutch drinking houses, as the genre paintings attest. Thirty-six pounds of tobacco and "some tobacco pipes" are listed in the Jansz inventory. This suggests that pipes and tobacco were both available for purchase or use at de Vrouw Maria. It is also likely that many patrons supplied their own smoking equipment. The archaeological record is instructive in this regard.

Extensive research on the pipe assemblage conducted by Paul Huey and Joseph McEvoy identified 7 separate marks among the 51 pipe fragments included in the assemblage (Table 5.4). Huey (1988a:479) noted that only 1 of the 5 heel marks from Stratum 77 was found elsewhere at the site, no Edward Bird pipes (common in other mid-seventeenth-century contexts, see Furlow herein) and no elbow pipes were recovered. Several of the pipe stems were relatively long and found at approximately the same depth and horizontal position within Stratum 77 (Figure 5.3).

Table 5.4. Tobacco pipe marks represented in the Stratum 77 assemblage

General Description	Type	Maker	Date	Huey Number
Fleur-de-lis	Stem	Unidentified	Unidentified	3
Fleur-de-lis	Stem	Unidentified	Unidentified	23
"HK" in Circle	Heel	Possibly Hendrick Claesz	Ca. 1650	45
"H" in Circle	Heel	Unidentified	Unidentified	47
"VO" below man riding a horse	Heel	Unidentified	1645–1660	46
"MPS" or "MTS" in circle with three dots	Heel	Possibly Maerten Pietersz Steijn	1637–1665	44
"SL" with fleur-de-lis	Heel	Unidentified	Unidentified	43

Source: Huey 1988a, 478–481, 735–740, Figures 113 and 114. https://www.claypipes.nl/merken/letters/vo/. Accessed October 13, 2020.

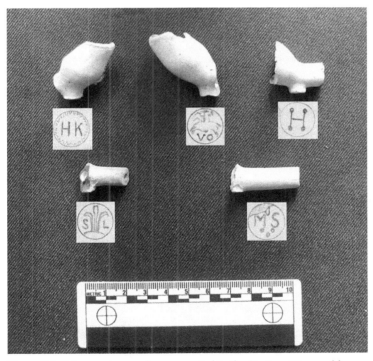

Figure 5.3. Tobacco pipe marks represented in the Stratum 77 assemblage. Drawings by Joseph McEvoy and Paul Huey.

Edward Bird elbow pipes were produced specifically for the American fur trade and resembled existing Native American forms (Bradley 2007:119; Furlow herein; Huey 1988a:466). Since de Vrouw Maria was strictly a drinking house, the absence of this form is not surprising. When pipes were supplied to customers, a relatively homogeneous assemblage might be expected. The variety of pipes could simply be the result of diverse clientele supplying their own pipes.

There is no direct reference to meals being served at de Vrouw Maria, or any other drinking house near Fort Orange. However, indirect historical evidence and the archaeological record indicates that meals were available to patrons. De Vrouw Maria property contained a cookhouse for preparing meals, and the presence of a hog pen suggests that pork was a likely source of protein. Seven hogs and one sow are included in the Jansz inventory. Huey's (1988a:468–469) initial summary of the faunal material from Stratum 77 suggests a reliance on pork with deer as the primary wild meat. Sturgeon and oysters were also present.

The small and highly fragmented ceramic assemblage from Stratum 77 provides little evidence of dining, and no ceramics, pewter, or utensils were sold by Jansz in 1655. Vessels represented include a minimum of one blue-painted Rhenish stoneware tankard or mug, one Dutch majolica plate, one unidentified blue-painted Dutch faience hollow vessel, one unidentified slip-decorated red earthenware hollow vessel, and an Iberian storage jug. Functionally, the sherds can be separated by coarse earthen wares for food preparation and storage ($n = 10$), majolica and faience tablewares ($n = 14$), and stoneware ($n = 7$) drinking vessels. Only stoneware drinking vessels figured prominently in the tavern paintings discussed earlier. While the ceramic assemblage is sparse and highly fragmented, the assemblage does suggest a well-furnished household.

Conclusion

The Cornelisz-Jansz-Goosen house was a product of time and place. It remains unclear how economically successful the drinking house was, but the name de Vrouw Maria was well known in 1655 when Henderick Jochemse purchased the sign for his own establishment. The historical and archaeological record clearly demonstrate what made de Vrouw Maria a distinctively Dutch place. First, the fact that beer was the main beverage stands out in comparison to seventeenth-century English drinking houses in the Chesapeake colonies, where rum and cider were the primary drinks (Lucas 2016). Second, as the glass assemblage from Stratum 77 and the tavern paintings attest, "Holland" beer was frequently consumed with delicate glass roemers and façon de Venise beakers. Third, although no gaming pieces were recovered from Stratum 77, a trictrac table was available at de Vrouw Maria. Perhaps less distinctively "Dutch" was the sale of tobacco at the house. Tobacco may have been sold at drinking houses in the New England colonies, however, in the tobacco-rich Chesapeake, there is little evidence of tobacco as a retail commodity. The available historical and archaeological information suggests that de Vrouw Maria was a distinctively Dutch establishment where patrons purchased and consumed tobacco, drank beer from fine glass vessels, played an occasional game of trictrac while seated at one of several rudimentary benches, and perhaps enjoyed a meal of pork, or venison.

De Vrouw Maria was also a product of a moment in time. During the 1640s and perhaps early 1650s, Fort Orange was prime real estate for a drinking house business. By the mid-1650s, the development of Beverwijck to the north and the steady decline of foot traffic to the fort for trade had lessened the value of the location. Perhaps this explains why no drinking houses appear to have operated out of the Jansz property after 1655. Van Leyden's drinking house would have captured travelers coming up from the south and perhaps depleted that source of patronage. Yet perhaps the most important reason for the decline in drinking houses near the fort was the growing population in Stuyvesant's Beverwijck, where town dwellers could walk to any number of nearby houses.

Of the many regulations implemented to manage drinking houses, the sale of alcohol to Native Americans was dealt with most harshly. It was also the most frequently prosecuted type of violation, comprising 40% of court cases related to alcohol (Salinger 2002:101). Fighting, drinking on the Sabbath, and other offenses were considered minor infractions. Even taxing and regulating the distribution of beer appears to have been a futile endeavor. For example, no punishment was issued to Maria Goosen or Adriaen Jansen van Leyden when they refused to have their cellars inspected. The final blow for de Vrouw Maria under Goosen's tenure was her prosecution for selling brandy to a Native American woman and subsequent year and a half prohibition from selling alcohol.

The artifact assemblage from Stratum 77 was discarded at a pivotal time in the history of New Netherland's northwestern frontier when the peripatetic center was shifting from Fort Orange northward to the community of Beverwijck. Drinking house keepers were flexible and shifted their operations to take advantage of these changes. The artifact assemblage, especially the glass drinking vessels, also suggests a drinking house that was very much a part of the Dutch cultural experience mapped onto the New Netherland frontier.

6

A Synthesis of Dutch Faunal Remains Recovered from Seventeenth-Century Sites in the Albany Region

MARIE-LORRAINE PIPES

Much of what is known about Dutch foodways in New Netherland comes from historical documents and paintings and from research conducted by archaeologists, food historians, and other historians (e.g. Chapman et al. 1996; Huey 1984; Jameson 1909; Janowitz 1993; Van Laer 1932b; Venema 2003). As with other frontier colonies in the New World, establishing successful subsistence practices was a critical priority. When initial efforts were less than successful, it was necessary to exploit locally available food resources, to trade with local people for food, and to even obtain food by force.

The heart of New Netherland was at the tip of Manhattan Island, where a fort and settlement were established. Situated at the south end of the Hudson River and New York Harbor, this settlement was located in a rich ecosystem abundant in wildlife resources. However, within a few decades the colonists had overexploited many of these local food resources, collapsed the local deer population, and ruined social relations with local Natives. Fortunately, their location on the seaboard facilitated both coastal and overseas trade, allowing the colonists to meet their food needs through trade and imports (DeVoe 1862:16–17).

The situation was quite different at the northern end of the Hudson River settlement zone, where the Dutch WIC set up a trading post at modern Albany and traded for furs with Natives. Fort Orange was built in 1624 and remained the center of the fur trade for decades. The patroonship of Rensselaerswijck's economic and political prerogatives partially overlapped with those of the company, but at least initially the patroon was driven by the desire to create agricultural plantations and a support a skilled labor force. Through time, however, trading became a prime driver of the patroon's activities (Bradley 2007).

This region was also rich in easily accessible food resources, which was important during the initial decades of Dutch settlement. A few farms were initially laid out close to the fort but were unable to provide enough food to support the population even though it was small. While the fur trade was the main economic focus, there was a great need to obtain food as well. Fishing along the river no doubt provided some food, but both hunting and fishing may have been somewhat restricted by the Native people who controlled hunting grounds and viewed by them as their own food resource base (Engelbrecht 2003; Van den Bogaert 1635, in Gehring and Starna 2013).

Other foods were supplied to the settlement from New Amsterdam via the Hudson River, but the supply system was interrupted seasonally in winter when the river froze (Venema 2003). In 1639, when the patroonship of Rensselaerswijck was founded, farmers and skilled craftsmen set up small-scale subsistence farms equipped by the patroon with housing, farming equipment, grain seed, and livestock. They were expected to repay some of the increase to the patroon within a specified amount of time. Grain crops included wheat, barley, and rye, and livestock included cattle, pig, sheep, goat, chicken, turkey, goose, and duck. Other domesticated plants and animals were brought and raised as well, for example, horses, dogs, cats, ducks, geese, beets, peas, potatoes, and onions.

In his description of New Netherland, David Pietersen de Vries (1642, in Jameson 1909). described Dutch colonial subsistence practices. Colonists raised cattle, goats, pigs, chickens, rabbits, turkeys, geese, and ducks. Many wild species were consumed, including buffalo (most likely elk, which were often described as *vache des bois*), raccoon, beaver, wild rabbit, and deer. He noted that the fish industry was not encouraged but that people caught fish by hook and line from the shore and docks. Deer, which were both hunted and bought from Natives, formed a significant part of the diet, as did wild turkey, also both hunted and bought. Deer was a seasonally available meat, brought for sale to the colonists during winter along with furs (Huey 1988a). Colonists also grew native crops including corn and tobacco and harvested wild hops, nuts, tree fruits, and berries.

Illustrations of upper-class Dutch tables show a highly diverse diet that included domesticated livestock and poultry, fish, and wild birds and mammals. Bread, fish, shellfish, dairy products, and grain gruels were foods commonly consumed, while smoked and salted meats were also popular (Janowitz 1993). Beef and pork were the most important sources of meat for the Dutch (Greenfield 1989; Janowitz 1993). Fresh meat was available for a limited time in late fall when pigs and cattle were slaughtered, although the bulk of the meat was preserved. Fish were also preserved by drying, salting, or smoking. The lower classes probably had a less diverse diet due to income. The greater settlement at Beverwijck was composed of a mix of upper- and lower-class people, many of whom were involved in the fur trade, regardless of social class. Life was hard in the settlement, and people had to depend on each other for survival. The reality of frontier life probably equalized some social differences. It is likely that class and economic differences in foodways were diminished for practical reasons.

Many colonists arriving in the settlement were less interested in farming and more in trading. This profitable endeavor hurt the settlement's ability to sustain itself. Still, some farms, such as the Schuyler Flatts, did produce crops and livestock and thrived. By midcentury the population had increased, and the town of Beverwijck expanded to include shops, bakeries, and taverns (Venema 2003). By the 1660s a well-established community with agricultural production was able to provide much of their food needs (Van Laer 1932a). Letters written by Jeremias van Rensselaer (1651–1671) reveal much about the state of agricultural production during this period. There were years when crop yields were poor (1657, 1660–1662, 1667) and others when they were abundant (1659, 1663). Livestock breeding efforts were stable, especially where horses and cattle were concerned. Horses were important in the settlement for transportation and traction, and they appear in great numbers in farm inventories (Van Laer 1932a), but archaeologically they are rarely recovered. When horse remains are found they almost never appear to have been butchered, as the Dutch in New Netherland did not eat them as a common practice.

On occasion, the settlement suffered disastrous events. The area was prone to flooding, which affected many people residing along the riverfront and the river islands. Late winter floods known as *freshets* devastated farms, houses, and other structures in the town of Beverwijck and in Fort Orange on several occasions, including 1648, 1654, and 1666. Livestock were washed away, and many lives were lost (Van Laer 1932a). The flood of 1664 destroyed half the town and resulted in the loss of many homes. Variable crop yields and environmental difficulties led to a continued need for support from both New Amsterdam and Natives. The dependence on trade, not only for furs but especially for food, may have been a major factor in the maintenance of relatively good social relationships between the colonists and local Native groups throughout most of the seventeenth century.

The most detailed source of information about subsistence practices, however, comes from faunal remains recovered from archaeological sites. Their significance is best interpreted with respect to the social context within which they were generated, and by considering the results of analysis in terms of subsistence models of known cultural practices. The Mohawks were subsistence agriculturalists. Their major crops were tobacco, corn, beans, and squash. They obtained meat by hunting, trapping, and fishing birds, mammals, turtles, and fish. Deer was their most important source of meat. During the seventeenth century, they hunted mammals for the fur trade, especially beaver and other fur-bearing species such as otter, mink, and bear (Van Laer 1932a). After these species were extirpated from the area, they brokered furs from Natives as far away as Hudson Bay. Dutch farmers grew crops like those grown in the Netherlands but quickly added New World crops. They raised domesticated livestock which they butchered and consumed fresh as well as preserved in a variety of ways including brining, smoking, salting, and drying methods (Rose 1989). They also hunted, most likely on their farms, deer and smaller mammals, birds, and turtles, and may have fished. Fishing may have been an age-based activity since no commercial fishing was done in the seventeenth century. Reverend Megapolensis (1644, in Jameson 1909) commented on the abundance of fish and his sons' plentiful catch. Many visitors noted the presence of a wide variety of fish (Jameson 1909; Snow et al. 1996).

The Dutch sites selected for examination in this analysis represent different segments of this small, complex society. The faunal assemblages are of varying sizes overlapping in dates from the 1630s to the 1660s. Each assemblage focuses on different social settings and actors of the past. The faunal deposits are representative of the diets of a large swath of colonists consisting of soldiers, businessmen, households, burghers, and farmers. They include special meals shared between colonists and Natives, probably important in sealing deals involving trade in pelts. These foods reflect not only the cultural identity of the Dutch but also the assimilation of Native foods into new subsistence practices. The Fort Orange assemblage is a complex set of deposits that span the seventeenth century and are associated with the military and company officials' occupations and traders conducting business at the fort. The Department of Environmental Conservation Headquarters faunal assemblage consists of two depositional components reflecting trade between a Dutch trader and a small number of Natives that was interrupted by a flood. The Quackenbush Square faunal assemblage consists of two occupational components belonging to different households living in a brickmaker's house built by the patron to lure prospective artisans to the colony. And the Schuyler Flatts faunal assemblage consists of a large midden, located outside the Van Curler house cellar and formed over the course of a decade.

All the faunal assemblages are similar in composition; each is composed of a mix of domesticated and non-domesticated mammals and birds, as well as fish. Aside from volume, the composition of the assemblages varied in terms of species diversity and relative abundance or importance of particular species in the diet. Species that appear in higher frequencies are those that presumably represent dietary staples. In many deposits, some species were always present in low numbers. In some cases, species present in low frequencies but may be underrepresented due to taphonomic factors. For example, the skeletal elements of boiled fish become soft and more subject to decay. In other cases, like fur-bearing species, the appearance of any element may be fortuitous since their pelts did not typically have many skeletal elements attached. For example, at Fort Orange mink appeared in three deposits and likely represents elements removed from pelts (Table 6.1). At one site, nontraditional foods were also identified, including butchered bear, horse, and dog. Unusual meat combinations likely point to important social interactions between Native and Dutch peoples and the social importance of food in establishing relationships within the context of trade, whether legal or otherwise.

Sites and Faunal Assemblages

Tables 6.1 through 6.4 summarize the range of species and number of skeletal elements for each site and its associated deposits. Fort Orange had the greatest potential for comparative analysis. The excavations yielded many deposits, several of which were sealed by the floods of 1640 and 1648. As such, these deposits offer a basis for comparing data from the other sites.

Fort Orange yielded a large faunal assemblage. Some of the deposits listed in Table 6.1 were compiled from multiple areas, for example general refuse from the fort and general occupation. Others were associated with four trader houses: Staats Van Twiller, Vos, Van Doesburgh, and Labatie (Huey 1988a). The faunal remains from these analytical units will be discussed further. Within the boundaries of the future town of Beverwijck,

Table 6.1. Fort Orange, pre- and post-flood deposits by location and associated houses, total number of bone fragments (TNF) and minimum number of bone units (MNU)

Class/Species/ Size-Range Category	Spanned Structure 1640	General Occupation Pre-1640 Flood	Labatie Pre-1648 Flood	General Refuse Bastion and Entrance 1648-1664	Staats-Van Twiller 1655-1668	Van Doesburgh 1651-1668	Vos? 1657-1664
	MNU	MNU	MNU	MNU	MNU	MNU	MNU
MAMMAL							
Bear	-	-	-	5	-	-	-
Beaver	-	-	-	1	-	-	-
Cat	1	-	-	1	-	-	-
Cattle	9	9	19	136	4	187	-
White-tailed Deer	35	52	25	208	29	89	3
Dog	-	-	-	2	-	-	-
Mink	1	1	-	1	-	-	-
Mouse	-	-	-	-	-	1	-
Otter	-	-	-	3	-	-	-
Pig	11	14	13	97	14	84	3
Raccoon	2	-	-	-	-	-	-
Rat	1	1	-	2	-	3	-
Sheep	3	-	2	36	-	38	-
Sheep/Goat	-	-	-	4	-	14	-
Squirrel	-	-	-	-	-	1	-
Woodchuck	-	-	-	-	-	1	-

Unidentified Mammal	13	4	19	51	12	58	3
Subtotal TNF/MNU	*76*	*81*	*78*	*547*	*59*	*476*	*9*
BIRD							
Cardinal	-	-	-	-	-	1	-
Chicken	-	2	-	4	-	17	-
Duck	2	5	2	9	-	19	3
Goose	3	9	4	9	1	28	-
Owl	-	-	-	-	-	1	-
Pigeons	1	2	1	10	2	44	-
Turkey	1	7	1	2	-	6	-
Unidentified Bird	6	5	5	5	2	38	1
Subtotal TNF/MNU	*13*	*30*	*13*	*39*	*5*	*154*	*4*
FISH/REPTILE/AMPHIBIAN							
Catfish	-	-	-	-	1	3	-
Salmon	-	-	-	-	-	2	-
Smallmouth Bass	-	1	-	-	-	-	-
Striped Bass	1	-	-	11	-	1	-
Sturgeon	-	1	-	-	-	1	-
Walleye Pike	-	-	-	-	-	1	-
Unidentified Fish	11	28	11	56	-	245	3
Unidentified Turtle	-	2	-	2	4	4	-
Amphibian	-	-	-	-	1	3	-
Subtotal TNF/MNU	*12*	*32*	*11*	*69*	*6*	*260*	*3*
TOTAL TNF/MNU	101	143	102	655	70	890	16

two sites yielded faunal remains. One of these assemblages was recovered during excavations at the DEC Headquarters site (Hartgen Archeological Associates, Inc. 2002). It represented two occupations at the same location. A small earth-fast structure was identified which was built in the Dutch style with a wood-lined cellar. Faunal remains from a midden washed into the cellar during the flood of 1648. The faunal data suggest it was a meeting place for the Dutch trader and Natives. After the flood, the artifact data suggest a Native camp was located on the same spot. The second assemblage was recovered during excavations at the Quackenbush Square site, located about 650 feet north of the DEC Headquarters site (Hartgen Archeological Associates, Inc. 2005). This site was the location of the first brickmaker in the settlement. The site consisted of a yard and tenant house built in 1630. The patroon had serious difficulties in getting a brickmaker to the colony. It is possible that the tenant house was occupied for a time by Arent van Curler. Only the faunal deposits associated with this occupation are considered here. The Schuyler Flatts is located 4 mi north of the settlement closer to the confluence of the Mohawk River. Van Curler built the farm in 1643 to siphon furs away from the fort (Huey 1987, 1988a). Archaeological excavations at the site revealed that occupation spanned thousands of years into the pre-contact past. Excavations located the Van Curler farmhouse, which included a large attached barn. Another structure is referred to in a letter called a workers' house, but it has yet to be located. The Schuyler Flatts farm was frequently visited by Natives. Visitors to the Schuyler Flatts mention the presence of Dutch men and household servants (Father Jogues in Jameson 1909; Raddison 1858). Evidence of the Dutch occupation associated with Van Curler was distributed in the yard area and slumped inside a wood-lined cellar, possibly deposited during a flood episode. Other faunal deposits found at the site are not discussed here.

FORT ORANGE

The fort was built in 1624 and occupied by WIC military personnel and licensed traders until 1639 when a period of free trade began. In 1648 a severe flood destroyed a large portion of the fort, including eight trader houses. Governor Stuyvesant ended free trade in 1648 and rebuilt the fort. The excavation of Fort Orange uncovered several deposits many of which could be dated temporarily by correlating silt deposit with flood episodes and other documentation. Seven analytical units were created based on

Huey's (1988a) dissertation research, some of which have been assigned to trader houses and others to more general areas.

General Occupation, Pre-1640

The general occupation debris, dated 1624–1640, yielded a small deposit (143 MNU). It provides insights, however, into early subsistence practices. Identified species included chicken, turkey, duck, goose, passenger pigeon, pig, cattle, mink, deer, sturgeon, smallmouth bass, and turtle. Deer was the most abundant species and was represented by skulls and mandibles and a variety of meat cuts. Meat cuts included stew meats from the neck, rib, brisket, and shanks, roasts from the chuck, and hindquarter. Age at death profiles indicated the presence of at least one juvenile, several mature adults, and one elderly individual. The range of body parts suggested the processing of whole animals. Pig was the second most frequent species and included a skull and pair of mandibles. Butchered skulls and mandibles are evidence of tongue and brain extraction as well as the removal of facial muscles. Until recently, these were commonly eaten, often incorporated into processed meats such as sausage and cold cuts. Meat cuts included rib-end chops, Boston butt ham, ham hock, and shank hams. The range of cuts was limited. These remains came from older individuals, including one aged at three and a half years or more at death. Cattle remains were limited to short ribs, a rump roast and two round roasts, and a stew cut from the foreshank. These three large mammal species represent two types of meat. Deer was butchered onsite and consumed fresh. Pork and beef were most likely preserved. Bird body part distributions were limited as well. Most were represented by the breast, leg, and wing. Chicken included a skull. It was not possible to determine if duck and goose were domesticated species or not. It is assumed that the turkey was wild. One fur-bearer was indicated by the mandible of a mink. Fish were well represented. Sturgeon was indicated by a scute and smallmouth bass by a skull element. Only one vertebra was present. Other unidentified fish elements included cranial elements, branchiostegals and rays, and spines.

This faunal material is significant because it suggests that during the earliest phase of the fort's history, the military relied on preserved meats and hunting deer to supplement its diet. As shall be seen in the general refuse deposits, deer were more likely to be represented by haunches of meat, while large-bodied domesticated mammals were represented by a wider range of body parts and by younger animals.

Spanned Structure, 1640

This deposit predated 1640. Identified species included turkey, duck, goose, passenger pigeon, cat, sheep, pig, cattle, brown rat, raccoon, mink, deer, and striped bass (101 MNU). Deer was once again the most frequent species. An almost complete range of body parts was represented. There were two heads, one from an immature individual. Except for this individual all other remains were from mature adults. Meat cuts included roasts from the chuck and hindquarter, and stew meats from the neck, fore- and hindshank, and discarded feet. Pig was represented by several loose teeth, a trotter, and two Boston butt hams. These came from individuals aged around one and a half years. Sheep was indicated by a partial mandible and a roast from the forelimb, which included the upper and lower elements. Cattle was limited to stew meats from the fore and hind shanks and one short rib. Medium and large mammal remains consisted of a small number of rib and longbone fragments. In addition to meat-bearing mammals, furbearers were also recovered in low frequencies. There was at least one raccoon indicated by a canine and a penis-bone, and a mink by a skull. Two commensal species were present, a cat represented by a skull and a brown rat by a mandible. Bird body parts were limited to the wing, leg, and breast. Striped bass consisted of a skull element and unidentified fish of skull, brachiostegals (rays that support the gills), and spine fragments.

Labatie House, Pre-1648

The Labatie house deposit probably predates 1648. Identified species included turkey, duck, goose, passenger pigeon, sheep, pig, cattle, deer, and sturgeon (106 MNU). Deer was the most abundant species. A minimum of three heads were present, all of which were mature adults. Meat cuts included stews from the neck, foreshank, and hindshank and roasts from the chuck and hindquarter. Beef was the second most abundant meat. One mandible was present. Meat cuts were limited to stew meats from the neck, rib, and hind shank and two roasts from the chuck. Two partial feet were present. Pig consisted of a skull, several loose teeth, a Boston butt ham, two picnic hams, and a shank ham, all from individuals aged around one and a half years at death. Medium and large mammal remains included a few rib, foot, and longbone fragments. Birds were infrequent. They were represented by the wing, breast, and leg. Sturgeon was the only identified fish. Other fish remains were infrequent and consisted of branchiostegals, skull elements, and a scale.

General Refuse: Bastion, Moat, and East Entrance, Post-1648 Flood to 1664

A large amount of bone was recovered from the bastion, moat, and east entrance (889 MNU). This material was the most diverse of the fort deposits. They most likely represent waste from the military mess. Assuming this is correct, they primarily indicate food remains prepared for soldiers. However, some of the remains clearly resulted from fur-trade activities as in the case of mink and otter. Identified species included chicken, duck, goose, passenger pigeon, cat, dog, sheep, pig, cattle, bear, mink, otter, and sturgeon. Many bone specimens were too fragmented to identify beyond class.

Most of the bone consisted of dietary refuse. Sheep were represented by stew meat from the neck, forelimb, and hindlimb and roasts from the shoulder, rump, and leg, and there was one butchered mandible resulting from tongue extraction. Sheep included adults as well immature individuals. Pigs were well represented. There were least four butchered heads and several loose teeth. Meat cuts included a variety of hams including Boston butt, picnic, shank, and butt hams. There were no trotters or hocks present. Pigs were generally aged between one and one and a half years, though some were less than a year. Like sheep and pigs, cattle were represented by cranial elements, some of which exhibited butcher marks. At least three individuals were indicated by mandibles. Meat cuts included stew meats from the neck, rib, and shanks. Large roasts came from the loin, prime rib, clod, round, rump, and sirloin. Stew meats were more abundant. Most beef cuts came from adults; however, there was at least one calf, based on a hindleg and foot. Except for this specimen, no other foot elements were recovered. Deer remains were abundant and represented by a range of elements, such as those of large-bodied domesticated mammals. Many of the bones exhibited butcher marks. Skulls and mandibles were processed for brain and tongue extraction. Deer brains were one of the ingredients for tanning hides, though there is no other evidence for that activity. Most of the individuals were adults, but one juvenile was indicated. There were many meat cuts, the majority of which were from the hindquarter, along with a few forequarters. There were only a few foot elements. Medium and large mammal refuse consisted mainly of longbone and small numbers of vertebra, rib, and cranial fragments.

Birds were represented by the breast, wing, leg, and thigh. No vertebral, skull, or foot elements were present. Fish remains were primarily branchiostegals and spines. Six sturgeon scutes were present as well. The lack of vertebrae may indicate fillets were obtained. The range of body parts possible for all classes and species was incomplete. Body part distributions were limited primarily to elements associated with organs and meat cuts which suggests the discarded refuse of prepared foods.

In addition to dietary refuse, butcher waste and incidental refuse was also present. As already noted, there was a mink skull and two paired otter mandibles. Bear was indicated by a foot consisting of two metapodials and a claw. One dog canine tooth was recovered. Large canine gnaw marks were observed on some of the specimens pointing to the presence of dogs.

Staats Van Twiller House, 1655–1668

A small faunal assemblage was associated with the Staats Van Twiller house composed primarily of dietary refuse (63 MNU). Identified species included goose, passenger pigeon, pig, cattle, deer, and catfish. Deer was the most abundant species, but it was represented by a narrow range of body parts. There were two butchered heads and a mandible from mature individuals. Most of the venison cuts were from the hindquarter, consisting of at least four haunches that included upper and lower elements, feet attached. There was one forelimb haunch, which also included upper and lower elements, foot attached. In addition, there were two chuck roasts. Pig was the second most frequent species. It was composed of several upper and lower teeth from a minimum of one individual aged at one and a half years. In addition, there was a single trotter. Cattle remains consisted of a short rib, chuck roast, and rump roast. Medium and large mammal remains included a few cranial, rib, lumber vertebra, longbone, and metapodial fragments. Identified birds included goose and passenger pigeon, which were represented by a wing and breast respectively. Catfish was the only identified fish species indicated by a pectoral spine. Unidentified fish included one vertebra and a couple of branchiostegals. Deer foot elements represent trimming waste removed before the meats were cooked.

Van Doesburgh House, 1651–1668

The faunal deposit associated with Van Doesburgh house was the greatest concentration of the Dutch-period contexts (890 MNU). This deposit differed significantly from others in several ways. The range of species was greater, cattle was far more abundant than other species, and there were immature chickens indicating the rearing of fowl. Identified species included chicken, turkey, duck, goose, passenger pigeon, cardinal, owl, sheep, pig, cattle, mouse, brown rat, squirrel, woodchuck, deer, salmon, catfish, walleye pike, sturgeon, striped bass, turtle, and frog.

Mammal remains differed considerably from the other deposits at the fort. Aside from the great abundance of cattle, no valuable fur-bearers were represented. Mouse, brown rat, squirrel, and woodchuck are potentially commensal species. People can eat them, but they tend to be starvation foods as well game acquired by kids. Mouse and rat consisted of hind legs, squirrel of an incisor, and woodchuck of a partially articulated spinal column. Small mammal remains included several ribs and a few crania and foot bones.

Cattle remains included veal and beef cuts. Cranial elements included three mandibles and upper and lower teeth from mature individuals. Veal cuts were limited and consisted of stew meats from the shanks. Beef cuts were abundant and varied. They included stew meats from the neck, rib, chuck, clod, and fore- and hindshanks, and roasts from the prime rib, loin, sirloin, rump, round, and chuck. Deer was the second most abundant species followed closely by pig. There were at least four deer skulls and associated mandibles from mature individuals. One senile individual was indicated by extremely worn teeth. Venison cuts included a few stew meats from the neck. There were minimally 12 haunches primarily from the hind leg which included the thigh and shank; no feet were attached. There were cuts from the forelimb dominated by chuck roasts, of which there were 11. These may have been part of haunches that consisted of upper and lower foreleg bones. In addition, there were a few butt-end leg roasts. Most venison cuts came from mature individuals though at least one juvenile was indicated. Pig remains were dominated by cranial elements. There were minimally ten heads represented by heads and mandibles, which included mostly subadults aged between ½ and ¾ years and at least one neonate. The presence of a neonate is significant because it is the indication of pigs being raised locally at the fort. Meat cuts included stew meats from the neck, hock, and trotters, rib and loin-end chops, and hams from the Boston butt, picnic, shank, and butt. Sheep were the least abundant large mammal species even though they were well represented. There were a few loose teeth, upper and lower, from older individuals. A lamb was represented as well by unfused phalanges. Most of the cuts came from individuals older than one and three-quarter years. Mutton cuts included stew meats from the neck, and fore- and hindshanks, feet attached. Most of the cuts were haunches from the hindquarter. In addition, there were a few roasts from the chuck and loin chops. Medium and large mammal remains included vertebra, rib, skull and mandible, and longbone fragments.

Passenger pigeon was the most abundant bird species, followed by duck, chicken, goose, and turkey. These species were represented by a wide range of body parts, including the wing, breast, leg, thigh, back, and foot. Except for a small bird beak, no other bird skulls were present. There was a minimum of two immature chickens. This is a clear indication that they were raised at this location. It is also the only case of immature chickens found at the fort. All the other birds were represented by mature individuals which suggests the likelihood that they were wild species. However, the Dutch brought ducks and geese to the settlement. Cardinal and owl were both represented by a single wing element. It is very unusual to see an owl in an historic deposit, which leaves open the possibility that it was brought by Natives to the farm. Fish species were varied. Identified species were mainly identified by cranial elements except for sturgeon. There were few vertebrae in the deposit. Most fish consisted of skull, branchiostegals and rays, and spines. A few large fish vertebrae fragments were bisected suggesting steaks. Neither turtle nor frog were present in large numbers.

Possible Vos House, 1657–1664

The remains of a house that may have belonged to Han Vos were located. A small faunal deposit was recovered which consisted of dietary refuse (16 MNU). Identified species included duck, pig, deer, and an unidentified fish. Bird remains included a wing breast. Pork was indicated by tongue, neck, and trotter. Venison was represented by roasts from the foreleg and thigh. Other cuts from large mammals included a stew cut from the lower leg, which may be part of the deer forearm, and a shoulder blade. Fish consisted of a branchiostegal. Though small, the deposit reinforces the continued importance of trade for meat at the fort.

Summary of Fort Orange Faunal Remains

The comparison of deposits from the pre-1648 and post-1648 periods at Fort Orange revealed similarities and differences in dietary patterns between military personnel and private traders. Domesticated animals and wild mammals were present in all deposits, revealing the continued importance a diversified diet. Earlier deposits may have included preserved pork and beef, whereas the composition of later remains suggests locally butchered livestock. The range of pork and beef body parts were limited in the earlier deposits suggesting that these meats were rarely consumed fresh and further indicating they were preserved meats. The importance of venison in the diet of both military and private citizens remained constant over time. However, a gradual trend was indicated in increasing frequencies of domesticated mammal and bird species. The nature of the fort as a trading post likely played a role in the range of species observed. It is likely that game animals were also traded by Natives for finished goods. Fish appear to have increased in frequency over time.

The presence of calves, lambs, neonatal pigs, and chickens in the later deposits signals a shift in subsistence. The earlier deposits lacked clear evidence of livestock rearing whereas later deposits contained remains of mature and immature animals. This indicates that by the third quarter of the seventeenth century, livestock production had stabilized enough so that fresh meat from domesticated livestock was continuously available.

DEC HEADQUARTERS, 625 BROADWAY

The DEC Headquarters site excavations uncovered an area along the former bank of the Hudson River that had two occupational sequences separated by the 1648 flood and capped by the 1654 flood. The lower component consisted of a small earth-fast structure with a wooden floor and wood-lined cellar. The structure has been interpreted as a trader's hut built probably between 1640 and 1648 before the town of Beverwijck came into existence. It was used to trade for furs probably during the period of free traders. The flood of 1648 wiped out the structure and washed in part of a surface midden which contained large amounts of shellfish as well as artifacts and faunal remains. The artifacts consisted of Dutch and Native materials. The combination of faunal remains from the lower level and flood episode are of great interest because they diverge from traditional Dutch foodways and suggest a ritualized meal occurred. The upper component consisted of a Native camp and hearth, very likely Mohawk. This component yielded historic and Native artifacts generated by the Dutch and their trading partners. The location of the camp suggests the location continued as a trading place. The deposits were sealed by the 1654 flood. The faunal data are presented in Table 6.2.

Flood Trader's Hut, Pre-1648 Flood

The faunal remains from the trader's hut and 1648 flood were combined, as were the post-1648 and post-1654 flood deposits (Table 6.2). The combined data from the first occupation are larger than the second (65 MNU). The

Table 6.2. DEC Headquarters, Trader's Hut, and Mohawk deposits and flood events, minimum number of bone units (MNU)

Class	Class/Species	Trader's Hut, Pre-1648 Flood Event MNU	Mohawk Camp, 1648–1654 Flood Event MNU
Mammal			
	Bear	1	-
	Cattle	11	2
	Dog	1	1
	Horse	2	-
	Pig	6	-
	Sheep	1	-
	White-tailed Deer	15	2
	Unidentified Mammal	12	1
	Subtotal MNU	49	6
Bird			
	Duck	2	-
	Unidentified Bird	1	1
	Subtotal MNU	3	1
Fish/Reptile			
	Catfish	2	1
	Sturgeon	1	-
	Unidentified Fish	8	-
	Unidentified Turtle	2	-
	Subtotal MNU	13	1
	TOTAL MNU	65	8

deposits were composed of domesticated mammals and wild mammals, birds, fish, and turtle. Domesticated mammals included dog, pig, cattle, horse, and sheep, and wild mammals, namely deer and bear. These remains were butchered. Deer and cattle were the most abundant of dietary-related species.

Much of the deposit was composed of dietary refuse, often of lower-quality cuts used for stews or soups, such as the foot bones of horse, deer, cattle, and sheep. Many of the cuts were associated with tongue extraction. There were head and mandible fragments of pig, cattle, and deer. Meat cuts included venison roasts from the fore and hindquarter as well as stews from the neck and shanks. Beef cuts were similar in range to venison. A single dog upper leg bone exhibits a deep slice mark at the proximal end, which shows the animal was butchered. This individual was between one-half and one year in age. Other small mammal bones came from the thorax, loin, and foot. Bear was represented by elements from a lower foreleg and hip, also bearing butcher marks. Duck was the only identified bird species, which consisted of a wing and leg. Other birds were indicated by longbone fragments. Fish elements were composed of skull, branchiostegal and rays, and sturgeon of scutes. One turtle was represented by carapace fragments.

The faunal remains are an interesting mix of foods specifically consumed by Dutch and Natives. Fish and bird remains were like those found at other sites. Most meats consumed at this location were typical of those eaten in the rest of the community. Deer was clearly important, though the high frequency of cattle relative to other mammal species is unusual for this period. While the Dutch were accustomed to bear being served by Natives, it was not their practice to eat horse or dog. Even bear was not commonly eaten by the Dutch in the settlement. On the other hand, butchered bear has been previously found at Mohawk sites (Funk and Kuhn 2003). The only other site in this study that yielded meat cuts from bear was the Schuyler Flatts. The only bear at Fort Orange consisted of a paw, perhaps from a pelt. Therefore, it seems likely that these foods in particular were brought by Natives to the trader's hut. The other domesticated mammals were likely provided by the Dutch trader. Considering the overwhelming absence of horse remains at most sites, it is a curious under what circumstances the horse was obtained.

Mohawk Camp, 1648–1654

The bone refuse found in the second occupation was located inside a hearth. The flood component is assumed to be closely related to this occupation. The combined hearth and flood faunal deposit was very small (8 MNU). Identified species included cattle, dog, deer, catfish, and unidentified bird. Though not identified by species, the medium and large mammal remains were butchered meat cuts. Cattle was indicated by a tooth and stew meat from the neck, and deer of two stew meats from the shank. Catfish and bird represent food remains as well as those of dog. The presence of dog in the later deposit is interesting and suggests a continued dietary practice in which this species played a role.

QUACKENBUSH SQUARE

Seventeenth-century deposits were recovered from the cellar and yard areas around a house identified as one that Kiliaen van Rensselaer had built in 1639 to house a brickmaker. He hoped to interest a skilled artisan in coming to the settlement to provide better building materials for housing. No such person arrived until midcentury. Until that time the house was used by tenants, and one of the earliest may have been Arent van Curler. He is known to have lived in the settlement and later moved to the Schuyler Flatts in the 1640s. Excavations uncovered two occupational sequences separated by the flood of 1654 and the faunal remains are presented in Table 6.3. Both occupations span long periods of time.

Occupation I, 1630s–1654

The faunal refuse associated with the first occupation is larger in size. There is a lot of overlap in terms of species between the two assemblages (327 MNU). Identified mammal species included cattle, chipmunk, pig, raccoon, rat, sheep or goat, and deer. The relative abundance of the larger mammals is weighted in favor of domesticated livestock. This suggests that these remains date to the end of this occupation since by then colonists were less dependent on venison for meat. Pig was the most frequent mammal species followed by cattle, sheep or goat, and deer. It was represented by a single head and several loose teeth from a minimum age ranging from a quarter to one and a half years. Meat cuts included stews from the neck, hocks, and trotters and hams from the picnic and shank. Cattle consisted of a mandible and upper and lower teeth from one mature individual. Meat cuts included stews from the neck, short rib, and hindshank and roasts from the prime rib and round. One subadult was indicated. Sheep and goat, mostly sheep, also consisted of teeth from a mature individual. Meat cuts included a chop, stews from the fore- and hindshank, and a chuck roast. All considered, most of these are poor-quality cuts of meat. Deer was represented by a mandible. Meat cuts included a chuck roast and three hindquarter haunches. Medium and large mammal remains consisted of skull, vertebra, rib, and longbone fragments. Two small mammal species were indicated, chipmunk and rat. The only other site that yielded a chipmunk element was the Schuyler Flatts. It is curious to consider that Van Curler might have kept them as pets. Rat was a commensal species. Raccoon was indicated by two teeth suggesting the discard from a pelt. Other

Table 6.3. Quackenbush Square Brickmaker's House deposits, first and second occupations, minimum number of bone units (MNU)

Class	Species	Occupation I, Flood 1630s–1654 MNU	Occupation II 1655–1686 MNU
Mammal			
	Cattle	21	17
	Chipmunk	1	-
	Pig	22	16
	Raccoon	2	-
	Rat sp.	1	3
	Sheep/Goat	15	9
	White-tailed Deer	11	4
	Unidentified Mammal	31	18
	Subtotal MNU	104	67
Bird			
	Blue-winged Teal	-	4
	Chicken	11	4
	Duck	12	8
	Goose	2	-
	Passenger Pigeon	2	1
	Turkey	1	-
	Unidentified Bird	23	16
	Subtotal MNU	51	33
Fish			
	Bass sp.	2	-
	Catfish	-	15
	Perch sp.	10	1
	Rock Bass	14	9
	Striped Bass	1	-
	Walleye Pike	10	-
	Yellow Perch	2	3
	Unidentified Fish	131	66
	Subtotal MNU	170	94
	TOTAL MNU	325	194

small mammal remains included canine, vertebra, and fore- and hindlimb elements.

Birds included chicken, duck, goose, passenger pigeon, and turkey. Chicken and duck were very common. Body parts included breast, wing, thigh, leg, and foot. No heads were recovered, and none of the birds were immature. Several fish were present including catfish, perch, rock bass, striped bass, walleye pike, and yellow perch. Fish were very abundant and were primarily represented by cranial elements, branchiostegals, fins, and spine rays. In general, vertebrae were rare in all the deposits across sites. This consistent pattern suggests that fish were cleaned elsewhere. Perhaps there was someone selling fish. It is also worth noting the great diversity of fish is like that at the Schuyler Flatts.

Occupation II, 1655–1686

The second occupation was like the first in terms of domesticated animals. But it lacked small fur-bearers like raccoon and had a smaller range of wild birds and fish (185 MNU). Cattle and pig were the most abundant species, followed by sheep and goat and last by deer. Cattle consisted of a partial mandible and teeth from a minimum of two individuals, one a mature adult, the other elderly. Meat cuts included stew meats from the neck, short rib, shank, and foot and roasts from the clod and round. Pig was also represented by teeth from two individuals, one a juvenile and the other a subadult. Meat cuts consisted of hams from the Boston butt and butt and stews from the trotters. Sheep or goat, likely sheep, consisted of a head from an adult, and stew meats from the fore- and hindshanks. No immature individuals were present. Deer was represented by a small number of upper teeth and a shank-end roast. Black rat was the only identified small mammal. It was represented by two forelimbs. Other small mammal elements came from the head, rib, and hind legs. Birds included blue-winged teal, other duck, chicken, and passenger pigeon, all of which were indicated by meat-bearing elements including the wing, breast, thigh, or leg. No heads or immature individuals were noted. Fish included catfish, walleye pike, rock bass, and yellow perch, most of which were represented by scales. Unidentified fish were represented by branchiostegals, spines, rays, and a few vertebrae. This was the only instance where fish processing was clearly indicated.

The bone refuse from the second occupation presented a more established picture of the settlement. Domesticated livestock production was more stable, and consequently reliance on deer for food decreased. Though there is very little bone data related to the fur trade, the presence of venison cuts points to continued trade for food.

THE SCHUYLER FLATTS

The Schuyler Flatts faunal deposits were recovered in and around the cellar of Arent van Curler's household. This farm and trading post were built in 1643 and occupied by Van Curler until 1659. It was abandoned around 1666. Though the Van Curlers did not have any children, his household included domestic servants, and his farm included a hired foreman and his family and periodic indentured laborers, as well as enslaved African people. Aside from raising crops and livestock, the farm served as a trading outpost actively engaged in exchange for furs and meat with Native people.

The Schuyler Flatts yielded the largest faunal assemblage of the four sites (3,118 MNU), detailed in Table 6.4. The refuse was generated over the course of 17 years and deposited around the outside of the house cellar. The Van Curlers left the Schuyler Flatts in 1659. Some of the bone eventually slumped into the cellar hole over time, possibly due to flooding. The faunal assemblage was in an excellent state of preservation that facilitated the identification of species, skeletal elements, and bone modifications. The faunal assemblage was composed of a wide range of species. There was a minimum of 39 bird, mammal, fish, and reptile species. Mammal and fish remains were by far the most common, followed distantly by bird, while reptile and amphibian remains were virtually absent. Most of the mammal remains were identified by species, whereas fish remains were not, because 85% of fish bones consisted of spines and rays.

Identified bird species included pigeon, turkey, chicken, duck, and goose. Bird species were grouped by domesticated and non-domesticated species. Except for turkey vulture all identified bird species represented food remains. Turkey vulture was indicated by a single wing element. It is possible that the wing represents a household item as feathered bird wings have long been used as decorations as well as whisks to clean out hearths. Pigeon was the most frequent bird species. Pigeon remains were most likely passenger pigeon. Historical accounts speak of the passenger pigeon as having been extremely abundant in the Northeast during colonial times and note that it was a very popular food (Fuller 2014). Body part distributions included the breast, wing, thigh, leg, and a few feet. No heads or necks and few backs were recovered. One clavicle exhibited a healed fracture. Turkey was infrequent and represented by a limited range of body parts. One ulna was

Table 6.4. Schuyler Flatts, Van Curler deposits, faunal summary, total number of bone fragments (TNF) and minimum number of bone units (MNU)

Class	Species	1643–1660 MNU
Mammal		
	Bear	22
	Beaver	3
	Cat	7
	Cattle	407
	Chipmunk	8
	Dog	5
	Eastern Gray Squirrel	11
	Elk	1
	Goat	2
	Horse	1
	Mouse	6
	Pig	351
	Rabbit	1
	Raccoon	8
	Rat	17
	Red Fox	10
	Sheep/Goat	142
	White-Tailed Deer	219
	Woodchuck	11
	Unidentified Mammal	382
	Subtotal MNU	1,614
Bird		
	Chicken	37
	Duck	31
	Goose	9
	Passenger Pigeon	103
	Turkey	18
	Turkey Vulture	1
	Unidentified Bird	60
	Subtotal MNU	259
Fish/Reptile/Amphibian		
	Bass	17
	Catfish	15
	Freshwater Drum	1
	Pikes	2

(continued)

Class	Species	1643–1660 MNU
	Rock Bass	8
	Smallmouth Bass	4
	Striped Bass	20
	Sturgeon	116
	Walleye Pike	1
	Yellow Perch	4
	Unidentified Fish	1,037
	Snake	1
	Turtle	7
	Snapping Turtle	4
	Frog/Toad	7
	Subtotal MNU	1,244
	TOTAL MNU	3,117

polished and may have been a tool. Body parts included the breast, wing, thigh, and foot. Domesticated bird species included chicken, duck, and goose. They were present in relatively low frequencies, chicken being the most abundant. There was a minimum of three individuals: one juvenile and two adults. Body part distributions included the head, breast, wing, back, thigh, leg, and foot. One leg bone exhibited slice marks. Duck was represented by a minimum of two adults. Goose was represented by a minimum of one adult individual. Body parts included the breast, wing, thigh, and foot. Many bird specimens were not identified by species. Within this group body parts included the skull, rib, breast, wing, back, thigh, leg, and foot. A few of these bones exhibited pathologies. Some longbones had medullary bone, indicating the presence of egg-laying hens.

Domesticated mammal species included cat, dog, horse, goat, cattle, sheep, and pig. Only cattle, sheep, and pig were present in high frequencies. Cat, dog, horse, and goat were infrequent and represented by a limited range of skeletal elements. Cat was represented by a minimum of three individuals, two adults and a juvenile. Body parts included a skull, three mandibles, two forelegs, a hip, and lower hind leg. The hip was arthritic, indicating an aged individual. Dog consisted of a mandible, incisors, and a foot bone from at least one subadult individual. The mandible was short and heavyset indicating that it came from a robust breed of dog. The small number of cat and dog specimens suggests their remains were treated differently. They were possibly buried as opposed to thrown onto the midden.

Horse was represented by a single shed incisor. This tooth indicates the animal was aged at two and a half years or more at death. The lack of other horse remains is interesting. A cultural bias against eating horses is suggested by the lack of horse bones. The farm was known to have specialized in horse breeding. Records reveal that Van Curler traded with Virginians for horses. Despite the great difficulties experienced by the colonists the lack of horse remains on archaeological sites strongly suggests that they did not eat their horses. Goat was rare. It consisted of a mandible from a very old individual and an articulated hind foot. The teeth were heavily plaqued and worn.

Cattle, sheep, and pig were the most frequent domesticated mammal species. These species, along with deer, represent the most important sources of meat at the Schuyler Flatts. Cattle was the most frequent mammal species though pig was nearly as abundant. There was a minimum of 13 cattle indicated in the assemblage. Cattle were represented by three age groups composed of three juveniles, three subadults, five adults, and two senile individuals. Mature individuals formed the largest age group. The smaller numbers of immature individuals probably represent the culling of males from the herd. Differences in size and stature were also observed that signal different sexes. Regardless of age or sex, all cattle were processed similarly. Only two horn cores were recovered suggesting that most cattle were either hornless or polled. Heads were processed for the removal of organ meats and facial tissues. Rib cuts were the most frequent, followed by the head. Hindquarter cuts were more abundant than forequarter cuts. While foot elements were well represented, there were less than the total number of cattle represented in the deposits. Most of the limbs were processed into large joints of meat. Stew meats were obtained from the lower limbs and spinal column.

Sheep were far more common than goat. There was a minimum of eight sheep represented. They fell into four age groups and included two neonates, two subadults, three adults, and one senile individual. Sheep body part distributions were not as comprehensive as cattle. There was a preponderance of upper foreleg and lower fore- and hindlimbs. The spinal column was poorly represented. Crania were virtually absent while mandibles were common. These exhibited butcher marks indicating the tongues were removed. The lower foreleg was the most frequent body part represented. There were fewer articulated feet than the number of sheep indicated. The uneven representation of body parts may indicate that mutton and lamb meat was shared with or marketed to other people, only certain parts being reserved for consumption at the farm.

Pig was represented almost as frequently as cattle. There was a minimum of 20 pigs. Most of these individuals were killed between the ages of one and one and a half years, though three neonates, one adult, and six more of unknown age were also indicated. During colonial times it was common to slaughter pigs as subadults. Pigs were slaughtered in the late fall (Rose 1989). It was the only time of the year normally that fresh pork was eaten. The bulk of the meat as well as the organs were preserved using a variety of methods, including pickling in brine, salting, and smoking (Rose 1989). There was a high frequency of heads, which were butchered for the removal of the brains, tongue, and facial tissues. There was a preponderance of meat cuts from the forequarter. Most skeletal elements were present in varying frequencies, indicating that some pigs were raised, slaughtered, and consumed at the Schuyler Flatts. Hams were extremely abundant; the most abundant type was the Boston butt ham from the upper foreleg. Additional hams from the butt and upper hind leg were present. The disproportional representation of hams suggests that hams and or other forms of preserved pork flesh were brought as units of meat to the farm.

A wide range of wild mammal species was recovered. Identified species included chipmunk, mouse, rat, woodchuck, rabbit, squirrel, raccoon, beaver, elk, bear, and deer. Except for bear and deer, wild species were uncommon and present in low frequencies. Some species may represent intrusions into the midden deposit. Chipmunk was represented by two individuals, and squirrel, mouse, and rat by a minimum of one individual each. Each species was indicated by mandibles, teeth, and a few limb bones. Beaver was infrequent consisting of an upper incisor, a first molar, and a butchered humerus and femur. Fox was also infrequent. Elements included a skull, three mandibles, an atlas, and two tibias. Raccoon was represented by a single individual consisting of teeth, a scapula, two ulnae, and a femur. Only one elk bone was identified, a butchered distal ulna. While it is possible that other elk bone was present, the large quantity of cattle remains may have obscured them due to heavy longbone reduction for marrow. Bear was not abundant though it was a pervasive throughout most of the excavation units. There was a minimum of two individuals indicated. One was larger in stature than the other. Skeletal elements included two mandibles, two incisors, five canines, a molar, three ulnae, a radius, three phalanges, a metapodial, a femur, a tibia, and a fibula. The mandibles and most of the longbones were butchered. The presence of bear may be tied to ritual feasting involving Native American and European interaction.

Deer was the third most abundant mammal species. There was a minimum of 16 individuals, including one juvenile, one subadult, three adults, and one senile individual. A deliberate selection process is indicated by a majority of adults. The selection of animals fully grown is typical of a hunting strategy. Deer body part distributions reveal a great disproportion in skeletal elements. There were very few skulls, though mandibles were common. Vertebrae were also infrequent. The hindquarter, especially the lower leg, was extremely abundant. Feet were abundant but did not reflect the number of individuals indicated. Overall, the data suggest that a small portion of the deer component may have resulted from localized hunting but that most of the remains represent haunches of venison. These consisted of leg joints from which the feet were removed prior to cooking. The presence of deer haunches may have been obtained by trade with Natives.

In addition to identified species, a large portion of the bone was classified as small, medium, and large mammal. This distribution reveals that a large volume of bone has been lost due to post-depositional factors. A wide range of skeletal remains is represented in all three categories, including the head, spinal column, rib, shoulder, butt, limbs, and feet.

Fish were extremely abundant and highly varied. All identified species were freshwater and anadromous fish. Historic accounts relate that fish was an important food source for Natives as well as the Dutch. Eel and salmon were most often mentioned though neither of these species was recognized in this assemblage. At least 10 species of fish were represented in the assemblage including bass, catfish, freshwater drum, pike sp., rock bass, smallmouth bass, striped bass, sturgeon, walleye, and yellow perch. Most fish elements consisted of gill, fin, and ray bones, while only a few vertebrae were recovered. Striped bass was the most abundant species. However, sturgeon represented the most meat. The size of recovered sturgeon scutes indicated the presence of massive fish, at least 10 ft or more in length. The skull bones of some fish species exhibited chop marks. The body part distributions indicate that most of the remains represent processing waste. The heads and fins were removed prior to cooking. The presence of burning on some of the skull and fin bones indicates that some fish were cooked whole.

Amphibian remains were represented by two partial toads. Body parts included three forelimbs, a hip, and two hind limbs. Reptiles included snapping turtle and an unidentified snake. Snapping turtle was represented by enormous carapace segments indicating it would have measured more than 3 ft in length. The snake consisted of a single vertebra.

The faunal assemblage from the Schuyler Flatts was large and highly varied in terms of species and meat cuts consumed. The analysis revealed much about animal husbandry, butchering patterns, dietary traditions, and trade practices relating to the economic and social interactions of the Van Curler household. A wide variety of mammal, bird, fish, and reptile species were consumed. Mammal and fish species provided most of the flesh consumed, though birds were also commonly eaten. Cattle, sheep, pig, and deer were the most eaten species.

Animal husbandry practices were focused on rearing cattle, sheep, and pigs. The relative importance of these species is hard to assess. Each species provided different kinds of resources. Animal consumption and exploitation patterns at the farm followed a set pattern. Cattle and sheep were reared for multiple reasons including milk, wool, labor, and meat, whereas pigs were raised for meat. Though horses were also raised the archaeological record revealed almost no trace of them.

The ages at which cattle, sheep, and pigs were slaughtered varied. Cattle were generally slaughtered as adults though there were several immature animals, likely males. The predominance of older cattle probably reflects an emphasis on dairying. Two oxen, draft animals, were identified. Sheep were mainly slaughtered as adults, though a few younger animals were present. They would have been raised for wool as well as for meat and possibly milk. Pigs were generally slaughtered as subadults. Preserved pork was eaten as well as fresh pork. The presence of a high number of hams suggests that preserved meats were brought to the farm as a food commodity. Deer were well represented but probably not hunted regularly. Harmen van den Bogaert's narrative revealed that the Dutch were "invited" to hunt (Van den Bogaert, in Jameson 1909). Perhaps opportunistic kills happened when deer ventured into crop fields. The high frequency of haunches suggests that venison was an important food commodity exchanged at the Schuyler Flatts by Natives.

Butcher patterns were similar for all the large mammals. The skulls and mandibles were processed for the removal of organ meats and facial tissue. The carcasses were split, and the limbs cut into large joints of meat. The lack of vertebra suggests a couple of explanations. It is possible they were fed to the dogs. But it is also possible that sides or quarters of carcasses were obtained from other farmers in the area. Any animal that died or had to be put down was consumed. A large animal could not be consumed by a small group of people nor could it be preserved in hot weather, so it is likely that people shared meat when a large animal was slaughtered. Large joints of meat serve as a reminder that many people shared the same meals even if they ate them in different places and at different times.

Discussion

During the first couple of decades the New Netherland colony struggled to establish an agricultural basis that could supply its needs. By the mid-seventeenth century, however, agricultural production had gained a foothold, and though the colonists were far from self-sufficient, they were more stable. Toward the end of the century they achieved the ability to meet their food supply needs. Wildlife resources remained constant throughout the century. Food played an important role in maintaining social relationships between colonists and Natives, with venison being a major trade commodity. Other foods were likely traded as well, including fish and fowl. Archaeological evidence for the fur trade is ephemeral, which is not surprising since prepared skins would not have had many bone elements attached to them. Still, traces of fur-bearers were apparent at Fort Orange, DEC Headquarters, and the Schuyler Flatts. The clearest evidence for intense trade, however, was seen in deposits at the trader's hut, where butchered dog, horse, and bear were found. The Schuyler Flatts also had butchered bear, though the remains were casually discarded in the midden. These unusual examples show the presence of Natives engaging with colonists in close quarters, sharing foods that they may have brought. The faunal assemblages from the four sites revealed patterns of continuity and change among Dutch people living in the Albany area over the course of several decades of the seventieth century. The Dutch struggled to establish a foothold in this remote location and did so by adopting new foods, maintaining good social relationships with Natives, and eventually giving attention to agricultural pursuits.

The archaeological evidence recovered from Fort Orange, DEC Headquarters, Quackenbush Square, and the Schuyler Flatts provide information about early colonial foodways not otherwise recorded. The mundane details of daily meals are often missing in the immense historical record. Cookbooks suggest possibilities but do not necessarily document realities. Diaries and inventories do not clearly document of dietary practices. When such written records are found, they rarely discuss in detail what was consumed or what was perceived as taboo. Archaeology fills in, then, a major gap in our knowledge of this early and period of complex cultural change and adaptation by both Dutch and other European immigrants, as well as resident Native peoples, who were introduced to a new set of animals from the Old World.

7

Woman the Trader

Native Women in New Netherland

Anne-Marie Cantwell and Diana diZerega Wall

This essay focuses on exchanges between Native women and Europeans in New Netherland that included not only trade but also intimate encounters. Although the latter occurred primarily during the earliest period of Dutch settlement, when there were relatively few European women in the colony, they persisted into the later years of the colony as well, according to the limited documents available (Jacobs 2005:4). Here we are not discussing the vital roles of Native women who were actively engaged in their settlements, nor their equally vital roles in preparing beaver pelts, corn, or wampum for exchange in the fur trade, nor their roles in inciting mourning wars, adoption, or local politics (Engelbrecht 2003; Goddard 1978; Loren 2008; Mann 2000; Nassaney 2000, 2004, 2015; Romney 2014, 2016; Rothschild 1995, 2003; Snow 1994; Tooker 1984).

Instead, our focus is on direct exchanges that by and large did not take place at Native settlements but rather occurred when Native women crossed that social space from Indian country into the European and African zone that was the colony of New Netherland itself. We argue that when they did, they usually did it not as wives, servants, or concubines but as independent agents often acting for themselves. Their relationships with Europeans were, we argue, part of a continuation and expansion of traditional societal practices of exchange and gift giving, and the Europeans, probably unknowingly, conformed to those practices. In fact, the arrival of the Europeans and the introduction of the fur trade may, in those early years of the colony, have offered them more opportunities. These exchanges between

Native women and European men cannot be seen in isolation but must be seen in the context of the roles of the European and African women who also inhabited that colony. The actions or non-actions of all these women impinge upon each other. All of their roles may in fact be affected by the *absence* or the *presence* of one or the other of these groups of women—the absence of the European women during the early years and the presence of African women throughout this period.

We hope this analysis will go beyond the often-criticized "add gender and stir" approach (e.g., Lugones 2010) and contribute to the discussion of the early years of settler-colonial societies, founded when modern European nation-states were first emerging and slavery was first being introduced to northeastern North America. Colonial enterprises differed, but it was often Native societies that gave them their essential shape, an important point too often overlooked (Hinderaker and Horn 2010:429). We also hope that this study will contribute to the interpretations of archaeological sites of that era, since it challenges many stereotypes of Native women. These stereotypes are based on the assumption that in New Netherland, European men stayed in their trading posts and settlements along the rivers, while Mohawk and Algonquian women stayed at home in their longhouses or wigwams, isolated from interactions with the newcomers. Then it is assumed only Native men crossed back and forth between these two worlds when they brought furs to the posts to sell. These stereotypes also ignore the presence of Africans and the effect of their presence on Native-European relationships. A corollary of this assertion, often assumed, is that Native women did not participate in exchange with Europeans: they did not engage in the fur trade themselves and had very little intimate contact with European men during this period. Although not explicitly stated, it is implied that European goods found in Native archaeological sites and the Native goods found at European sites all arrived through the agency of Native men.

WOMAN THE TRADER

A close scrutiny of the records shows that Native women did not always stay home, cloistered from a larger world that included Europeans and Africans as well as members of other Native societies. In fact, right from the beginning they took part in trade with the newcomers. Hints of this come from one of the earliest documents we have. Robert Juet, Hudson's first mate, wrote that when they arrived in New York Harbor on September 5, 1609:

> Our men went on Land there, and saw great store of Men, *Women*, and Children, who gaue them Tabacco at their comming on Land. . . . This day many of the people came aboord, some in Mantles of Feathers, and some in Skins of divers sorts of good Furres. Some *women* also came to vs with Hempe. They had red Copper Tabacco pipes, and other things of Copper they did weare about their neckes. (Jameson 1909:18; emphasis ours)

Seven days later, as they sailed a few miles up the Hudson, "there came eight and twentie Canoes full of men, *women*, and children" (Jameson 1909:20; emphasis ours).

Following the establishment of the colony, American women, both Algonquian and Iroquoian, went to the European settlements under many circumstances and for many reasons. Some came with their families, for trade, treaty, or land negotiations; to seek protection; to visit; and even out of curiosity. However, some also came on their own or with other women to participate in the newly formed Atlantic trade in their own right; like many of their Northern European women neighbors, they were also active in the fur trade. The documentary records are scanty in their accounts of Native life and often do not mention the gender of the actors, let alone their names. Much of the evidence comes to us in the form of court records, suggesting that much of what went on that did not wind up in court is not revealed to us (c.f. Fabend 2003:272). These records frequently do not mention Native tribal affiliations, which the Europeans may not have even known; this means we sometimes have to use the more generic terms "Native" or "American," although we realize, obviously, that there are significant differences among the various groups.

Even with this flawed documentary record, there are some clues to help us understand the role of Native women in the emerging Atlantic world. Some come from the minutes of the court at Fort Orange dealing with incidents when the law was broken. For example, one case in 1654 notes that a Native woman gave wampum to a European woman in exchange for brandy in a small pewter bottle (Gehring 1990:154; see also Gehring 1990:263). There is also an account of a 1660 court case at Fort Orange involving a woman trader, probably Mohawk, and Adriaen Jansen van Leyden, the defendant. The Native woman was accosted by an agent of

Van Leyden while bringing furs to her preferred trader in Fort Orange, given wampum, and brought to the defendant's home. Once she was there, "she refused to trade and insisted on going to Volckert Jansens," whereupon her beavers were retained and she was pushed outdoors by the defendant's servant, the door being then locked" (Gehring 1990:523). The woman was not cowed and filed a complaint with Johannes la Montagne, an officer of the court, who presented her case for her and then ordered Van Leyden to restore her furs. Van Leyden's wife refused to do so, and the Native woman was forced to trade there. The case returned to court, but its resolution is not documented.

This last account raises a host of issues. It suggests that Native women were traders; were not awed by European men; and, even though they lived outside the colony, were savvy enough in Dutch ways to address the wrongs done to them in the Dutch court. It further suggests that this woman, at least, was an accomplished trader who had established a trading relationship with a particular preferred European trading partner: Volckert Jansen Douw, a prominent magistrate and trader. The remains of his house were found during the excavations by Hartgen Archeological Associates at the KeyCorp Site in Albany in the 1980s. Excavations revealed evidence of Douw's trading stock which included such preferred items as blue tubular beads, knives, mouth harps, European smoking pipes, and lead bars, among other things (Bradley 2007:120; Fisher 2008: 15–16; Pena 1990:100–101).

Obviously, we don't know whether the Native woman who was heading for the well-stocked Douw house when she was intercepted was interested in acquiring some of these particular goods or something else entirely. Nonetheless, this incident raises questions as to who was responsible for the acquisition of trade goods that archaeologists have recovered in Native households. Archaeological excavations at the homes of European traders such as Arent van Curler at Schuyler Flatts and Hendrick and Marietje van Doesburgh at Fort Orange also recovered evidence of their stock for Native traders. Van Curler, who was friendly with Mohawks, had been involved with a Mohawk woman, and had a child by her, may have learned through her what would comprise good stock. At Schuyler Flatts, Paul Huey recovered European ceramics, some of which may have been intended for the Indian trade, funnel bowl clay smoking pipes made expressly for the Indian trade, glass beads, brass mouth harps, tinkler cones, iron knives, and gun parts (Bradley 2005; Huey 1998:28). Huey's excavations at the Van Doesburgh house in Fort Orange also uncovered trade items, including funnel bowl clay pipes, wampum, glass beads, and gun parts, as well as fragments of Native pottery, perhaps left by a Mohawk woman trader (Huey 1988a:352, 414–416, 466, 594).

So women clearly bridged the social space between their settlements and those of their European neighbors. Furthermore, it seems that this may have been part of a long-standing pattern of women trading among Native groups and that the arrival of the Europeans simply presented Native women with an opportunity to expand already established patterns of exchange and gift giving for their own advantage and that of their lineage. We have already noted that Algonquian women were among the parties greeting Hudson on his arrival here, hoping for trade or rather an exchange of gifts. And Van den Bogaert on his trip into the interior in 1634–1635 noted that three women, perhaps Seneca, had come to Mohawk country to exchange fish and tobacco (Gehring and Starna 2013; see Waterman 2008:139, 143 for Iroquois women trading in later periods).

Many settlers in Beverwijck had special accommodations for visiting Natives, probably including women. These outbuildings were referred to as "little Indian houses" (Venema 2003:92). This may also have been the practice in New Amsterdam, where Sara Roeloffse, wife of the surgeon Hans Kierstede, is reputed to have had a shed built in her yard to accommodate Native traders who had come to the settlement. It is said that "under its shelter there was always a number of squaws who came and went as if in their own village" (Grossman 2009; Van Rensselaer 1898:26). They were not trading furs (which had already been hunted out in that area) but were reported to be making baskets and brooms to sell at market, stringing wampum, and sewing and spinning, as well as selling maize and venison. This evidence that Native women visited Dutch homes requires that we rethink the analysis of assemblages from these homes so that we can look for the presence of these women there.

As a final note, Ruth Trocolli (1999:57) has offered insights that might be helpful in looking at the archaeological record. She suggests that "the separation of the so-called domestic sphere from the public sphere is an analytical model that is not applicable to all societies." In speaking of Native North American peoples, particularly those living in matrilineal societies, she argues that "these women's existential identities are not tied to notions of passivity, lack of personal power, dependence, and childishness—qualities associated with women in Western culture. . . . [Instead, t]hese women accessed roles that in Western society are gendered and limited to, or reserved for, men. Such roles are not defined by gender in their own societies;

instead they are circumstantial" (Trocolli 1999:56). We agree and argue that trading is one of those roles that is not inherently defined by gender but instead is circumstantial. Further, we argue below that sexual freedom for some Native women differed significantly from seventeenth-century (not to mention twenty-first-century) Western notions and may not have been understood for those very reasons.

INTIMATE EXCHANGES

In 1638, just before the company removed its monopoly on the fur trade, it proscribed sexual relationships between Native and African women and European men: "Furthermore, each and everyone shall refrain from fighting; from adulterous intercourse with heathens, blacks or other persons" (Van Laer 1974b:4). Both the existence of this ordinance and a close reading of the documents show that even though the Europeans tended not to write about them, such relationships between European men and Native women certainly existed in New Netherland. Most of the documented relationships took place during the early period, before the arrival of large numbers of European women in the colony (Rink 1986:146–147, 166–167).

Colonist Adriaen van der Donck (Gehring and Starna 2008:75), in his paean to New Netherland, described the situation between Native women and European men clearly: "their womenfolk have an attractive grace about them, for several Dutchmen, before many Dutch women were to be had there, became infatuated with them." We argue that at least some of these relationships were consensual, involved customary gift giving, and provided women with power, a power neither intended nor understood by the European men who contributed to it. The Europeans did not understand either the workings of matrilineal societies or the sexual codes of the Americans (Mann 2000:275–277). Furthermore, the Europeans also did not understand the difference between commodity exchange and gift exchange or the Native concept of gift giving (Murray 2000:15–47).

We do not have enough information about African women to determine whether these relationships were consensual for them, but we can only suspect they were not. Although many African women also came from matrilineal societies, most of them were now, unlike Native women, living enslaved within a European colony. Even though they did, presumably, have support from the African community and many had established strong kinships relations in the colony (Evans 1901; Purple 1890; Romney 2014:191–244), they did not have the support of their homeland kin. In the early years of the colony, the nature of enslavement was quite different from what it would become in the middle of the century (see Cantwell and Wall 2015; Jacobs 2005:380–388), and Africans were able to join the Dutch Reformed Church, where many were married and had their children baptized (Cantwell and Wall 2015:35; Evans 1901; Purple 1890; Romney 2014:208–213). Baptism provided godparents for their children, vital relationships for building kin networks in an environment where people had been enslaved and stripped of their families.

Documentation on transient sexual relations between European men on the one hand and indigenous and African women on the other often appears in the record in the form of evidence used to undermine the character of male witnesses or defendants in cases brought before the company's council. There are reports that women, African and Native alike, sometimes spent the night with European soldiers at a guardhouse in New Amsterdam. For example, in 1638 Nicolaes Coorn, a sergeant, was charged with theft and adultery; part of the charge was that he had several times had "Indian women and Negresses sleep entire nights with him in his bed, in the presence of all the soldiers" (Van Laer 1974b:33, 44–45, 122; see also Lipman 2015:175, 309n16; Romney 2014: 177–181; Williams 2001:68). None of the testimonies contained mention that Native or African women were forced against their wills. However, of course, coercion though not recorded may certainly have occurred.

Although some scholars invariably see sexual relations between European men and Native women in New Netherland as instances of dominance or coercion (see Foote 2004 as well as Anderson 1991 for neighboring New France; but see Mann 2000 and Williams 2001 to the contrary), and some contemporary European men describe the behavior of Native women as "whorish" (Jameson 1909:174), neither description is accurate, and the situation seems more complex. As Kurt Jordan (2016:69) has argued, "indigenous systems provide a vector of difference that indigenous populations drew upon in social action." The seventeenth-century sexuality of Native Algonquian and Iroquoian women should be examined in the context of Native culture and not western culture (Lugones 2010; Troccoli 1999; see also Jordan 2016:69–70). In most cases, according to the documents available, the women were neither coerced nor "whorish"; they were simply following traditional models of gift giving and exchange. By no means do we imply that there was no coerced sex. Far from it. The absence of court cases does not mean an absence of events. But it seems that at least some of these liaisons were ones into which unmarried women entered willingly for their own purposes, for pleasure, power, prestige, or wealth. Although for the Natives adultery on the part of married women was frowned upon except under special circumstances, it was acceptable for young unmarried women to have sexual relationships with men of their own choosing, whether European or Indian. Furthermore, exchange in the form of gift giving on the part of the man to the woman formed an important part of these trysts. Adriaen van der Donck (Gehring and Starna 2008:86; emphasis ours) recounts that

> if the woman is single or . . . unattached . . . *she may do as she pleases, provided she accepts payment. Free favors they regard as scandalous and whorelike.* She is not blamed for what else happens to her, and no one will later scruple to propose marriage to the woman concerned. It also happens that a free woman cohabits with someone for a time so long as he satisfied her and gives her enough, whom she would nevertheless not wish to marry. They are *actually proud of such liaisons* and as they begin to grow old, boast of having slept with many chiefs and brave men. I was amazed to hear how sedate and steady women, of the worthiest among them, *thought highly of themselves when speaking of such conduct on their part, as if it were praiseworthy and glorious.*

Other documents confirm the importance of Native customary gift giving in these relationships, although they may see it through the lens of their own European sexual codes. For example, Domine Megapolensis in 1644 described such liaisons thus: "The women are exceedingly addicted to whoring: they will lie with a man for the value of one, two or three *schillings*, and our Dutchmen run after them very much" (Jameson 1909:174). A more concrete example comes from an incident in the 1650s, when a Mohawk woman, described as having a "beautiful figure," is reported to have had sex with Jacob van Leeuwen, a merchant who frequently visited New Netherland, in the Fort Orange courthouse attic during church service. At some point during their encounter, Van Leeuwen gave her a necklace made up of blue and red beads that she was seen wearing as she came down the courthouse steps after their tryst. Evidently the gift pleased her because she was often seen wearing it later on (Venema 2003:168). In her society, gift giving played an important and necessary role in sexual relationships for unmarried women, and that necklace was her due (Jacobs 2005:396; Venema 2003:169; for additional comparative studies of intimate encounters, see Loren 2012; Rothschild 1995, 2003; and Voss and Casella 2011).

In sum, the records indicate that through the gifts given by European men (who were perhaps unwittingly adopting traditional Native exchange), these women, on their own accord and through the power of their own sexuality, also actively entered the emerging Atlantic economy. Through this exchange, they obtained wealth in money or trade goods, as well as power that added to their own or their lineages' prestige. As Van der Donck reported, older women often boasted of their youthful affairs. Furthermore, these gifts may have been part of a process used by Native women to maintain power in the changing circumstances of colonization (c.f. Sorenson 2000:175). Although a colonizer may see a Native woman as "a potential convert and labourer, wife, concubine, slave, part of social exchanges and political alliances, a fleeting unwilling sex partner or an object of abuse and degradation" (Sorenson 2000:173), that does not, we argue, mean that the Native woman saw herself as the colonizer did. From her perspective, the colonizer may be a source of the new material goods she desires; a way of maintaining her status and that of her lineage; a source of power, pleasure, and perhaps prestige for her children; or an access point to a wider exchange network. In other words, she might benefit from such a relationship in many ways. Gender, as Jordan (2016:63, 69–70) pointed out, is also a "category in motion."

Since unmarried women were free to explore their sexuality as they pleased, we wonder if in addition to the novelty of European gifts that they valued and received from their encounters, the novelty of European men was also an appealing factor and may have played into their fantasies. Such contacts may have been explored for any number of reasons, including desire. No records that we know of from oral traditions or European sources say one way or another. Yet we cannot but wonder if some Native women may have found some European men attractive while others did not or were indifferent. European men, after all, were very different in appearance than Native men. They were hairier on face and body, and their eyes were not all the same color. As Evan Haefeli (2007:426, referencing Moogk 2000:25–27) noted in another context, hairiness was associated with animals and "the multicolored eyes of Europeans only had counterparts among dogs and wolves." Some women may have found these "animalistic" qualities ambiguous, seductive, or magical and therefore highly desirable. Others, of course, may have not. Furthermore, Marie Sorenson (2000:177), in talking about the "newness" associated with contact, reminds us how "the outsider, or that which is new or from far away, can be an object of imagination and desire" and how contact can be an exploration and a highly charged one.

We should not leave desire and curiosity, from the perspective of Europeans or Africans or Native peoples, out of the equation of intimate encounters. In regard to the allure of sexual fantasies from the European perspective, Cornelis van Tienhoven, the company's secretary, was reputed to have run around dressed as an Indian, "with a little cloth and a small patch in front, from lust after the whores to whom he has always been mightily inclined" (Adriaen van der Donck, quoted in Jacobs 2005:396).

Parenthetically, we should note that we have no evidence of intimacies between European women and Native or African men, although there is an intriguing account given by Pierre Esprit Radisson in which a Dutch farm woman shows curiosity about whether such intimacies have in fact taken place. Radisson was escaping from the Mohawks, who had captured and adopted him. He then decided to escape and was posing as a Mohawk fur trader and was hiding at the Dutch farm from his Mohawk captors. The woman's husband was away at Fort Orange looking for help for him. Radisson reports that the woman, thinking he was Mohawk, "shews me good countenance as much as shee could, hoping of a better imaginary profit of me. Shee asked me if we had so much liberty with the ffrench to lye with them as they; but I had no desire to do anything, seeing myselfe so insnared att death's door among the terrible torments, but must shew a better countenance to a worse game" (Snow et al. 1996:92).

These liaisons did not go unnoticed in the metropole. In addition to the company ordinance against sexual relationships between Dutch men and Native and African women, mentioned above, in 1643 Kiliaen van Rensselaer, the patroon of Rensselaerswijck (his private colony near Albany), who lived in the Dutch Republic, imposed a series of fines on the men in his colony who cohabited with "heathen" women. The fines ranged from 25 guilders for "unchastity with heathen women and girls," to 50 guilders if the woman became pregnant, and to 100 guilders if the woman gave birth (Van Laer 1908:694). His bothering to implement these fines indicates not only that was cohabitation an ongoing issue but also that he was troubled by the possibility or the actuality that an Indian woman might become pregnant and bear a child fathered by a European in his employ. As James Homer Williams (2001:65–66) points out, Hugo Grotius, the foremost Dutch judicial scholar of the time, saw adultery as a form of behavior against personal honor and reputation. Related to this were fears that extramarital sex led to illegitimate children that resulted in threats to public order and the sanctity of marriage. Van Rensselaer had grounds to be concerned. As mentioned above, Arent van Curler, one of his employees who was also a kinsman, fathered a daughter with a Mohawk woman (Wilcoxen 1979). Van Curler was not alone, and there are other references to the children born of these relationships. What Van Rensselaer and other Europeans did not understand, however, was that because American peoples in New Netherland were by and large matrilineal and matrilocal, reproduction rights rested in the mother's lineage (Snow et al. 1996:44). All children were members of their mothers' matrilineage, regardless of who their fathers were, and were raised by their mothers' people. From the Native viewpoint, in the early years of colonization, constructions of identity were not made by Europeans either in the metropole or colonial settlements. They were made in Native settlements, and there was no stigma attached to the circumstances of a child's parentage as there might have been in the European colony. In fact, Radisson notes that when he was living with the Mohawks, his best friend there was courting a young Mohawk woman "who by report of many was a bastard to a flemish. I had no difficulty to believe, seeing that the coulour of her hayre was much more whiter then that of the Iroquoits. *Neverthelesse, shee was of a great familie*" (Snow et al. 1996:91; emphasis ours).

Native women themselves do not appear to have made demands on their former lovers for themselves or their children, though in 1659 a Mohawk delegation went to Fort Orange with a number of demands, including "that when any one of their people dies and the Dutch is her mate, he ought to give to the relatives of the deceased one or two suits of cloth" (Gehring 1990:454). Unfortunately, the court minutes do not mention the outcome of this particular demand (Gehring 1990: 453–460). Nonetheless, the fact that this demand was presented at a formal court session at Fort Orange underlines the ubiquity and the knowledge of such relationships, the fact that marriage or cohabitation was not part of them, and the important role of gift giving in them.

Many studies of intimate relationships in colonial encounters seem to focus on the "sexual politics of colonial institutions" (Voss 2008:192). In looking at New Netherland, it is obvious to us that the sexual politics of *indigenous* institutions is just as important and has been too long ignored. In this case, Native women are not responding to colonial institutions but rather to their own. In fact, they are making the colonizers respond to them by their insistence on exchange and gift giving. In so doing, the women may be expanding on traditional mores for their own advantage. So although in many colonial societies, to be sure, "concubinage, slavery, and servitude were likely to have been the most common means through which colonists incorporated Native Americans and Africans of both genders into their households" (Voss 2008:192), this was not the situation in all European colonies throughout their histories. Natives were not in all cases incorporated into colonial households, nor were they cloistered in their own settlements with little contact with Europeans. The situation with African women in New Netherland is quite different, as we discuss below. But Native women in many instances not only acted according to their own cultural norms but were able to make European men follow those norms as well.

It is these instances, we argue, that have not received sufficient scholarly attention (c.f. White 1999). What Gilles Havard (2003:50, quoted in Cohen 2008:21) argued for Native people of the Great Lakes could also be argued for Native women in New Netherland: "far from seeing themselves as actors on the European periphery, [they] believed themselves to be at the center of the world." It is important to incorporate Native and African archaeology and history into colonial archaeology and history to realize that non-colonials have their own worlds and perspectives in which sometimes Europeans play only a peripheral role (e.g. Cohen 2008; DuVal 2006; Richter 2001; Trigger 1984; Van Zandt 1998, 2008). It is only through considering their worlds that a true understanding of colonialism—one of the most dramatic, painful, complex events in world history, with effects continuing to this day—can be understood. These ignored worlds, including the agency of women, challenge the traditional, romantic, and self-congratulatory narratives so common to settler societies (Stasiulis and Yuval-Davis 1995:4; see also Greene 2007:235) and reshape American history and other histories as well. As a final note, Sorenson (2000:181) has pointed out that although contact does not always benefit women, it is a mistake to think that it *never* benefits them or that they are passive in their encounters with Europeans. It is also important to remember that the roles of women (as well as those of everyone else) in colonial situations are never static but are constantly changing as they adapt to new circumstances. As we said above, gender is a category in motion (Jordan 2016:70).

ENGENDERING NEW NETHERLAND

We have tried to show that Native women in New Netherland were not simply "an appendage to colonial history" as Bruce Trigger (1984:32) argued in another context. Nor do they fit into the triad that researchers have suggested for Native women living elsewhere in settler societies in North America: intermarriage, concubinage, or servitude. In fact, in New Netherland, Native women had agency and power in their interactions with

Europeans. They appear to have followed their own established traditions and expected Europeans to conform to them as well. They may have used the Europeans to improve their own status and standing and initially such contact may have benefited them. Europeans may have misunderstood and not realized that they themselves were, in fact, doing what the women expected them to do. As in many colonial situations, all sides, compelled by their own patterns of culture, acted with little knowledge of, or interest in, what that interaction meant to the other. European men may have thought that the Native women were prostituting and degrading themselves, but for Native women it seems to have been a simple matter of traditional exchange and gift giving in a customary sexual context that was appropriate for unmarried women. Of course there may very well have been coerced sex that was not recorded in court and other records, but we do not have evidence of that and therefore do not know.

The preliminary implications of our study, looking at New Netherland from the vantage point of Native women, are twofold. The first relates to a rethinking of the archaeological record. Archaeologists have tended to assume that most European goods found in Native contexts arrived there through the agency and design of Native men—they were the fur traders, they were the ones in contact with the Europeans—while the women, by and large, stayed home. But what we have shown challenges that view. Native women were certainly in contact with Europeans in New Netherland in various exchange contexts where they too obtained European goods. The fur trade and the arrival of the Europeans offered new opportunities for women, opportunities that they seized. What this means is that we as archaeologists must now develop new ways of interpreting the European trade goods that have been found in Native contexts, and of understanding who acquired them. Furthermore, we need to rethink the assemblages found on European sites. Native goods would not necessarily have been left by Native men who were trading. Native women were also trading there. And we cannot assume that European traders chose the trade goods archaeologists have recovered on their sites for trade with men exclusively. Nor can we give a facile explanation for the goods that we have recovered from European homes.

In other words, we must rethink the patterns of interaction and exchange between and among all the various groups in seventeenth-century New Netherland as they, with varying degrees of power, built the new Atlantic world. To elaborate upon what Natalie Zemon Davis (1994:85) has argued, we must "insist on the absolute simultaneity of the Amerindian and European worlds" and look for interactions "in the colonial encounter other than the necessary and overpolarized two-some of 'domination' and 'resistance' and attribute the capacity for choice to Indians as [well as] to Europeans." That capacity for choice also, obviously, includes Native women. Although we may never be able to sort out just who left particular artifacts behind—Indian, African, or European, male or female—we should at least not assume that they all arrived solely through the agency of European or Native men. We need to think of the activities of Native women outside their households as they bridged the social distance between Native and European worlds and how this might affect household assemblages in Native and European households. In addition, there is the larger question of how their efforts led to a creation of the new entity that became colonial America as all groups tried to maintain and expand their own worlds. This and other questions will provoke new ways of looking at archaeological assemblages and stimulate the formulation of additional questions. Further, understanding the roles of and exchanges between the men and women of all of the cultural groups living in or on the outskirts of colonies will also provide a greater understanding of colonialism itself.

The second thrust of our study relates to the role of women in the earliest years of a colonial encounter. Ann Stoler (1989:154) has noted that "early colonial communities commonly produced a quotidian world in which the dominant cultural influence in the household was Native." However, this was certainly not true in New Netherland, a colony that persisted only during the earliest stages of colonialism in North America. Native women there had autonomy and entered the colony on their own terms, then returned to their own households and settlements and kin groups. They were not recruited to work, willingly or unwillingly, in European kitchens or nurseries either before or after the arrival of European women in the colony. And although they may have slept with European men, it seems to have been mostly of their own choosing.

Unfortunately, we have found no specific mention in the documents of who cooked for the European men during the early period, when European women were scarce. Jaap Jacobs (2005:382) suggests that enslaved Africans, probably female, were used in domestic tasks, and the only hints that we found support his interpretation. However, those hints are scanty. There is a reference to a young African girl, Maria, "belonging to the honorable West India Company." Company director Kieft leased her to Nicolas Coorn in Rensselaerswijck for four years (Van Laer 1974b:223–224). (This may well be the same Nicolaes Coorn whom we mentioned above, who was charged by the company's council with spending nights with Native and African women.) Another source mentions three older African women who were given their freedom in the early 1660s on condition that one of them come and clean the home of Director General Petrus Stuyvesant every week (Jacobs 2005:382). Jan Gerritsen is known to have had a woman slave, but it is not clear whether she was a domestic slave or worked in his brewery or both (Williams 2001:68; for further discussions of Africans in the colony, see Cantwell and Wall 2015; Romney 2014; Van Zandt 1998, 2008; for European women, see Fabend 2003; Romney 2014, 2016; Shattuck 1994). Certainly, enslaved African women in these colonial households were in a very different position than contemporary Native women, and they were certainly far from being free agents.

This raises an important point. We speculate that Native women might have escaped domestic roles in European homes in New Netherland (unlike in many other colonial situations), not only because they lived in matrilineal and matrilocal societies with settlements at a remove and thus were able to engage Europeans on their own terms, but also because that role was filled by enslaved African women, both in the early days, when European women were in such short supply, and afterwards. In other words, perhaps Europeans were *not* making claims on the domestic labor of Native women in the European settlements because they had coopted the labor of enslaved African women instead. Much of the Indian country that became New Netherland was not densely populated, and the indigenous peoples there lived in small-scale, non-hierarchical societies. Some historians studying similar topographical and cultural environments in Latin America suggest that it is in such conditions (unlike those, say, in populous, hierarchical central imperial Mexico, where indigenous labor was easier to coopt) that Europeans were more likely to depend on enslaved African labor (e.g., Hinderaker and Horn 2010:429). This might also be a factor in the case of New Netherland and should be given more consideration. We should not forget the important role that Native societies and their ecosystems play in shaping colonial worlds.

Clearly more attention needs to be applied to colonial situations where there are both free and enslaved non-European women present and where the Native populations are matrilineal and matrilocal. It is also important, in studying colonialism, to remember that the roles of one group of women (or men) cannot be studied in isolation from the presence or the absence of other groups of women (or men). Their lives (in this case Native, African, and European) are entangled with each other, whether or not they ever met. It is that tangle that raises intriguing possibilities in understanding the working of colonies such as New Netherland.

As we have tried to show, although colonialism may be universal, it is by no means uniform. It is composed of many local entanglements, such as those described here, which must first be understood before their aggregate can be appreciated. There is no place on the globe today that has not been touched by colonialism in one way or another, and studies of it and the inequality that inevitably follow in its wake remain central not only to archaeology but to our understanding of the modern human condition.

III

The South River

8

Tamecongh, or Aresapa, to New Castle

LU ANN DE CUNZO

Beginning early in the twenty-first century, scholars started to reexamine the Delaware Valley's early colonial history. They have challenged models of structural hierarchies in which European homelands and colonies dominated indigenous populations and appropriated resources (e.g., Lightfoot 2004:209). In the seventeenth-century lower Delaware Valley, Europe could not provide colonists and soldiers in the numbers and with the means needed to take control. In 1654 at least 4,000 Lenape lived along the Lenapewihittuck (later South, then Delaware) River along with about 400 Swedes, Finns, and Dutch; by 1671 the number of Europeans had barely doubled (Soderlund 2015:86, 115).

Recent revisions accept that Native peoples had greater agency and determinacy than historians and archaeologists had previously acknowledged. Mark Thompson (2010:105) argued that European and Native traders, settlers, merchants, and officials negotiated the contest for the Delaware Valley by constructing transnational or "cosmopolitan" affiliations with diverse actors maintaining connections through communication and daily practices. Native traders shrewdly shifted among European nations when discontent, affording them power and control. Jean Soderlund (2015:4–5) concluded that, in fact, "the Lenapes dominated trade in the Delaware Valley and determined if, when, and where Europeans could travel and take up land." She concurred with Thompson that the Lenape maintained their sovereignty through diplomacy, strategic localized alliances and violence. Daniel Richter (2016:272) disputed Sonderlund's position, describing the lower Delaware Valley instead as the "periphery of a landscape that the

Iroquois and Susquehannocks dominated from the headwaters of the Hudson, Delaware, and Susquehanna river systems."

Here I query the nature of Native-European relationships through the lens of one fortified Dutch settlement in this Lenape homeland and European colonial borderland between the English Chesapeake and the New Netherland colonial center. I share Christopher Gosden's (2014:481) perspective that "colonial encounters were about danger, experiment, ambiguity, and shock, where the values that all parties brought to the encounter were put at risk and often overturned. . . . The colonial past was made up of a number of intersecting dimensions of strangeness." Susan Romney's (2014:18) project to understand the "intimate networks" that constituted the Dutch Atlantic economic empire in New Netherland also informs my approach. These "webs of ties . . . developed from people's immediate, affective, and personal associations and spanned vast geographic and cultural distances." Material practices have received little attention in past studies, except the imposition of European town plans and privatization of property. "How people lived, ate, worshipped, and dressed" were contested objects of uncertainty and anxiety in colonial contexts, and warrant our consideration (DiPaolo Loren 2012:106, 2014:256). Referencing time and space to traditional frameworks and philosophies, finding a way to "reflect alterity and not modernity" is difficult but essential to accessing Native meanings of material culture in colonial settings (Vitelli 2011:177–178).

In this chapter, my larger purpose is to assess the usefulness of borderlands theory to understanding the lower Delaware Valley between 1650 and 1664. Borderlands are dynamic landscapes fraught with "tensions and . . . conflicts, control and friendly relations." Borderlands "empower, creating possibilities to act in ways impossible or difficult to do in other places" (Naum 2010:102, 127). They are liminal places: multivocal, multilocal, shifting, situational places ripe for deployment of strategic identities. In borderlands, rituals of power and boundary-marking or of self-deception about one's powerlessness become essential to forging and maintaining alliances through symbols of cooperation and integration (Donnan and Wilson 1999:63–86; Fur 2009:16–18).

Actors accommodated difference in colonial encounters through their interactions and negotiations, creating hybrid transcultural forms, affiliations, and meanings (Silliman 2014:490). The process of hybridity created cultural entanglements through the dynamics of creativity, innovation, experimentation, fusion, commercialization, mimicry, mockery, and reflection (Deagan 2013:261, 274; Liebmann 2013:41; Silliman 2013:493).[1]

HISTORICAL CONTEXT

Lenapehocking was the early seventeenth-century homeland of several autonomous political groups in the Delaware Valley. Lenape favored inland villages accessible to the waterfront, moving seasonally between woods and coastal settings to plant, hunt, gather, and fish. By 1632 groups of Minquas (later known as Susquehannocks) from the Pennsylvania interior traveled down to the river laden with furs, attacking Lenape to secure the fur trade (Fur 2009:7).

The private Dutch West Indies Company, founded in 1621, secured a monopoly on trade, governance, and navigation to New Netherland (Johnson 2005:5). The WIC created a landscape of small forts built in low-lying waterfront areas along the North and South Rivers to protect them from European invaders. Explorers determined that the South Bay offered good harbor and anchorage, trade and commercial potential, as well as fertile fields (Gehring and Starna 2008:7, 10). Under Peter Minuit's instigation, the Swedes established New Sweden, headquartered at today's Wilmington, Delaware in 1638. Petrus Stuyvesant, who became director general of New Netherland in 1647, perceived that the English would take advantage of the colony if divided by the Swedish incursion. Stuyvesant opted for bold military action, and in 1651 relocated Fort Nassau across the South River to a place the Lenape called Tamecongh or Aresapa, naming it Fort Casimir. The Swedes retaliated, recapturing the fort. In 1655 Stuyvesant headed a large military force to defeat the Swedes and overthrow their colony (Shorto 2012). Less than a year earlier, Peter Lindeström mapped 23 Swedish, 4 Dutch, and 2 English forts and blockhouses along the roughly 35 mi of river from today's Salem, New Jersey, to Philadelphia.

Stuyvesant had wisely chosen to act when emigration to New Netherland was on the rise due to slow economic growth at home between 1649 and 1664 (Jacobs 2009:32). Most came as soldiers, one-third from the seven Dutch republics; the rest left homes in Germany, Scandinavia, France, and England. They often brought their families, and their interests facilitated more formal imperial efforts (Jacobs 2009:38–39; Romney 2014:120).

Fort Casimir, a typical Dutch colonial trading settlement, became home to many of these families, at least for a time (Cantwell and Wall

2008:318–319, 322). Established at Santhoek, it featured a moated hill jutting out into the water and surrounded by marshes. The point stood high above a sandy beach, and the water line curved toward the mouth of a stream entering the river where small boats would have safe harbor. Located downstream from the Swedish Fort Christina, the spot had the necessary defensive and commercial advantages. It sat at the first place where the river channel approaches the western shore and just above the river's first major bend. The site also offered access to portage across the peninsula to the Chesapeake Bay and control of the overland north-south route through the Middle Atlantic (Jeannette Eckman papers, Delaware Historical Society, Boxes 104–108; Heite 1978:4–6).

In 1656 the City of Amsterdam assumed control of the area from the overextended WIC, as payment for use of a warship and soldiers. The city named the colony within a colony New Amstel. It extended from the Christina Kill to Bombay Hook, operating as a node in the Dutch Atlantic World (Gehring 1992:10). The settlement's trading opportunities increased enormously in 1663, when the South River was granted the right to function as an independent port of entry. Unfortunately, this action came too late.

In 1664 Charles II granted his brother James, the Duke of York, much of New Netherland. Through military action, the English took control and administered the colony from New York until 1680. William Penn received his proprietary grant of Pennsylvania, including the three lower counties "on Delaware" in 1682.

This narrative explores exchange, alliance, identity, power, and conflict and the process of hybridity it engendered in the cultural landscape, food, dress, and other material culture in Tamecongh–Fort Casimir–New Amstel. It proceeds in a generally chronological format to highlight process and intersectionality.

FORT CASIMIR TO NEW AMSTEL

In July 1651 Petrus Stuyvesant met with Lenape sachems, including Mattahorn, Sinquees, and Peminacka, who sought to help the Dutch establish a more "secure and strategically located trading fort." Susquehannock sachems witnessed the deed, "indicating their interest in better access to Dutch trade" (Soderlund 2015:77–79). Native occupants retained hunting and fishing rights. From 1651 to 1654, Dutch activity centered on Fort Casimir, surrounded by marsh at the northeast end of the village (Figure 8.1). Below a valley south of the fort, Stuyvesant planned two rows of roughly

Figure 8.1. Fort Casimir, ca. 1656 (Tantillo 2011:83).

60-by-300-ft house lots along the riverbank and inland. The settlement was home to about 26 families and 22 houses two years later (Johnson 1930:188; Roberts 1987:6). My demographic research (Table 8.1) has identified 24 men and 5 women residents, including at least 11 Dutchmen, 2 Germans, 2 Swedes, and 1 Norwegian. Most men were military officers, soldiers, or seamen or worked for the WIC, but their number included builders, smiths, a brickmaker, a tavernkeeper, and a doctor. Many also engaged in the fur trade (Craig 1999; Gehring 1981; Jacobs 2005).

Table 8.1. Demography, Fort Casimir–New Amstel, 1655–1664

Identified Individuals	173
Male	142
Female	31
Children	51
Marriages	17
Identified Origins[a]	
Dutch	32
German	4
Swedish	9
Walloon	2
Norwegian	1
Pole	1
Spanish	1
African	3

[a] First- and second-generation colonists' Old World origins ascribed based only on direct statements in historical documents.

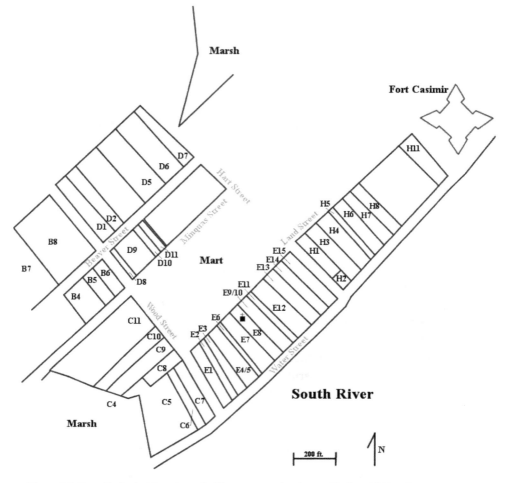

Figure 8.2. Fort Casimir–New Amstel village, properties granted before 1664 and owners (prepared by Andrea Anderson based on Heite 1978 and De Cunzo research). No street names were assigned before 1664; names in light gray are earliest documented.

Key to lot owners, 1651–1664:

B4: Dirck Albertson, 1659

B5: Giles Barrett, 1659

B6: James Wallem, physician, 1652

B7: Alexander Boeyer, Indian guide, translator, 1651; Jan Hendrickson van Stuckhousen, 1656

B8: *Smithy:* Gerrit Jansen van Beck, smith, 1651

C4: Cornelius Wynhart, 1664

C5: Jacob Alrichs, director general, 1657; Dirck Albertson, 1658; William Tom, soldier, 1664; or William Beekman, governor, 1664

C6: Jacob Alrichs, director general, 1657; William Tom, soldier, 1664

C7: Jacob Alrichs, director general, 1657; Martin Rosemont, trader, 1657

C8: Martin Rosemont, trader, 1657

C9–11: Philip Janse Ringo, 1656; Barent Jansen van Swol,

1657; Nicholas de Ringh, 1659; Aemilius and Mattias de Ringh, readers, Dutch Church, 1664

D1: Roeloff de Haes, soldier, 1651; descends through de Haes family, 1657

D2: Andrew Cectle; Roeloff de Haes and family

D5: Jan Gerritsen, seaman, 1657

D6: Harman Reynertson, trader, by 1664

D7: *Bakery and brewery:* Hendrick Kipp, brewer, 1659; Reynier Reynerson Vanderculin, baker and innkeeper, 1664

D10–11: Jan Eeckhoff, 1657

E1: Martin Gerritson, 1664

E2: *Tavern:* Cornelius Mauritson, tavernkeeper, 1651; John Arskine, 1664

E3: Constantinus Gronenburgh, soldier, 1651; Claes Janse, 1655; Constantinus Gronenburgh, 1656; Thomas Bruyn, 1662; John Henry, soldier, 1664

Political instability and strategic alliances characterized the dynamic when the Dutch reclaimed "control" after the brief Swedish occupation. In September 1655 Director Jean Paul Jaquet issued more specific instructions to expand and protect the community. Settlement should concentrate south of the fort, avoiding grants of building or farm lots on the valley edge between the river and fort or behind the fort. To accommodate growth, another inland street should be laid out behind the houses already built, with lots 40 to 50 by 100 feet (Heite and Heite 1989:16). Upon acquiring the South River colony, the City of Amsterdam promised to "fortify [the town] with a ditch without and a wall within; and divide the inclosed land into streets, a market, and lots suitable for the use as well of traders and mechanics as farmers" (Heite 1978:55). The administration promoted tobacco production to encourage settlement (Gehring 1981:75).

The administration divided and granted at least 46 lots. Most lay along the two streets paralleling the river. The settlement extended 2,000 ft (0.35 mi) along the waterfront, the core bounded by east-west streets leading inland less than a quarter-mile: Hart to the north and Wood to the south. Every lot in this strand block was granted and almost certainly occupied, and some were regranted. The church and burial ground stood on the inland portion of two mid-block lots. Further inland, lots lined the north side of Beaver Street south of Hart. Here, at the southern boundary with the woods, smith Gerrit Jansen van Beck and guide and translator Alexander Boeyer and their families settled. Minquas Street was inserted parallel to and east of Beaver, forming the western edge of the 300-by-500-foot central open mart. Three lots occupied this block; Dr. James Wallem, surgeon, lived on the corner lot until he died in 1691 (Figure 8.2).

E4–5: *Inn:* Reynier Dominicus, house carpenter, 1651; Foppe Jansen Outhout, innkeeper, 1655; Jacob Vander Veer, soldier, farmer, trader, 1662

E6: Peter Harmanson, 1651; Alexander Fenix, 1656; Peter Harmanson, 1657

E7: Harman Jansen, trader, 1651; Andreas Hudde, commissary, surveyor, secretary, sheriff, 1656; Alexander Fenix, 1657

E8: *Dutch Church:* Andreas Hudde, commissary, surveyor, secretary, sheriff, 1656; Jacob Alrichs, director general, 1657; Alexander Fenix, 1659

E9–10: Jan Andrieson, soldier, blacksmith, 1651; Jacob de Hinse, 1656; Jan Andrieson, 1657

E11: Alexander Leendertsen, 1657; Foppe Jansen Outhout, innkeeper, 1662

E12: William Tailler, 1651; Isaac Tayne, soldier, 1655

E13: Thomas Bruyn, 1651; William Maurits, tobacco inspector, alcohol dealer, 1655; Jacob Alrichs, director general, 1657; Harmen Jansen van Jevern, 1659

E14–15: William Maurits, tobacco inspector, alcohol dealer, 1655; Jacob Alrichs, director general, 1657

H1: Gerrit von Sweringen, commissary, sheriff, 1656; John Carr, English captain, 1664

H2: Roeloff de Haes, soldier, 1652; Gertruyd de Haes Crabbe, widow, 1656

H3: Claes Petersen, smith, 1652

H4: Jan Schut, 1652; Luykas Dirckson, corporal, 1657

H5: Aerian Jacobs, 1657

H6: Cornelius Steenwyk, trading agent, Amsterdam merchant house, 1657

H7: Ryer Mol, 1656; Harman Pietersen, 1657

H8: Peter Laurenson, soldier, leatherworker, 1652

H11: *Magazine*

I have enumerated 142 men and 31 women who inhabited Fort Casimir and New Amstel village sometime between 1655 and 1664. They came primarily from northern Europe, spoke different languages, and knew different religions, laws, and customs but shared a common Protestant social order (Cantwell and Wall 2008:316). The household formed the foundation of early modern Dutch society. Husbands and wives were responsible for their children and servants, and household members engaged together in production and consumption (Romney 2014:5–6). Colonists reproduced these principles of marriage and family throughout New Netherland. In Fort Casimir–New Amstel, at least 38 immigrants arrived as couples, some with children, and another 17 couples married between 1655 and 1664. Among these, 4 women had lost their husbands and remarried. Three marriages joined children of original settlers. In the community, marriage allied the Albertson, Egbertson, Gerritson, Andrieson, deVos, Linborg, deRingh, Dirckson, Jans, Maurits, Bruyn, and Pieters families and the Jacops, Jansen, and deHaes families.

It must be noted that the Dutch patronymic naming system complicated genealogy efforts. In this case, I considered only family interrelationships that I could document existed or were created within the community in the nine-year study period.

Table 8.2 summarizes the occupations of male colonists. Documents report 34 different occupations for 73 men, include 8 military ranks (44% of individuals) and 7 civilian and 3 religious positions (25%). Another 12 percent practiced trades and professions. These data are incomplete, and notably excluding women. Dutch colonization was "grounded in the petty financial motives and schemes of individual men and women who pursued their agendas" (Romney 2014:18). Many settlers, including soldiers, legally and illegally traded with Natives and each other. Later documents reference women laundresses and seamstresses, work likely also performed by women in this generation. Throughout the Dutch empire, landladies and innkeepers created households for sailors and other working men (Romney 2014:34). In New Amstel, Cornelis Maurits and his wife Styntje Pieters boarded men in their inn at the corner of Wood Street and The Strand.

These years represent a short but crucial period of fluid negotiation as various groups struggled to establish relationships of value favoring their goods (Fur 2006:110–111). In December 1655 Lenape sachems met with Vice Director Andries Hudde at the fort. They sought assurance that recently negotiated higher prices would be honored and requested the customary gifts to confirm their new treaty. Both European and Lenape valued

Table 8.2. Occupations, male inhabitants, Fort Casimir–New Amstel, 1655–1664

OCCUPATIONS	1655–1664
Military	Commander
	Commissary/Surveyor: 3
	Sergeant: 2
	Corporal: 3
	Lance Corporal
	Gunners: 3
	Soldiers: 16
	Cadets: 2
Civil Officials	Director General: 2
	Vice Director
	Secretary
	Justices: 4
	Councilors: 3
	Sheriff
	Court Messengers: 3
Religious	Dutch Pastor
	Church Warden
	Schoolmasters: 2
Professionals	Doctor
	Surgeon
	Merchants: 3
	Trader
	Tavernkeepers/Liquor Dealers: 3
Craftspeople	Carpenters: 2
	Smiths: 2, Blacksmith
	Cooper
	Turner
	Leatherworker
	Brewer
Transportation	Translator, Indian Guide
	Waterman/Trader
	Seaman
Service	Servants
	Enslaved

the legitimacy of these ritual acts of diplomacy (Fur 2009:22). A scribe recorded such a ritual 20 years later involving the English governor, representatives of the Swedish nation, and Lenape sachems:

> The first Sachem rises up and walkes up and downe taking notice of his old Acquaintance[s]. . . . Then taking a band of Sewant, he measured it from his neck to the length downeward and . . . his heart should bee so long and so good to the Go[vernor]. And the Christians, and should neer forget the Go. So presents the belt of Wampam, throwing it at the Go. Feet. The next rises up and professing much friendship and thanks to the Go. For his kind Expressions presents another belt of Wampam. The Go. Tells them the two belts shall bee Kept as bands of friendship betweene them. The belts of Sewant [wampum] were written upon, to bee kept in token of a continuance of Peace. The first belt was 15, t'other 12-wamp: high. The Go. Presents them with 4 Coates and 4 lapp Clothes. They returne thanks and fall a Kintecoying [lively social gathering with dancing] with expressions of thankes: singing Kenow, Kenow. (Gehring 1977:71–72)

Such rituals of exchange familiarized strangeness through creative misunderstanding. In 1655, fearing unrest and commercial disruptions, Hudde conceded to most Lenape requests. He then immediately banned sale of guns and liquor to the Natives, a decree just as immediately broken. Before long, the council at Fort Casimir realized the peril of agreeing to inflated prices (Fur 2006:224–225). In January 1657, 33 traders in and around town signed a new internal price agreement (Gehring 1981:77–78; Johnson 2005). The director general also evaluated the Native political landscape before initiating new strategic alliances. He identified 12 individual "nations" in the region surrounding New Amstel (Fernow 1877:186), another indicator of the complex entanglement of sovereignty, diplomacy, and negotiation in the local trading landscape.

Between 1657 and 1662 New Amstel received three major shipments of colonists and supplies from the homeland. The first year, the city ambitiously budgeted to sustain 100 new New Amstel colonists in security and an approximation of home. Dress would highlight cultural and social identity and provide an external skin of familiarity. Men's shirts, colorful stockings and hose, and shoes and boots would arrive from Europe along with fine and coarse linen and woolen cloth to tailor men's suits and sew women's petticoats and neckcloths and children's clothing. Shipments of food rations (listed greatest to least quantities) would deliver customary nourishment from meal, salt, beef, dried codfish, peas, pork, beans and groats, a bit of cheese, and butter. Special allocations of hams, smoked beef and tongues, Spanish wine, brandy, French wine, oil, vinegar, and mustard seed would pleasure colonists' cultural palate and distance them from Lenape foodways. Weapons and ammunition, blankets and double carpets, candles, and wooden storage containers completed the homeland administration's list of New Amstel's material needs (Linn and Egle 1878:806).

The director general's reports underscored the colony's perilous circumstances, a life on the edge of survival. Recent arrivals to New Netherland suffered the shock, estrangement, and dangers of an alien environment and climate. In 1660 Willem Beeckman grumbled about "storm, wind, frost, snow-drifting . . . [and] floating ice." Violent storms and hurricanes also eroded the sandy fast land, summer heat, humidity, and marshy wetlands bred biting insects, and each late summer fevers afflicted the settlers (Jacobs 2009:238; Linn and Egle 1878:720).

Hunger plagued the soldiers and colonists for several years. Maize, beans, and meat often took priority over skins for trade, but New Amstel never had enough cloth such as red and blue duffels, blankets, linen, guns, gunpowder, lead, imported liquor (wine, brandy, anise), and local brews to trade (Fur 2009:16–18). The precarious food supply dislocated social relations in town. In fall 1656 trader and liquor dealer Cornelis Maurits charged Adam Onkelbach, a soldier, with stealing 23 cabbages from his garden one night. He even watched Onkelbach cut the cabbage into his kettle in his quarters. Stealing bred distrust, threatening the fragile order in town. Due to the severity and potential escalation of the threat Onkelbach's actions posed, the commandant decided to imprison him and take the extreme step of sending him to Manhattan for adjudication (Gehring 1981:71).

The spring following the cabbage theft Director General Jacob Alrichs described the company livestock as mostly "lean and feeble," only two cows giving little milk and a few wild pigs. He requested that Stuyvesant send bacon, wheat flour, gray peas, barley, butter, and oats for the horses. Desperate soldiers resorted to stealing company muskets and exchanging them with the Natives for food (Gehring 1981:71–72). In the spring of 1659, the director general reported New Amstel's troubled state: colonists harvested no grain, having spent the first year clearing land, hauling materials, and building houses (Fernow 1877:236). In October 1662 Vice Director Willem Beeckman was still pleading with Stuyvesant to ameliorate their dire situation (Fernow 1877:415).

Table 8.3. Documented conflict, Fort Casimir–New Amstel, 1655–1664

Military	14
Murder/Violence	4
Indians/Liquor	8
Indians	6
Estate probate	1
Trade/Debt	20
Servants	2
Other	2
Total	*57*

An unstable economy, competition, conflict and violence characterized the first years of New Amstel. The court settled 57 of these disputes, 60 percent of them involving trade, debt, and military misconduct. Table 8.3 illustrates documented conflicts over the 1655–1664 period. In 1658 Director General Alrichs reported to Stuyvesant "many petty quarrels . . . , misunderstandings . . . , and licentious acts committed by soldiers" (Fernow 1877:206). That spring Stuyvesant visited New Amstel, observing firsthand rampant smuggling, fraud in the company's customs, duties and stamps missing, and other violations disrupting the attempt at order in the colonial borderland (Fernow 1877:212). A year later, smuggling goods on ships sailing between New Amstel and New Amsterdam continued; the traffic in guns was of special concern (Fernow 1877:316).

Anxiety, isolation, mistrust, and need fueled insubordination among the troops and conflict against authority. Given the European culture of honor, the community view of one's character distinguished "citizens" from "others." Slander, insult, gossip, and lack of deference to authority triggered violence and portended chaos in the western imaginary of order (Jacobs 2009:238). In one instance in January 1656, Jurriaen Hanouw, "the Pole," refused an order. Swords were drawn and disaster narrowly averted. Soon after, a drunk corporal unfit to stand guard came to blows with the commandant (Gehring 1981:52–54).

The settlers deployed the courts as a tool in their quest for economic advantage, restitution, compensation, and protection from challenges to legal and traditional practice. Laurens Pieters and Tomas Bruyn offer one example in this competitive environment. In 1656 they sought adjudication after failure to agree on the obligations and rights of servitude led to violence. Pieters challenged Bruyn's taking tobacco he raised on Bruyn's land. Bruyn claimed "ownership" of Pieters's labor and its products as a right of their servitude contract. Pieters then asserted his entitlement to compensation for his labor and challenged Bruyn's right to beat him so badly he could not work. The court held Bruyn responsible for Pieters until he could work and ordered Bruyn to provide the servant contract. The same day Bruyn faced charges of "vilifying" and "raging" against the Dutch nation (Gehring 1981:54, 59–61). He was not alone in raging against the constraints imposed by the colonial administration. Many colonists undertook economic initiatives to press the unstable borderland situation for their own aggrandizement.

In 1656 Commissary Elmerhuysen Cleyn had entered the fort and found Natives ready to exchange beavers, but the company had insufficient duffels on hand, so Cleyn brought his own goods to trade. His competitors, neighbors Cornelis and William Maurits and Constantinius Groenenburgh, trading from their houses along the strand south of the fort, assaulted Cleyn and threatened to break into his house and claim the beavers, unfairly won (Gehring 1981:67). These tensions worsened when a glutted Amsterdam beaver market in the late 1650s depressed prices, and local traders sought skins of deer, elk, otter, fox, lynx, and raccoons from Native hunters (Jacobs 2009:111).

Stuyvesant and New Amstel Director Jean Paul Jacquet responded quickly as greed edged competition toward eruption. They understood how places—containment, separation, and access—empower and constrain agency and mobility. Jacquet assembled the community and agreed to a pricing schedule because deerskin prices had risen by one-third. First-time violators lost their trading license for a year, and the third violation resulted in banishment. Residents promised to surveil their neighbors and report violations to the authorities. Jacquet also took steps to isolate Native traders and contain and control trading within the fort. He forbade inhabitants from bringing goods to the Natives or meeting them at the colonists' homes for trade. Native traders were ensured unrestricted travel with their goods (Gehring 1981:77–78). Stuyvesant ordered "a house of bark [be built] outside of the Fort as lodgings for those In Natives, who are not great Sachems" to stay during trading visits (Soderlund 2015:96).

A January 1657 court case detailed a transgression of these boundaries imposed on the colonists and their ambivalence toward the "intimate strangeness" alcohol stimulated among Natives and colonists, servants and masters, military and civilian, and new families created by marriage. A year after his court dates with Bruyn, Pieters complained that his brother-in-law, liquor dealer Cornelis Maurits, sold Natives a pail of beer that they drank at Pieters's house. Maurits and his wife, Pieters's sister Styntje, operated a tavern in their house on a corner lot in the first row, at the opposite end of town from the fort. The five Native men, two or three women, a big boy and a child became drunk and insolent at Pieters's, and he asked his sister not to tap more beer for them. Her husband nonetheless sold them another 5 pints. They returned to Pieters's house. Afraid of trouble because he and his wife were alone in the house, Pieters went to the fort and complained to the commandant (Gehring 1981:78).

The court revoked Maurits's license to tap but later reinstated it so Maurits could provide for his family. As an example to others, the justices condemned Pieters to company work for six weeks without pay. Concerned about the drunken misconduct of the residents *in concert with* the Natives, they acted to maintain distance between them, which the intimacy of sharing drink threatened.

In Amsterdam the colonial administration continued to grapple with funding essentials to grow the settlement. Two lists prepared in 1659 included carpenters' tools, cross-cut saws, hard brick, roofing tiles, lime, hinges and other fasteners for buildings, smiths' coals, iron and steel to forge and maintain ironware, iron pots and kettles for cooking and laundry, and gunpowder for defense. Baize jackets, farmers' cowhide shoes, and English caps were detailed, along with a variety of colorful, striped, and checked linens, duffels, cloth, and notions to offer colonists' flexibility to craft clothing and linens as needed (Fernow 1877:316–318; Linn and Egle 1878:371). In 1663 the last ship arrived from Amsterdam carrying a consignment of clothing and other textiles for the soldiers (Fernow 1877:415; Gehring 1981:428–429).

These lists indicated the priorities for establishing a viable colonial settlement, but little about the domestic and personal items colonists valued in this southern New Netherland outpost. Director General Alrichs died in 1659; theft and other connivances by his successor, Alexander d'Hinijossa, left Alrichs's family with mostly books, company papers, maps and prints. D'Hinijossa did not, however, appropriate Alrichs's memorabilia from his time as WIC receiver general in Brazil because they lacked meaning for him. These items included plates decorated with teakwood, 45 carved coconuts, and a teakwood gold weight. These exotica were likely deployed with prestige objects like the Wan Li majolica and bright red earthenware chargers, roemers, metal-lidded Rhenish stoneware tankard, and the alcohol

bottles and clay tobacco pipes archaeologists recovered near the fort. Together they contributed to creating a singular, creatively hybridized setting
in the fort appropriate for the ritualized meetings with Native sachems and
other colonial officials (Catts and Lukezic herein; Heite and Heite 1989:40–
41; Leach, Catts, and Lukezic 2013:57, 61).

Meanwhile, soldier and settler action counteracted attempts to maintain propriety and accord in the trade with Natives. In 1660 Vice Director
Beeckman expressed his fear of the consequences of the "intimate strangeness" that Natives and colonists shared through drink. Jan Juyriansz Becker
sold soldiers brandy on account and ignored multiple warnings to stop
after nights of singing, brawling drunkenness in the fort. One day two soldiers, drunk on his credit, burned a Native canoe. In retaliation, six drunk
Natives descended on Becker's neighbor, Native translator and broker Alexander Boeyer, who lived at the southwestern border of town. The Natives
stole his company gun and the blankets from his bed. Another soldier met a
Native at wood's edge, and they drank a two-gallon jug of Becker's brandy.
The next morning the Native was dead in the woods with the jug, which
Beeckman recognized as Becker's. The Natives threatened to kill Becker
for poisoning their comrade. They laid him on a litter and set it up on four
large forked stakes in the thicket opposite Becker's house. Despite the danger, the soldiers remained devoted to Becker, foiling Beeckman's efforts to
catch him (Gehring 1981:184–185).

On another visit to New Amstel, Beeckman reported "seeing many
drunken Natives daily and [was] told that in some taverns they sit drinking
in public." While he was at Foppe Janssen's public house on the strand wel-
coming a visitor from Virginia, drunken Natives appeared before the windows, disgracing Beeckman in the presence of dignitaries. The same day
observers reported Natives drinking anise on the beach near the church.
Gerrit Jansen van Beck, the smith who lived at the edge of the woods near
the Boeyers, complained of trouble from drunken Natives every evening
and considered abandoning his house (Gehring 1981:205). These actions
document complicated deepening entanglements linking Native, settler,
and alcohol. Dutch settlers sold the Natives alcohol, drawing them to town,
even drinking with them. Yet embedded in that intimacy were acts of distancing, mutual surveillance, and often violence.

Violence among New Amstel residents, Lenape, Minquas, and the colony's local leadership escalated. In 1660 two former Alrichs servants murdered two Lenape and a Minquas on the Alrichses' farm. Fearing vengeance,
residents outside town fled to houses near the fort for protection (Gehring

1981:188). A year later, "River Indians" murdered three Englishmen and a Dutchman. The murderers came to Foppe Janssen's tavern and trading house to sell the dead men's clothing. The Natives threatened townspeople and were placed in temporary custody to prevent further violence (Gehring 1981:222).

In June 1662 sheriff (Schout) Gerret van Sweringen fatally shot cadet Van Deventer, who had been drinking with two friends at Foppe Janssen's. On their walk back to the fort, they passed the sheriff's house, singing. The sheriff took issue with this "disturbance of the peace," tempers flared, and Van Sweringen shot Van Deventer, who died from his wounds despite the colony surgeon's ministrations. To the chagrin of the director general, the local magistrates only temporarily discharged Van Sweringen from office (Gehring 1981:281–285, 302).

New Amstel became embroiled in a wider colonial conflict in 1663, when Seneca warriors blockaded Minquas in their Susquehanna valley fort. Townspeople hastily repaired the New Amstel fort and dispatched representatives from the military contingent at the fort to act as peacekeepers. The Minquas attacked, retook captives, and sent the Senecas fleeing, with a loss of 10 lives. The conflict never reached New Amstel village (Hazard 1852:347).

The last director general of New Amstel, Alexander d'Hinijossa, further disrupted the fragile order during his tenure. In 1663 Vice Director Willem Beeckman reported to Stuyvesant that d'Hinijossa was selling everything for personal gain, including houses, the brewery and other buildings in the fort, even powder and musket balls from the magazine. Later that month, the administration recalled d'Hinijossa (Fernow 1877:422, 427–428).

Of the approximately 175 Europeans who resided at Fort Casimir and New Amstel village between 1655 and 1664, some stayed only briefly, and others made it their lifelong home. Soldier Isaac Tayne and his wife, Sara Rosen, number among the latter. Protestant French-speaking exiles from the southern Netherlands (now Belgium), called Walloons, may have arrived with experience of colonial life at the Walloon settlement on Matinicum Island further upriver. Tayne acquired a double strand lot measuring 60 by 300 ft in 1655, on which he erected a house. Their children, Isaac, Mary, and Elizabeth, also married and remained in New Castle after their parents died in the late 1670s. The documents are otherwise silent about the family's everyday experience and interactions, and they did not enter court either as defendants or plaintiffs.

The house displayed urban Dutch architectural characteristics, comprised of a "long, narrow [frame] structure with gables facing the streets, one-and-one half stories high" (Zink 1987:280). The chimney consisted of hardy yellow brick *drielingen* as well as red brick. Driven and hole-set posts uncovered during archaeological testing identified a fenceline and possible outbuilding along the western boundary of the lot (De Cunzo 2018). The compressed seventeenth-century pollen record included insect-pollinated goosefoot, plantain, and other aster family plants that colonize soils disturbed by gardening. Flotation samples yielded charred and uncharred seeds from blackberries and raspberries, goosefoot, pokeweed, wood sorrel, and copperleaf, in addition to maize kernels and cob cupules. The quantity of charcoal from poor fuelwoods suggests local gathering of deadwood for fuel.

In a compact yard near the house, the household discarded food waste, including at least one haunch of deer, its long bones shattered to extract nutritious marrow, along with beef, goat, pork, raccoon, goose, and other local fowl, fish, oysters, and turtle, along with Minguannan ceramics and lithics. Almost 1,100 flakes and shatter from readily available jasper evidence a Lenape spending some time finishing or maintaining tools in the yard or teaching a colonist the craft. A single white glass barrel bead reinforces the link, and a larger number of Dutch and English smoking pipes (EB and Tudor Rose) remind us of the cross-cultural entanglements implicated by tobacco (De Cunzo 2018). The food and tools negotiated other intimacies of strangeness, a shared if contested experience of eating, smoking, and working.

In addition to native pots, the household used numerous vessels from the Atlantic world, including redware pots, an Iberian olive jar, a tin-enameled costrel, clear- and green-glazed buff-bodied earthenwares, two German gray stoneware jugs, and a Hohr stoneware jug, Dutch tin-enameled earthware, an olive wine bottle, a Dutch roemer, possibly a *vetro a fili* beaker, and Dutch mermaid and blue-on-white floral tin-enameled chargers. These objects would have negotiated exchanges of strangeness surrounding gendered labor and rituals of dining between Lenape and Walloon and communicated prestige among European diners in this era of political, social, and economic maneuvering for position and opportunity (De Cunzo 2018).

Intimate Strangeness in a New Netherland Borderland and Lenape Homeland

Postcolonial archaeologists urge us to interrogate the implications of and then to disrupt the dichotomy of colonized/colonizer in our exploration of places such as Tameconegh–Fort Casimir–New Amstel. Focus on shared experiences of danger, strangeness, innovation, negotiation, accommodation, reflection, and embodiment advances the project. The intersectionality of aspects of identity shaped individual experience of these phenomena, yet everyone experienced them. At Tameconegh–Fort Casimir–New Amstel between 1651 and 1664, colonizer and colonized shared priority concerns for security, sustenance, beneficial exchanges, and maintaining a power balance that ensured them. Many did not have their first cross-cultural experience in the community. Europeans had entered the region decades before. Many soldiers and colonists served and worked elsewhere in the Dutch Atlantic empire, Europe, or New Netherland before arriving at the fort. Many moved on; others stayed.

Humans embody their experience of each other through manipulation of space. The Dutch designed Fort Casimir–New Amstel on an intimate scale, with the palisaded fort upstream and across a marshy valley from the village. The City of Amsterdam administration intended to enclose the town with wall and ditch fortifications, but the project was not completed. Within the small community, the Lenape guide-translator, the smith, and a liquor dealer inhabited the wood's edge at the settlement's border diagonally opposite the riverfront fort.

Impulses to isolate, contain, separate, and distance colonists and Natives countered those to share and cohabit space in efforts to control trade. Dutch administrators sought to regulate colonists' movements outside the community and Natives' movements inside it, even ordering construction of a bark-covered building to house Native traders in a familiar and visually non-European setting. For profit, for companionship, and perhaps to subvert strangeness, Dutch settlers sold the Natives alcohol, drawing them to town, even drinking with them. These communal acts involved men, women, and at least Native children. Yet embedded in the intimacy of sharing drink were acts of distancing and mutual surveillance among all participants. Liquor also likely provoked acts of physical, sexual intimacy, mutually desired and forced. Administrators voiced concern over soldiers' "licentious acts," and cross-cultural sexual alliances among the Lenape are documented, if infrequently (Fur 2009:102; Soderlund 2015).

Natives moved knowledgeably and comfortably throughout and around the town, in homes and inns, disrupting Dutch administrators' and perhaps Lenape and Susquehannock leaders' efforts at controlling their encounters and exchanges. The Native people effectively surrounded, surveilled, intimidated, and threatened violence if warranted to assert their usufruct privileges. For them, the village margins at the woods' edge and the river's beach were "intensely liminal settings" in which the "importance of ritually crossing thresholds . . . to undergo or produce transformation" was heightened (Vitelli 2011:182). Here, for example, a Native died of alcohol poisoning, and his comrades responded with an act of material violation against culture broker Alexander Boeyer and laid the man on a ceremonial platform near the site of his death.

Within the settlement, inhabitants provoked disruption within as well as outside the fort: insubordination, appropriation of company goods and the built environment for individual gain, violation of the order of law, and dishonoring the person. Yet fewer than six cases of disorder, violence, and violation came before the court each year. Those that did also document conviviality, economic partnership, intermarriage, cooperation, and community as well as competition and surveillance of neighbors and Natives. Lenape, Minquas, Susquehannock, Dutch, Swedes, Germans, Walloons, Norwegians, and a few enslaved Africans experienced the differences and similarities among them, and selected from available materials to create a hybrid material world for purposes of utility, communication, and empowerment.

Lenape hybridized dress, attributing value to meaningful properties or qualities of materials such as the red and blue colors favored for duffels (Vitelli 2011:184). Colonists likely also incorporated Native materials into their dress due to limited shipments from Europe and New Amsterdam. Corn replaced most familiar European grains in the community's diet, as did local wild plants, animals, birds, and fish. Lenape and Susquehannock incorporated guns but did not replace hunting and warfare practices. Native women controlled some aspects of alcohol distribution within their communities, and its use in rituals both eased accommodation and provoked confrontation. Exchange practices and rituals of diplomacy incorporated European features while maintaining Native structures. Soldiers displayed collections of exotic memorabilia from Atlantic world travels as signs of prestige as Lenape did colorful wool coats, and Susquhannock buried acquired trade goods with their dead.

The perspectives and purposes of authors writing about Tamecongh–Fort

Casimir–New Amstel highlight competition, conflict, and death. Historians and archaeologists have gained some insights from close readings of records otherwise silent about Lenape and Susquehannock settlements, women and children, and the rhythm of daily experience. Archaeologists have yet had few opportunities and little success locating and investigating habitations from this period. We lack details of materiality and individual practice over time. Yet our findings suffice for me to concur with Donnan and Wilson (1999:62) that "borders are simultaneously structures and processes, things and relationships, histories and events," dynamic, dangerous, and fascinating.

NOTE

1. Previous in-depth research on seventeenth-century Fort Casimir–New Amstel undertaken by Jeanette Eckman, Edward Heite, Louise Heite, Craig Lukezic, Wade Catts, Daniel Roberts, and Laura Johnson made this project possible. I am also indebted to James Meek for making primary and secondary sources available on the New Castle Community History and Archaeology program website, and to Charles Gehring and his predecessors for their translation efforts.

9

Resetting the Starting Point

Archaeological Investigations of Fort Casimir in New Castle

WADE P. CATTS AND CRAIG LUKEZIC

Fort Casimir is an icon of Delaware history. For more than three centuries, the myth and memory of the fort has survived in the minds of the citizens of the state and of the city of New Castle. The fort site and the early life of the community associated with it are steeped in the history of colonialism, but that history has comparatively little physical evidence to mark its passing. In a public lecture summarizing his research and study of the fort, local historian Alexander Cooper (1905) declared Fort Casimir to be "the starting point in the history of New Castle."

Researching and writing during the colonial revival period, Cooper conveniently ignored the generations of Native people who used the location in his declaration. As De Cunzo demonstrates (herein) more recent postcolonial scholarly study of the relationships among the Lenape, Swedes, African, Dutch, and English settlers in the region is revealing the complexities of life in the borderlands. The renewed interest in the lower Delaware Valley's colonial past coupled with new perspectives and interpretations and the results of recent archaeological survey provide us with an opportunity to reset the starting point so that we interpret the archaeological remains of Fort Casimir as part of a broader Atlantic world.

This chapter reports on the recent archaeological investigations to locate Fort Casimir. It should be noted that additional productive investigations were conducted in the summer of 2019 under the direction of the lead author; however, those results are not yet available for detailed discussion here. No archaeological study exists in a vacuum, and we built on the research of past scholars and researchers, most especially the work of the late

Edward "Ned" Heite. In 1986 Ned and Louise Heite reported on the history of Fort Casimir and its site on Bull Hill and excavated several test units in an effort to provide archaeological evidence for the fort's location. Their research on the land use of Bull Hill and the soils of the testing indicate extensive ground disturbance during the last quarter of the nineteenth into the mid-twentieth century.

In 2012 it was conceivable that most of the remains of the fort no longer survived. If this was the case, the best we could anticipate discovering were surviving fragments and sections somehow undamaged during several centuries of construction activities at this location, particularly construction and landscape modification associated with the development and operation of the New Castle Pennsville Ferry established over part of the fort site in the mid-1920s.

DEFENDING TRADING INTERESTS ON THE SOUTH RIVER

In the seventeenth century the trade for beaver pelts was the principal economic driver of eastern North America (Emmer 2014). Competitive conflict arose among the Native suppliers and between the private European traders.

The South (Delaware) River was a border land between the Dutch colony of New Netherland and the English colonies in the Chesapeake Bay area (De Cunzo 2013; Naum 2010). The trading situation became more complicated when a Swedish colony, under the leadership of Peter Minuit, established itself in this neglected border territory. Originally from the Rhineland, Peter Minuit rose through the ranks of the WIC to the chief in New Amsterdam (Manhattan). With his intimate knowledge of New Netherland, Minuit traveled to Sweden and developed a plan for a Swedish colony (Johnson 1911:177). He was aware the South River was a thinly populated border area where the handful of Dutch soldiers were hard-pressed to keep out Swedish or English interlopers (Johnson 1911:185–186).

Dutch Director General Petrus Stuyvesant needed to improve the Dutch position on the southern border. Fort Nassau was positioned near present-day Trenton at the fall line of the Delaware River. Minuit also strategically positioned the Swedish settlement on the Minquas Kill, or the Christina River, on a narrow peninsula near the confluence of that river and the Brandywine Creek. While this strategic post did not control the Delaware River, it out-maneuvered the Dutch, whose Fort Nassau was on the east, or wrong, side of the river to trade with the Minquas. Following the same tactics seen on the northern border, the Dutch responded with another factory on the Schuylkill River, only to be cut off by a Swedish blockhouse (Jacobs 2015:39).

Fort Nassau was poorly sited to control river traffic from the competing Swedes. In 1651 the WIC closed Fort Nassau and moved the garrison, cannons, and the freeman's house to the Sand Hook. The relocated fort became Fort Casimir, and the WIC laid out the streets and lots for an associated village.

On May 31, 1654, a Swedish force under Governor Rising forced the small, unprepared Dutch garrison at Fort Casimir to surrender (Jacobs 2015:41). The Swedes renamed the fort Fort Trinity. Swedish engineer Peter Lindeström commented that the Dutch fort was in poor condition at the time of its capture. Lindeström and Lieutenant Sven Skute rebuilt the front, or river side, of the fort. In addition, the Swedes constructed a four-gun water battery along the shore.

In September 1655 a WIC 300-man task force pressured the Swedes at Fort Trinity to surrender. Through a financial arrangement in the Netherlands, the city of Amsterdam took control of the Fort Casmir community and renamed it New Amstel in May of 1657. However, the territory to the north was still a WIC colony, centered at Fort Altena (formerly Fort Christina). A succession of New Amstel commanders built up the community's economic base through illicit direct commerce with Maryland (Weslager 1987:183).

In autumn of 1664, a British force under Sir Robert Carr assaulted Fort Casimir and conquered the town. In the assault, the fort was severely damaged. By 1671 the fort was a ruin. The English built a blockhouse on the green in town and called it a fort, repurposing hardware and tiles from Fort Casimir. A cordwainer, Engelbert Lott, was granted the former fort site under the condition he level the remains of the fort in 1678 (Heite 1986:21).

Fort Casimir's Historical Context

In the seventeenth century, the term "fort" carried multiple definitions and was used by military and non-military authors in its broadest sense. In 1670 the term was used by the English to denote a palisaded blockhouse in New Castle by 1670 (Catts and Tobias 2006:84–87). *Fort* also defined a factory or trading station and warehouse. The factory was a Portuguese innovation adopted by the Dutch for their worldwide trading network (Schwartz 1987:18). Once the traders could establish and staff a secure warehouse, the ship no longer needed to stay in the anchorage for months to host trading activities but could offload its goods and sail on to make more profit (Klooster 2016:19). A fort could also be a complex fortress, a clearly military defensive installation. Forts of this type were designed to resist a European force, unlike those above, and its accompanying artillery. On the frontier, these fortresses were much more than a military installation (cf. Haviser 2010; Huey 2010). Forts served as the center of civil administration of a colony. Fort Casimir held the courthouse and governor, along with the stores for the colony. In addition to secular roles, Fort Christina contained the church for New Sweden. The military commander balanced his military obligations with the needs of other aspects of the colony in the same space. For example, in Europe, the commander kept all housing away from the fort to enable maximum observation of the surrounding terrain and clear fields of fire. While housing was forbidden adjacent to the fort, this was impractical for the multiple functions of the administrative center of a colony.

Fort Casimir was positioned to control the Delaware River, and Fort Christina controlled the Christina River. Therefore, both forts Casimir and Christina were meant to control a regional water route of transportation and hence European access to the region itself. While their purpose was thus the application of power within a specific locale, the reality of military control—projecting force against an enemy—was more problematic. The forts were not really designed to withstand significant application of force by a European military.

Peter Lindeström described Fort Casimir in 1654, noting that "the Hollanders have also fortified and built a fortress with four bastions. . . . However when we arrived in New Sweden, it had fallen into almost total decay" (quoted in Heite and Heite 1989:11). Lindeström drafted the elevation drawing of the fort which remains the principal contemporary image of available to researchers (Figure 9.1). Using the same scale drawing, modern estimates of the fort's dimensions vary from 160 ft (Tantillo 2011:39) to 210 ft in length (Heite and Heite 1986:14). Only an archaeological excavation can sort out these contradictions.

In the northern Netherlands, fort walls were made of turf. At Zwartendijksterschans archaeological work has documented sections of stacked turf in the wall (Van Westing 2012:34). This building technique was utilized at the Swedish forts Christina and Elfsborg, where earthworks were reinforced with wood (Jacobs 2016:34). However, the Dutch forts constructed around the world may not have strictly followed the pattern set out in the

Figure 9.1. Lindeström Elevation of Fort Trinity (Casimir). Thomas Campanius Holm, ca. 1670–1702. *Kort beskrifning om provincien Nya Swerige uti America: som nu fortjden af the Engelske kallas Pennsylvania* (Stockholm: J. H. Werner, 1702). University of Delaware, Special Collections Department.

Netherlands, as they were adapted to local conditions (Antczak et al. 2015; Haviser 2010; Huey 2010).

According to the Lindeström sketch, the curtain and bastion wall of Fort Casimir are depicted as smooth, compared to the vertical lines in the front battery wall. Therefore, Fort Casimir was probably an earthwork that may have been supported by timber beams and wooden planking. Earthen gabions were employed for the repair, and maybe in the original construction. Indeed, Willem Beeckman, the WIC representative at Fort Altena, was in charge of the gabion production for all of New Netherland (Jacobs 2015). "We are busy fitting the fortress with gabions and shall cut the decayed points down obliquely" (Gehring 1981:195).

In other contemporary forts in the Netherland, the base of the wall hosted a "palisade." These were wooden poles or pales which functioned as an abatis or obstacle to sudden assault, but not a solid barrier (Van Westing 2012:40).

According to the Lindeström drawing the bastions appear to be 42 ft in length along the front side (see Tantillo 2011:39). If Fort Altena can be used for comparison, Beeckman wrote on rebuilding the bastions or walls: "it is not necessary that the decayed batteries be built up with sod or beams. I have them here at hand from the dilapidated house on Cuyper's Island"(Gehring 1981:170).

This leaves us with the impression that sod (not generic earth) and wooden beams were the primary ingredients for the battery or bastion. The use of readily available natural materials to construct the walls and bastions of Dutch forts can be seen at the location of the fort defending the salt pan at La Tortuga Island; at that location, the space between the wooden walls was packed with coral (Antczak et al. 2015:204 205). At Fort Casimir sod may have been extensively used, as the site is surrounded by wetlands in a time before the current invasive flora of phragmites invasion. Further, there are numerous Dutch dikes in the region, and at least two within 300 yards of the fort that may have been constructed from sod (Catts and Mancl 2013; Mancl et al. 2014).

There is a suggestion of a military magazine for gunpowder in the documents. Lieutenant d'Hinijossa was observed locking two prisoners into a "dark powder hole." In forts of this period, locating the magazine buried or standing in the bastion was a common practice. Indeed, in May of 1657, Jacob Alrichs wrote that he constructed a powder magazine in the southeastern bastion:

The house is covered with oak shingles which are so shrunk, drawn up, and in part rotten, that scarcely a dry spot can be found when it rains. And as there was no place for the powder, and only from eight to ten kegs in the house, I have thought it best to have a powder house constructed under the southeast bastion of the fort for the greater security of about 36 or 40 kegs. (translated and transcribed in Jacobs 2015:43)

A number of support buildings were assembled inside and out of the fort. These structures were components of the administrative service center of the colony. According to a 1659 letter from Jacob Alrichs, five structures stood inside the fort. They include a large storehouse and dwelling, a guardhouse, a bakehouse, a commander's dwelling, and a commissary (O'Callaghan 1856:69).

In addition to the structures detailed above, it appears a magazine was constructed outside of the fort and did not initially perform a military function. It served as a storehouse, perhaps an official one for the WIC or the New Amstel colony. A land grant to John Moll places this outside of the fort, in or across the ravine from the fort (Heite 1978:130; New Castle Deed Book B-137).

Additional correspondence reveals the mercantile nature of this structure, and the location was the official sanctioned area for trade. Edicts were passed to ensure the protection of Native traders outside of a community and to have a supervised area of trade. Occasionally, Natives were victimized by alcohol or other "sharp practices" that fueled conflict and bloodshed. It was in the best interests of the city to have a sustainable trade in beaver pelts with the Natives. It seems the space in front of the fort, by the river and magazine, was this supervised market area and maritime activity area (Gehring 1981:22; Jacobs 2005:212). The magazine functioned as a store house that was adapted to various need of the colony. It may have demarked the edge of the strand or commercial waterfront, or perhaps separated the official beaver pelt trade market area from the commercial waterfront.

THE SAND HOOK LANDSCAPE

Understanding the topography and the changes to the landform are crucial to interpreting the location of Fort Casimir and whether any portions of the fort remain. New Castle, or New Amstel, was built on a landform called the Sand Hook, which was fast land. Bull Hill, a small lobe that separated the town marsh from the river, connected to the northeast side of Sand Hook. Both side of the Delaware Bay are fringed with wetlands, with serpentine creeks, so areas where a ship could land were scarce and prized. Sand Hook was prime land.

Over the centuries, the landscape was sculpted to serve many purposes. The marsh on the interior side of Bull Hill was drained by the Broad Marsh Dike beginning in 1675 (Mancl et al. 2014). Drainage continued to be an issue in New Castle. Topographical surveys of the town were completed in 1804 and again in the 1920s. Several researchers have analyzed these data to re-create the contours of the landform. In 1804 Bull Hill was an actual hill rising 8 ft above the marsh and river. It was subsequently cut down to create fill for the low-lying areas between 1804 and 1851 (Heite and Heite 1989:8; Leach et al. 2013; James Meek, NCCHAP website; Tantillo 2011:84).

From the historical land plats, we have a good idea where Fort Casimir stood. In 1678 the English government granted Engelbert Lott two lots, located adjacent to the current intersection of Chestnut and Second Street, one containing the fort, with the understanding he would demolish the fort (Heite and Heite 1986:8).

Searching for Fort Casimir: Archaeology

In 1905 local historian Alexander Cooper announced the remains of Fort Casmir had long eroded away. In his lifetime, he experienced the massive flooding from the hurricanes in the 1880s that devastated much of the region. However, archaeologists Ned and Louise Heite challenged these conclusions. In 1986 they completed a reconnaissance-level archaeological survey searching for the remains of Fort Casimir (Heite and Heite 1989). The Heites' analysis of stratigraphy and cultural materials concluded that a sealed seventeenth-century archaeological deposit was present. Artifacts recovered from the excavations included Dutch majolica, gray Rhenish salt-glaze stoneware, red earthenware, yellow bricks, and a few tiles. Other finds included pipe stems, glass, and iron artifacts. In concert, the Heites' datasets lead them to conclude that "Fort Casimir [had] been found" (Heite and Heite 1989:45). While they could not determine which part of the fort had been uncovered, the Heites speculated that other archaeological remains of the fort likely existed under the adjacent parking lot (Figure 9.2).

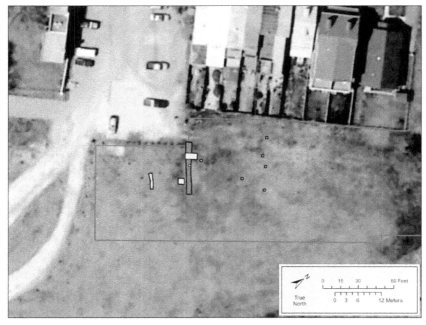

Figure 9.2. Test units of Fort Casimir in New Castle. Heite (1986) in light gray rectangles; 2012 trench in dark gray rectangles.

2012 INVESTIGATIONS

Building on the insights of the Heites, a team of professional archaeologists supported by a strong contingent of avocational archaeologists followed up with another campaign of excavations in 2012 funded by the Delaware secretary of state. The investigations combined geophysical survey (a ground-penetrating radar [GPR]), mechanical trenching, and manual excavations (Leach et al. 2013).

The results of the GPR survey indicated that the study area is filled with soil anomalies, or unexplained irregularities. One of linear zones behind, or southeast of the row houses along Second Street appears to be an early historic ditch (Figure 9.2). The eastern or riverside section of the landform consisted of late nineteenth-century or early twentieth-century fill. Similar fill zones appear to the north of Bull Hill. One can speculate this area was eroded away in the Gale of 1878, and subsequently filled with debris from around the region to reconstruct and possibly expand the landform. This chain of events would explain why the historian Alexander Cooper believed the ruins of the fort were washed away, as he may have witnessed the storm and the reconstruction episodes.

The project team consulted with Oscar Hefting and Hans van Westing of the New Holland Foundation, and determined to place a mechanically excavated trench to confirm the location of the Heites' test unit, centered on the rediscovered unit and extending toward the Delaware River (Figure 9.3). In the western section of the trench, several feature stains were discovered. In addition to a modern sewer pipe, two parallel trench or palisade lines appeared that were a little more than three feet apart. Within the trench features were post molds of circular, triangular and quadrilateral forms. The bases of these post molds were basin shaped that is common for a trench with set posts. No artifacts were observed in any of the associated soils. If these features were later nineteenth-century garden fences or other landscape features, one would expect to find a number of artifacts in the associated soils. As the soils were clean, the palisade lines were early features.

A filled ditch paralleled the trenches to the south, initially filled with nineteenth- and eighteenth-century artifacts. At 3.4 ft below the surface, another soil change was observed where the excavators found a white clay tobacco pipe bowl, cast into shape indicative of the mid-seventeenth century. Other artifacts dating to the period of New Netherland were recovered.

Artifact Analysis

The artifact assemblage collected during the trenching and hand excavations was intended principally to serve as a method of dating the eastern trench, but the recovery of early colonial artifacts from the lower strata of ER20 also helped the research team to confirm the intact presence of a mid- to late seventeenth-century infilled trench.

Brick and Tile

Fifteen nearly whole yellow bricks were retrieved during the excavations, along with a large number of brick fragments. The bricks recovered from the excavation of the trench appear to be of a small brick type of Dutch origin referred to as *drielingen*. This type of brick was specified in an early seventeenth-century law as a standard size for buildings in Amsterdam, and drielingen were soon used in other parts of the Netherlands and New Netherlands. Standardized measurements for drielingen were 6 by 3 by 1 in (current measure), and the nearly complete bricks found in the Fort Casimir excavations are extremely close to those measurements. Other

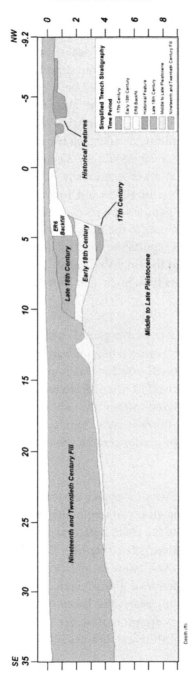

Feet Below Ground Surface

Simplified Trench Stratigraphy

Time Period
- 17th Century
- Early 18th Century
- ER6 Backfill
- Historical Feature
- Late 18th Century
- Middle to Late Pleistocene
- Nineteenth and Twentieth Century Fill

Historical Features

17th Century

ER6 Backfill

Late 18th Century

Early 18th Century

Middle to Late Pleistocene

Nineteenth and Twentieth Century Fill

Figure 9.3. Simplified profile of 2012 trench, facing southwest.

categories of Dutch yellow brick, such as the larger *moppen* and Vecht- or Utrecht-sized bricks were not present in the assemblage (Blackburn and Piwonka 1988:127). Drielingen are the most frequently reported type of brick found on seventeenth-century archaeological sites in Delaware associated with Dutch occupation and have also been reported in Maryland, Pennsylvania, New York, Virginia, and the Caribbean (Veit 2000:70). The brick was relatively water-resistant, resists wear and frost damage, and allows mortar to cure more fully. Overall, yellow brick was an excellent brick for exterior construction of building facades, roadways, and footpaths (Blackburn and Piwonka 1988; Meeske 1998:212–214). Similar brick has been recovered from excavations at other locations in New Castle, notably at the New Castle Courthouse Museum (Catts and Tobias 2006:71). Fragments of red ceramic roofing tile of pantile were recovered from the lower strata of the trench. Historical references to the use of roof tile at the fort are found in 1658 when Jacob Alrichs reports the construction of a bakery with a tile roof, and later in 1671 when the English Capitan John Carr orders the fort dismantled along with all its tiles, brick, and iron material.

Ceramics

Fragments of white undecorated tin-glazed earthenware were recovered in the excavations. A large fragment of a redware early charger form with a glazed interior and unglazed exterior was found in level XIVXV (E/F) or ER20, along with a fragment of Rhenish stoneware. From Feature 12.1 a small fragment of green-glazed earthenware was retrieved, which is tentatively interpreted as either Borderware or Saintonge. The Heites (1989:37–42) reported the recovery of similar ceramics from their excavations.

Glass

More than 30 fragments of window glass were found in level XIV XV (E/F), and two drinking glass rim fragments were also recovered from the same level. One of these is a clear, fluted glass rim, and the second appears to be a roemer (or römer) glass fragment (Willmott 2002:53 54). Likely made in the Low Countries or Northern Germany (and less likely Venetian), roemer stemmed glasses were common drinking vessels often found on Northern European sites. Based on their presence in continental art of the period, they appear to have been used in the consumption of white wine. As one English researcher has commented, the prevalence

Figure 9.4. Bar shot and grenade recovered in the trench.

of roemer glasses "in Dutch, and to a lesser extent German, art suggest that they were important cultural icons" (Willmott 2002:53).

Munitions

Three artifacts that may be associated with the military function of the fort were recovered during the investigations. A lead musket ball was found in ER 20 (ER6B location). A dropped ball (that is, not fired or impacted), it measures 0.612 in (15.545 mm) in diameter and weighs 20.6 g. The size and weight of this projectile suggest that it is either a pistol or possibly a carbine bullet (Foard 2012:57; 64).

A hollowed iron ball was retrieved from the base of ER21 (XIII). The ball may be an iron hand grenade (Figure 9.4). Hand grenades of the period could be made of glass, earthenware, or iron. Ceramic examples have been recovered from siege sites and battlefields, such as the English Civil War siege of Leicester (Courtney and Courtney 1992:69–76), Newcastle-upon-Tyne (Harrington 2004:112), and Gloucester (Atkin and Howes 1993:33–34), and on the battlefields of Aughrim in Ireland (1691), Killcrankie in Scotland (1689), Sedgemoor in England (1685). The example from Aughrim is made of iron and is similar to the specimen found at Fort Casimir (Foard 2012:92). The iron ball has been X-rayed by the Maryland Archeology Laboratory at Jefferson Patterson Park and Museum.

An iron cannon ball was also recovered from the excavations of ER21, level XXI (E2). The ball weighs 6 lbs and contains a metal spike driven through the center (Figure 9.4). This is an example of bar shot or cross-bar shot. Ten examples of cross-bar shot have been recovered from a circa 1590s shipwreck in Alderney, for example, excavated since 1993 by the Alderney Maritime Trust (2016). Cross-bar shot was intended for use as an incendiary shot, with propellant-soaked rags or clothes attached to the bar, so that upon firing the shot would hit a wooden surface, stick to it, and ignite. Bar shot also consisted of two iron balls linked by a bar, with a use intended for removing ships rigging or masts.

The recovered munitions artifacts may be testament of the English attack on the fort in 1664. It is possible the musket ball and the grenade are evidence of an infantry assault on the fort. The spike or bar shot could have been fired from a 3-lb cannon or minion, from the flagship *Guinea* in the attempt to ignite the fort into flames during the 1664 English attack.

INTERPRETATIONS AND CONCLUSIONS

The results of the 2012 investigation were both expected and remarkable. Not only did they confirm the Heites' findings, but they also show that their excavations only literally scratched the surface of an infilled trench or ditch likely associated with the former forts Casimir, Trefaldighet, and Amstel. They were remarkable too, in that besides the infilled ditch two other features were discovered only a few inches below the ground surface that may represent the remnants of palisade lines. Whether these features are associated with the forts remains to be determined (Figure 9.5).

The modern topography reveals much about the layout of the property, especially the former shoreline position, likely that of circa 1930. Earlier aerials support this conclusion as well, as do GPR results that revealed coarse fill deposits under made land, and the excavation and stratigraphy of the east trench. The west trench is directly beneath the location of a former

Figure 9.5. Reconstruction of Fort Casimir and environs by Len Tantillo (2011).

structure that a few local informants described as a two-story office building. This structure is visible on aerial photographs, including a few oblique aerials, from the 1930s to the 1950s. The excavations in the west trench uncovered two possible palisade trenches and revealed no anomalies suggestive of twentieth-century origins other than the terra cotta drainage pipe.

It is clear from the investigations that prior to the 1930s considerable shore erosion had occurred. Indeed, Alexander Cooper in his early twentieth-century attempt to located Fort Casimir was convinced that little if anything remained of the fort. Cooper placed the fort not on the parcel owned by Engelbert Lott but too far to the northeast, while mapping overlays completed for this work place the fort closer to the intersection of Chestnut and Second Streets. The mapping completed by Tantillo in 2011, which relied on the Heite and Heite archaeological report, places Fort Casimir too far to the northwest, almost on top of what would have been Bull Hill. This placement does not fit with the 1681 plat map of the windmill, which depicts the "fort lot" as situated a short distance southeast. Therefore, while we know that there is a seventeenth-century archaeological component in the area that is likely associated with one or more of the fortifications (Casimir, Trefaldighet, or Amstel), at this time we do not know precisely which portion of the fort(s) we have encountered—curtain walls, exterior ditch, water battery area, firing step, or shore line.

The munitions artifacts recovered during the investigations of Fort Casimir may be associated with the 1664 seizure of the fort by the English. In mid-autumn 1664 two English warships mounting 46 guns and an assault force of 130 men fired 2 broadsides into the walls and structures of Fort Casimir, at that time mounting only 14 guns and garrisoned by 30 men. The assault included not only ships' broadsides but an infantry attack from the land side of the fort. The Dutch garrison was overpowered, and nearly one-third of the garrison were casualties of the attack (Tantillo 2011:76; Weslager 1967:189–190).

Further archaeological investigations focused on the ditch feature and the possible palisade lines may be beneficial in providing verification of what part of the site is in this area. Additional geophysics in the parking area at the foot of Chestnut Street may also be useful. Based on the historical record and mapping, this is the lot purchased by Engelbert Lott that contained the fort. While disturbance caused by the ferry terminal did occur, geophysics has the potential to identify possible anomalies associated with the fort(s), and this could provide further evidence of what parts of the fortifications are still archaeologically present.

10

Wolf Traps in Seventeenth-Century Delaware

WILLIAM B. LIEBEKNECHT

In the early days of the county [New Castle County, Delaware] the settlements were infested with wolves.

J. Thomas Scharf, *A History of Delaware, 1609 to 1888*

At one time the gray wolf was widespread, covering two-thirds of the United States and thriving in a diversity of habitats. Wolves live in packs ranging from as few as 2 to as many as 15, with most packs having 4 to 9 members. Since the seventeenth century they were hunted ruthlessly and extirpated over most of their range. In recent times we have come to understand that the gray wolf plays a vital role in the health of the ecosystem. Gray wolves are canines with long bushy tails that often display a black tip. Their coat colors are typically a mix of gray and brown with buff-colored facial markings and undersides. They can also be solid white, brown, or black. Gray wolves look similar to a large Alaskan husky and vary in size depending on where they live. Wolves in the north are usually larger than those in the south. The average size of a wolf's body is 3 to 5 ft long with tails ranging from 1 to 2 ft long. Females typically weigh 60 to 100 pounds, while males weigh between 70 and 145 pounds. Wolves are carnivores, and in the wild they prefer to eat large mammals such as deer, but, they also hunt smaller mammals such as beavers, rodents and rabbits. When the opportunity provides itself they also will hunt domestic livestock. Adult wolves can eat up to 20 pounds of meat in a single meal. In the wild, wolves live in general from 8 to 13 years.

This chapter considers the wolf "problem" as it existed historically in early colonial Delaware and the interpretation of an unusual archaeological feature as a wolf trap.

ROOTS OF HATRED

Europeans have feared and hated wolves for centuries stemming from their reputation for killing livestock. They were convinced that wolves hunted humans, entering towns to kill children as they slept in their beds. This fear and hatred was proliferated for generations by fables and fairytales such as "Little Red Riding Hood," "The Three Little Pigs," "The Wolf and the Seven Little Kids," "Peter and the Wolf," and "The Boy Who Cried Wolf" by Aesop, Grimm, and Jacobs.

Were wolves a real problem? The answer is not quite so simple, as it was a matter of perspective. A Swedish traveler in Philadelphia in 1748s aid, "all the old Swedes related, that during their childhood, and still more in the time of the arrival of their fathers, there were excessive numbers of wolves prowling through the country, and howling and yelping every night, often destroying their domestic cattle" (Watson 1877:433). The same traveler reported that "In the early days, a horrible circumstance occurred for the poor Indians. They got the smallpox from the new settlers. It killed many hundreds of them. The wolves, scenting the dead bodies, devoured them all, and even attacked the poor sick Indians in their huts, so that the few who were left in health, were much bruised to keep them off." More often than not, Natives are thought to have revered and honored the wolf, and although they shared the same prey, they lived side by side for thousands of years. So why were wolves perceived to be a problem in the colonies? Was it a matter of prejudice proliferated by European fables and fairytales or did the population suddenly increase and if so, why?

Prior to the arrival of colonists to the New World, the wolf population was likely far lower than levels reported throughout the American colonies a century later. One of the first orders of business when arriving was to clear large areas of the forests to build houses and to carve out fields for agriculture. Colonists also introduced an important component into the ecosystem, domesticated livestock. Animals such as horses, cows, swine, sheep, and chickens were not native to North America. These animals were initially free-ranging, that is, not kept in pens, paddocks, corrals, coops, or barns, and thus were left unprotected from predators. Horses were usually were usually kept close to the house, chickens sometimes slept indoors, sheep roamed the yards, but cows and swine often grazed in fields and wooded areas on the periphery of the farmsteads where they were prime targets for wolves seeking an easy meal.

Wolves are opportunistic predators that prefer to attack old, young, and sickly prey. European domesticated animals represented new and easily acquired food to native wolves. Under these conditions, wolf populations likely proliferated to such an extent that they became a serious threat to livestock and thus a threat to the livelihood of colonists.

COLONIAL REALITIES

Whether wolf populations actually increased or were only perceived to have increased does not matter. From the seventeenth century on wolves were exterminated, pushing the species toward extinction in region after region. It was not until 1960s that their highly endangered status received attention from biologists and wildlife officials.

During the early colonial period, authorities recognized that the physical dynamics of free-ranging forms of various livestock, set against the backdrop of a wolf-laden wilderness, was or could be a costly nuisance. They ordered wolves hunted and trapped to mitigate the threat. The earliest recorded bounty on wolves was passed by the Massachusetts Bay Colony in 1630, followed by Jamestown, Virginia, in 1632. In 1645 the Massachusetts General Court decreed, "any person, either English or Indian, that shall kill any wolf or wolves, within ten miles of the Plantation of this jurisdiction, shall have for every wolf by him or them so killed ten shillings, paid out of the Treasury of the Country" (quoted in Kevin 2015). At this time in Middleboro, Massachusetts, John and James Soule farmed in the shadow of "Wolf-Trap Hill." A family tale relates that at dawn each day, one of the brothers hiked up the hill to check the pit trap they had dug to catch wolves (Coleman 2003:2).

In Maryland in 1644 John Lewger reported that out of a flock of 11 sheep belonging to Lord Baltimore, four had been killed by wolves the previous year. Also in Maryland, Thomas Glover observed that in 1676, "As to sheep, they keep but few, being discouraged by wolves, which are all over the Country and do much mischief amongst the flocks" (Glover 1904:19). In 1688 the Pennsylvania legislature ordered that the Natives be encouraged to destroy wolves in reward for an extra provision (Watson 1877:94). At the court held at Chester, Pennsylvania, on October 2, 1695, the grand jury recommended a levy to help pay for several wolves' heads turned in for bounty (Watson 1877:92). In 1706 a communication made to the governor and the Pennsylvania Assembly reported that "the wolves had increased in such a degree as to cause an apprehension for the safety of all the flocks of sheep in the immediate vicinity of Philadelphia" (Watson 1877:96).

In New Jersey a law passed in 1697 stated that any Christian who brought the head of a wolf to a magistrate would be paid 20 shillings. In 1730 the governor of New Jersey signed an act charging local officials with raising moneys necessary for defraying the charge of killing wolves and panthers. The sum of 20 shillings was paid for wolves and 5 shillings for wolf whelps (Acts of the General Assembly 1776:90–91). In 1751 the bounty was increased to 40 shillings for each wolf (Acts of the General Assembly 1776:90–92). Wolves were hunted with guns, a variety of traps (including metal spring traps), and poisons. However, it also appears that some Europeans adopted the wolf pit from the Native inhabitants.

Seventeenth-Century Delaware

In May of 1676, Sheriff Captain Edmund Cantwell of Appoquinimink (present Odessa) stated, "wolves being so over frequent and doing such daily damage to sheep, cattle and hogs that any person who brings in a wolf skin or head to the local magistrate be paid a bounty of 40 [Dutch] gilders from a public levy" (Fernow 1877:546–547). This order appears to have been ineffectual; on January 5, 1677, it was ordered that the inhabitants erect "woolf-pitts" along the streams before May 1, under penalty of 75 gilders, as follows:

> The Court taking into Conciederation the dayly & Continuall spoyle & damadge wch ye Woolves Committ upon the stockes of the Inhabitants, and that the said woolves (notwithstanding the former order of the Laest high Court allowing 40 gilders for each Woolfe head) are no wayes more destroyed than heretofore: Itt was therefore this day Resolved and ordered by the Court for the good of the Country in general that att or about the places, neighbourhoods & plantations hereafter mentioned by the Inhabitants thereof bee made and erected fitting woolfe pitts or houses wherein the said varim in may bee catched & destroyed, the same to bee made by the first of the month of May next uppon ye forfeiture and penalty of seventy and fyve gilders each partee neglecting the same: The severall Constables from tyme to tyme are to see that this order bee fulfilled and observed,

and alsoe that the said pitts or houses bee in good order well bayted & tended; They to lnforme agst the neglectors, and to haue halfe of theforfeiture for their paynes. (New Castle Court Records 1677)

From the records, it appears 54 Dutch, Swedish, and English planters constructed wolf pits in New Castle County, and in 1677 Garret Otto and Johannes DeHaes presented wolf heads to the court for bounty (Heite 1972:6). Johannes DeHaes, who lived in the vicinity of Odessa purchased Abraham Coffin's lands containing the old landing road (Figure 10.1) by sheriff sale in 1678–1679. In October of 1678 Governor Edmund Andros wrote in a letter to the justices at New Castle, Delaware, "Payment for Wolves and other necessary Charges, are to continue" (Fernow 1877:609).

Although not demonstrated conclusively, it seems that the adjacent lands of Roelof Janse and Adam Pieters are the lands Heite identified as Roeloffe Anderson and Adam Peterson. This provides the general location of six wolf pit traps near present-day Odessa (Figure 10.1). Hendrick Walravens's land borders the Wolfe Kill Swamp and lies southeast of "the Trap." John Taylor and Thomas Snooden owned adjoining land just west of the trap along a branch of Drawyers Creek. The trap also known as Mac-Donough is just north of Odessa, Delaware.

These wolf pit traps served to form a protective ring around Appoquinimink. The map compiled by Heite coupled with the knowledge that the traps were instructed to be erected along the streams provides researchers with vital clues to narrow down the search for the locations of these pits. Most of the locations are situated close to the wetlands would not normally be tested using standard archaeological survey models.

There are other less detailed indications from Kent and Sussex Counties in central and southern Delaware. A Kent County Court document from 1686–1687 ordered that any Christian who killed a wolf and brought the head to the Justice of the Peace would receive 50 lbs of tobacco while a Native would receive a pound of gun powder. Near Rehoboth Bay, in Sussex County, there are wolf trap indications in place-names such as Wolf Pit Pond, Wolf Pit Marsh, and Wolf Pit Creek (now known as Johnson Branch). Across the Delmarva region there are multiple wolf pit or trap and variant place-names mentioned in about 50 land patents. Colonists affixed wolf place-names to fields, meadows, brooks, swamps, and forests as a way to notify neighbors and travelers of the location of wolf trap pits in the area (Coleman 2003:3). Wolves may have indirectly the cause of other place-names such as Hog Island; islands in the tidal marshes with strong currents

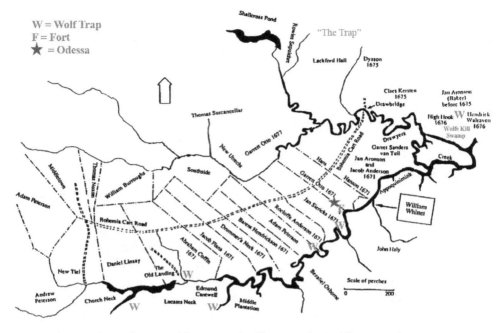

Figure 10.1. General projected locations of wolf traps in the Middletown-Odessa area in the seventeenth century. The base map was compiled by Louise Heite and altered by De Cunzo in 1993 and by the author in 2016 to show projected locations of wolf traps based on the current available data (De Cunzo 1993:27; Heite 1972).

would have provided safe havens for livestock away from predators such as wolves.

WOLF TRAP PITS

We know wolf pits were legislated, but what did they look like? What could archaeologist expect to find in the field? To answer this question a variety of sources were consulted focusing in on Europe, the American colonies, and Natives.

European Forms

Our research of wolf traps identified many variations on the theme (metal traps, snares, deadfalls, etc.). Similar to researching mouse traps expecting to find the one you have in hand, you end up finding everything but the one you have in hand. Changing the focus to wolf *pits*, however, produced a much more manageable array of types.

In Sweden, Norway, Hungary, and Germany, they use what is referred to in Norway as an *ulvestuer*, or catching trap. These trap pits have diameters ranging between 5 and 10 m with a depth of 2 to 3 m. The pits were baited with meat beaten into the bottom of the pit trap. The top of the pit at ground level was covered with light vegetation to camouflage the opening. An additional piece of meat or even a live bird such as a goose was placed on a small platform supported by a long pole in the middle of the pit. When a wolf came by and pounced on the bait, the weak covering would then collapse, causing the wolf to fall into the pit and be impaled on stakes at the bottom or be trapped until it could be disposed of later (Balassa and Ortutay 1979).

Early American Forms

Although numerous place-names refer to wolf pits, there very few that have been positively identified in the eastern United States. Wood-lined wolf pits were reportedly constructed on a farm in Fairfax, Virginia. An animal carcass was drug for a mile or so through the woods to create a scent trail leading to the pit. A wooden plank was balanced over the pit and baited. When the wolf went for the bait, the plank and the wolf would fall into the pit. The creek running through the farm was named Wolf Trap Creek (shown on deeds as early as 1739), and the farm became known as the Wolf Trap Farm, the present site of the Wolf Trap National Park for the Performing Arts.

In 1728 W. Byrd of Virginia stated, "The inhabitants hereabouts take the trouble to dig abundance of wolf-pits, so deep and perpendicular, that a wolf is once tempted into them, he can no more scramble out again than a husband who has taken the leap can scramble out of matrimony" (Young and Goldman 1944: 294). Another description of a colonial wolf pit states the haunch of venison or a dead sheep was usually placed in the pits, which were 8 ft deep, broadest at the bottom so as to render it impossible for the most active animals to escape from them (Young and Goldman 1944:293). A seventeenth-century account relates that wolf pits were to be constructed of solid and strong earth and lined with boards on the inside, so the entrapped wolf could not escape by scraping and digging with his paws (Young and Goldman 1944:290).

Although unspecified as to the location within the United States, Ranger (1866:27) reported that wolf trap pits were constructed in the mid-nineteenth century by placing a thick stick or pole across the top of a pit. The pole was fastened a plank, which covered the top of the pit. Attached to one end of the plank was a piece of venison, and on the other a large counterbalance stone. This allowed the wolf to come to the venison, and just as it got on the plank to eat it, the plank would turn, causing the wolf to fall into the pit. The counterbalance weight on the other end would raise the plank up again, remaining baited for another wolf.

Native American Forms

Native Americans also had their methods for trapping wolves and coyotes by setting "heavy stakes in the ground in a circle, about the carcasses of one or two buffalo. The stakes were placed at an angle of about 45 degrees, a few inches apart, and all pointing toward the center of the circle. At one place, dirt was piled up against the stakes from the outside, and the wolves, climbing up on this, jumped down into the enclosure, but were unable to jump out" (Grinnell 1892:240–241).

ARCHAEOLOGICAL EVIDENCE

During archaeological investigations conducted in advance of the construction of a new alignment for U.S. Route 301 outside of Middletown, Delaware, for the Delaware Department of Transportation, many historic cultural features were discovered. These included the typical range of early historic features from cellar holes to smoke. These features are familiar to the archaeological community and have often been documented across the Middle Atlantic region.

In the summer of 2012 at the Elkins A Site (7NC-G-174), a team of archaeologists from Hunter Research, Inc. uncovered what appears to be an entirely new or at least previously unrecognized feature type in this region: a wolf trap. While stripping the plowzone with a backhoe during the data recovery excavation, a distinct circular feature was noted. The large circular feature measured approximately 15 ft in diameter and based on soil auger tests it was determined to extend 2.5 ft below the top of the subsoil in the center (Figure 10.2).

The fill of the pit was a mixture of a variety of silty loams, very compact clays, and some gravel. The colors of the fill ranged widely from a dark yellowish brown (10YR 4/4) to a light reddish brown (5YR 6/4). When the pit was bisected it was noted that although there were distinctly disturbed soils, there were no cultural materials present. This pit would not have held water because of a band of sandy gravel situated near the base of the pit allowing for rapid natural drainage.

An array of brown linear staining was noted throughout the fill. This

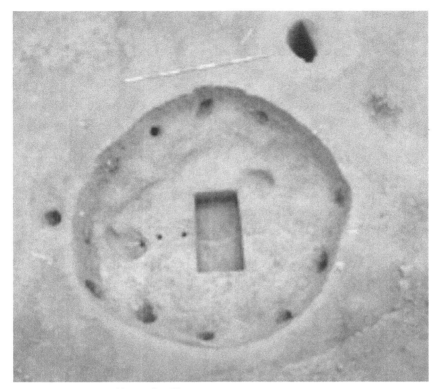

Figure 10.2. Excavated base of wolf pit.

type of staining is indicative of decayed wood, thought to be possible posts, smaller branches of various sizes, or vines that had fallen into the pit following its demise in no distinctive pattern.

Resting in a vertical position were 263 tabular slabs of sedimentary stone weighing 202.5 lbs that were mainly located in the center of the feature fill. Cross-mending of the slabs revealed they may have originated from one to three slabs.

The slab or slabs could have been used either as a dead fall, where the weight of the rock would crush or injure the wolf once it had fallen into the pit, or more likely was part of a counterbalance weight to a baited plank. If this were the case, when the wolf would come to devour the bait, the plank would tip inward, causing the wolf to drop into the pit. The weight of the stone at the other end would then cause the baited plank to return to its original position, ready to lure another wolf. The weight of the stone slab or slabs (202.5 lbs) is about the weight of an adult eastern white-tailed deer (*Odocoileus virginianus*), which may have served as the bait.

The base of the pit was irregular and unprepared. If the base had served as a floor for a domestic structure or outbuilding there would have been a flattened compact surface. The only sign of activity at the base of the pit were three irregular shallow but distinct pits, which may have been dug by an animal such as a wolf or fox. It is probable that an animal trapped inside the pit would have attempted to dig its way out, but the dense clay soils would have made this an impossible task.

Following the removal of the very compacted fill, it became apparent that there were 11 evenly spaced post holes around the upper inner circumference of the pit (Figure 10.2).

A position for a twelfth post, at position was a possible based on spacing, although no physical evidence in the form of a soil change or stain was observed at the time of excavation. Each post hole measured 1 ft in diameter, with post molds of diameter ranging from 6 to 7 in. These posts were spaced on average 2 feet apart. Four of the posts had stones wedged in under the interior face of the base of the post. The stone acted as a support to maintain the angle at which the post was originally positioned. The posts all exhibit a distinct cant, angled toward the center of the pit varying between 10 and 30 degrees, converging above the center of the pit forming a cone. The posts were likely secured by weaving smaller sticks or vines forming a basket-like construction. The excavated rectangular section in the center of the pit shown in the photograph was a test excavation to make sure sterile-undisturbed soils had been encountered. Accounting for the removal of the plowzone and regional soil deflation, the pit could have been as deep as 4.5 ft at the time of construction. The soils that were removed from the pit during construction appear to have been packed against the sides of the cone shape, creating a camouflaged mound-like enclosure rising about 3 ft from the surface of the ground. If the posts were positioned in a 30-degree angle, the estimated length of each post would range between 9 and 10 ft. The estimated interior height of the construction would have been between 6 and 7½ ft.

During the initial excavation, a darker stained area was noted which was slightly off-center to the northeast. This darker area may be a reflection of the position of the opening at the top of the mound/cone. The opening would have allowed for organic materials to fall in over time, thus leaving a darker stain behind. The stain, which measured 7 by 9 ft, is likely to be a little larger than the original opening due to the hollow nature of the construction. The position of the slabs may suggest the counterbalance was purposely discarded within the pit once the trap was no longer functional

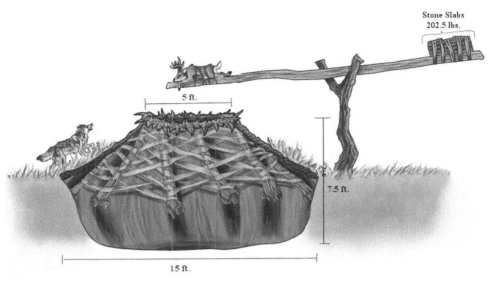

Figure 10.3. An artist reconstruction depicts what this pit trap may have looked like based on the available archaeological evidence.

so that it would not be a hazard to plowing. In addition to the interior posts near the rim of the pit, there was a post hole immediately adjacent to the northeast side of the pit that was revealed at the top of the subsoil. This post had a 1-ft diameter and contained large amounts of charcoal. This post is thought to have served as an anchor for the plank or pivot system, which would have been weighted by the stones as a counterbalance similar to a wells sweep. That system would have made it possible for multiple wolves to be caught in a single evening as it would allow the baited plank to spring back up into position over the opening. When the next wolf walked out over the plank in pursuit of the bait, its weight would cause it to fall and then the counterbalance (rock) would return the baited plank to the ready position (Figure 10.3).

Over time or from neglect, the posts would eventually decay, causing the up-cast soils packed around them to drop back into the pit. The plank and posts would also eventually decay and fall into the pit as well. It appears that from the pattern of the pit's fill, the stone slabs were dragged or pushed into the slumped pit. This type of construction using natural materials would leave no dateable or diagnostic artifacts behind.

Initial interpretations and suggested interpretations included a well, a privy, a spring house, a cistern, a root cellar, a windmill, a wolf trap, some sort of prehistoric ritualistic feature, or any of a variety of other indeterminate functions. Without diagnostic artifacts leaving us traditional clues, we had to view this feature ultimately through the characteristics of form, function, and distribution. The pit lies 42 ft north of a stone-lined root cellar, which presumably was situated under a house at the Elkins A Site, circa 1740–1780. There were no artifacts dating to this period (or any other period) recovered from the fill of the pit, suggesting the pit had been constructed, used, and filled in prior to 1740. Given this scenario, it may have been no longer detectable by the time the house and root cellar at the Elkins A Site were constructed circa 1740.

The process of elimination left two possibilities for this feature complex: first, a very large root cellar located far from the nearest known structure likely dating prior to circa 1740, or second, a wolf trap segregated from the domestic nucleus on a large parcel of land situated near a small steam. The more likely scenario seems to be that of a wolf trap pit dating to circa 1677, when such traps were mandated to specified large landholders in New Castle County. These traps were ordered to be constructed near streams, and logic dictates that they would have been located a reasonable distance from any dwellings as the objective was to draw the wolves away from dwellings to the pit using bait. Figure 10.3 is a reconstruction of what this pit trap may have looked like based on the available archaeological evidence.

ARCHAEOLOGICAL EVIDENCE OF WOLVES

There have been some archaeological finds of wolf remains and evidence of the activities of wolves. At the Rumsey/Polk Site (7NC-F-112) in New Castle County, Delaware, the remains of a wolf were recovered from a subfloor pit dating to the mid-eighteenth century. These disarticulated remains exhibit cut marks in locations consistent with skinning (Heinrich personal communication, February 28, 2014). Similar discoveries were also made at the Strickland Plantation Site (7K-A-117) in Kent County, Delaware, as well as at a seventeenth-century Native village site, the Buffalo Site (46-Pu-31) in West Virginia (Catts et al. 1995:79; Guilday 1971).

A feature discovered during excavations at the Cardon-Holton Site (7NC-F-128), circa 1720 to 1740, consisted of a small circular pit, which contained the partially articulated skeleton of an adolescent pig (Hunter Research, Inc. 2013b). The pit was located adjacent to another refuse pit near a fence line separating the core living area of the site from disposal areas. The pig skeleton lacked butchering marks, and the rationale for disposing of a seemingly perfectly fine piece of meat in the field was puzzling. Henry

Miller (1986:3–12) encountered a similar feature in Historic St. Mary's City, Maryland, at the St. John's Site in the 1970s. The St. John's Site feature, which dates to the second half of the seventeenth century, contained the burial of an articulated sheep with a portion missing. The partial skeleton lacked any evidence of butchering or gnawing, and it was concluded that a carnivore, most likely a wolf, had carried off the hindquarters. The action of disarticulating a prey animal might not necessarily leave marks on the bones left behind.

ARCHAEOLOGICAL EVIDENCE OF WOLF TRAPS

So how would an archaeologist recognize a wolf pit in the field? If a wolf trap pit were encountered in a typical site location survey shovel test, it would likely consist of a mottled soil profile devoid of artifacts. Further evaluation would be unlikely if the same feature or no artifacts were recovered from additional tests. Various configurations of wolf trap pits would result in their being multiple archaeological signatures, most of which would likely be devoid of artifacts. How many such features have been overlooked in the past?

During a site location study by Gardner and Stewart (1978) in the Odessa area, it appears that they may encountered such a pit on the former lands of Jan Siericx or Siericks, near the boundary with Garret Otto, who were known to have been jointly instructed to erect a wolf trap pit. They encountered a large feature consisting of "somewhat patterned soil disturbed involving the removal of earth from certain areas and mounding of it in other locations." They described the feature as 8 ft square with highly organic soil devoid of artifacts (Gardner and Stewart 1978:16–17). Their final interpretation was that they had encountered a settling pond for a tannery and additional excavation was not felt to be justified (Gardner and Stewart 1978:26). Given the relatively undeveloped state of historical archaeology at that time when the survey was conducted, this interpretation is perfectly understandable. In many ways unfortunately it would still be a valid interpretation in many states.

SUMMARY: HOW TO LOCATE THESE HIDDEN FEATURES ON THE PERIPHERY OF CIVILIZATION

Our current models for archaeological site location testing us keeps us out of the wetlands and buffer zones. As such, we rarely get a glimpse of what lies within these areas. In New Castle County, where we have a good idea of where they should be, those areas should be targeted when future projects are planned for those properties near and along the Delaware River and Bay.

If cultural resource consultants and reviewers are made more aware of this type of feature, they will be less likely to dismiss potential evidence of such manifestations. In an effort to manage cost in the competitive world of cultural resource management, site evaluation test units have grown smaller in size, from 5 ft square to 3 ft square, thus reducing the odds of identifying a wolf-pit-type feature. Larger excavation units still would likely miss or misidentify this artifact-free type of feature. Only removing the plowzone in block units or stripping larger areas is likely to reveal these unique cultural features. Even stripping, which is more often focused on the core of a historic site, will undoubtedly miss ephemeral features such as wolf trap pits situated on the outer periphery of a farm. The Elkins A Site wolf trap pit was a fortunate chance discovery which will be difficult to duplicate. It was and is a remarkable example of cultural interaction in the early decades of colonial Delaware.

The author would like to first thank Glen Mellin, who was most helpful in figuring out the function of this feature. Glen has a knack for thinking outside of the box and continually asking thoughtful questions. Next I would like to thank the Hunter Research, Inc., field crew, Monica Weetman, Tim Hitchens, John and Sue Ferenbach, Jack Cresson, Dawn Cheshaek, and Joelle Browning. I would like to thank Patrick Harshbarger of Hunter Research, Inc. and John Bansch for their assistance in researching this topic. I would also like to Matt Miller for his skilled work with the backhoe; Angelica Dennis for her depiction of how I envisioned the appearance of the wolf trap; and Ian Burrow, Chris Espenshade, and Wade Catts for their constructive comments. I would also like to thank David Clarke and Kevin Cunningham of the Delaware Department of Transportation for encouraging us to look outside the box and the Staff of the Delaware Historic Preservation Office for their useful comments when visiting the site.

11

Fort New Gothenburg and the Printzhof

The First Center of Swedish Government in Pennsylvania

Marshall Joseph Becker

Archaeological sites dating from the seventeenth century remain relatively rare in the mid-Atlantic region despite the documented rapid expansion of European settlements throughout that area during that time. Despite significant efforts to locate traces of the early Swedish colony, the Printzhof complex (36DE3) remains the only physically verified site known to date from that period. This Swedish intrusion into Dutch controlled territory began in 1638 with the construction of Fort Christina, now Wilmington, Delaware (Becker 1999). No physical evidence of that fort or from any of the contemporary buildings has been identified. The location of the Printzhof, erected in 1643 by the third Swedish colonial governor, Johann Printz, had been long known from oral traditions that were initially confirmed by archaeological excavations in the 1930s (Figure 11.1).

Three historical elements render this site of particular importance. First, the Printzhof complex became the de facto seat of government for the colony and thereby the first European capitol in what was to become Pennsylvania. Second, "America's first international tribunal" was convened here in 1643 by Printz in response to criticism of his conduct in the trial of the pelt trader George Lamberton of New Haven (see Johnson 1930:206, 243–247; Underhill 1934:810). The third important point is that the "special day of Thanksgiving" celebrated there in October of 1646 was the first to be held in this part of the New World (Johnson 1911:36).

Archaeological investigations at the Printzhof complex were led by the author in in 1976, and again in 1985 and 1986, revealing numerous features (Figure 11.1). The following review provides an update of earlier summaries

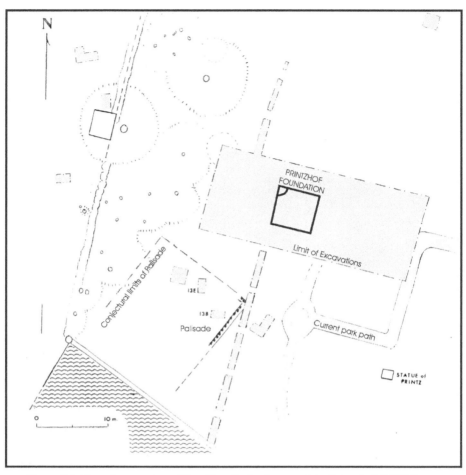

Figure 11.1. Plan of excavation of Fort New Gothenburg and the Printzhof (36DE3).

of what was known about this site (Becker 1999, 2011a), with emphasis given to what we now know about Fort New Gothenburg. Excavations in the 1980s conclusively demonstrate that a small (approximately 16 m square) palisaded fortification was erected at the waterside on the southwestern edge of Tinicum Island.

FORT NEW GOTHENBURG AND THE PRINTZHOF

When Lieutenant Colonel Johann Printz, arrived in the New World in 1643 to take up his post as the governor of the Swedish colony, he decided to establish his own home, which could be used as a trading post as well, on

Great Tinicum Island, situated some 30 km up the South (Delaware) River from Fort Christina and just downstream from the mouth of the Schuylkill River (Becker 1979, 1987, 2011a; Johnson 1911). The Schuylkill was used in the spring season by the Susquehannock to bring peltry from their home range around present Lancaster, Pennsylvania, to the trading stations on the South River.

The Printzhof, as Printz's American residential complex is generally identified, included a small cluster of buildings constructed in a fashion that could be described as a *storgård*, the Swedish term for a substantial farm. Among the expected structures would be a large residence, barns, and other outbuildings. Various maps on which Fort Nya Göteborg (Fort New Gothenburg) appears and documentary references to Printz's estate leave the details of the complex somewhat poorly understood. Printz appears to refer, at times, to his property as Fort New Gothenburg, but this usage may reflect a wish to emphasize his role as a military governor. The ship *Fama*, which arrived from Sweden on March 11, 1644, carried a document giving Printz title to Tinicum Island. Johnson (1930:34) translates the relevant Swedish text as a "Capital donation of that place called Tinnaco or New Gothenburg for Printz and for his lawful heirs." This suggests that the island was characterized by the fortification, but not with Printz's residence and other structures. The report of Andries Hudde "Dated N[ew] Gothenburg, Sept. 30, 1646" indicates that the name of the fort and the name of Printz's holdings on Tinicum Island were used interchangeably. In a report to the Swedish West India Company "Dated at New Gothenb[urg], February 20, 1647," Printz himself demonstrates the equivalence. I suggest that the name of the fortification was used for official business that transpired on Tinicum Island, although the activities described must have taken place within the residence. However, Johnson's map (1930: fac. 44) depicts and labels "New Gothenburg" as separate from the Printzhof, to the northeast and another structure to the northwest. This suggests that a separate "fortification" had been erected, providing protection for the residential buildings or complex. The documentary sources for Johnson's interpretation are not known. Other maps suggest that only a single complex, perhaps a fortified farmstead, was present.

Printz's first log structure, built as a residence and trading post in 1643, burned during November of 1645, together with many of the outbuildings. Only the barn is recorded as having survived that event (Johnson 1930:130–131). The principal house was rebuilt at once, as a somewhat larger log construction that stood for 180 years. During the winter of 1645–1646, the storehouse was repaired and a church built nearby. From other records we know that a separate brewhouse also formed part of the original complex (Baron 1962). Magnusson (2003:223–227, Fig. 2) provides important data from another Swedish outpost of the same period. The Swedish manorial estate of Kunda in Estonia (ca. 1647), with its log house and four log outbuildings, could be similar to the Printzhof complex on the South River. The two floors and tall attic of the Kunda house could be described as having a ground floor plus one and one-half floors *above* it. Of particular note are the three extremely tall chimneys on the Kunda house, which would explain the discovery of considerable numbers of small, yellow bricks used in the construction of the Printzhof (Becker 1977).

ARCHAEOLOGICAL EVIDENCE

In 1937 Donald Cadzow was chosen by the Commonwealth of Pennsylvania to direct an archaeological excavation at the Printzhof as part of the extensive Works Project Administration initiative of the federal government. A complex series of seventeenth-century and later foundations were revealed (Johnson 1938), the artifacts recovered in this process including many dating to the middle of the seventeenth century. Written records and artifact descriptions from these excavations were never published (see Craig 1992:3 for the Cadzow plan).

During the summer of 1976 the William Penn Memorial Museum, now the State Museum of Pennsylvania, provided funding to reexcavate the area of the 1937 project to confirm earlier findings and to conclusively demonstrate which of the foundations belonged to the Printzhof as distinct from those of later structures or additions. This project confirmed that the work of Donald Cadzow in the 1930s had indeed located the foundation of a large Swedish cabin. Correspondence between features of the foundation and Printz's reports, plus the associated artifacts confirmed that this was the structure built by Governor Printz in 1643 (Becker 1977, 1979). Of particular note was the identification of evidence for the rebuilding of that structure in the manner that Printz had described in his 1645 report to the Queen (see Johnson 1911).

The discovery of the palisades of the original fortification was an exceptionally important discovery. Furthermore, many artifacts recovered in the 1976 and later excavations duplicated those recovered by Cadzow that had been preserved at the American Swedish Museum. In fact, some of those newly discovered pieces of European-made clay pipes could be matched with pieces of these artifacts that had been found 40 years before.

Valuable clues to Native American activities at this location both before and after the arrival of Printz were also revealed. Features reflecting Native occupation in this area attracted our interest as well, providing clear evidence that Natives were active at this colonial trading post, camping almost literally on Printz's doorstep (Becker 1993). Since much of what we excavated that first season had been disturbed by the 1937 project, we were eager to examine some of the undisturbed features revealed in our excavations.

The success of the first season of modern excavation at the Printzhof led us to return in 1985. Excavations in 1976 included a 1-m-wide test trench extending from the large excavation at the center of the principal area of interest, around the house, to the modern sea wall. This narrow test trench exposed a cluster of three features that appeared to be the margins of Native burial pits of a pre-contact date. Since Cadzow noted that he located some Native burials in 1937, we were not surprised to find that what seemed to be burial features had been stripped of any human remains and artifacts. Cadzow did not indicate what had been discovered within these features, but some of the finds that survived in storage suggested to us that a pre-contact Native cemetery might exist in this area near the Printzhof proper. After consultation with the appropriate Lenape representatives in Oklahoma during 1983 and 1984, the following year we arranged to test the specific area to the south of the Printzhof, where Cadzow had found what appeared to be at least two burials, and where we thought a cemetery might exist.

The 1985 season at the Printzhof began by locating the three features found earlier that we believed might reveal a cemetery. Testing the westernmost of them, a feature only partially exposed in 1976, indicated that the feature did not represent a pit for a flexed burial. What appeared to be a corner of a grave, turned out instead to be part of the exterior angle of a right-angle turn in a long ditch or trench for an historic period fortification. More significantly, this feature was revealed to have been a very well-dug feature that held a series of posts set into it all along the western side of the north-south leg. After following the north-south leg for several meters we found that it took a sharp turn to the west that we followed for about 1 m. The posts in this east-west leg were set on the north side of the trench, but three particularly large poles were found on the opposite side of the ditch.

The European-dug trench and the posts driven into its floor are clearly the remains of a palisade (Becker 1997). Wooden stake defensive walls are known from Dutch colonial sites along Delaware River and Bay both from excavations as well as from old drawings and maps (Bonine 1956:14–15). These defenses were primarily meant to deter attacks by other Europeans.

The palisade at the Printzhof is nowhere noted in the known contemporary literature. This apparent omission may be because the construction of a palisaded defensive wall was an automatic part of establishing any encampment at that period. Such basic features of these early outposts may not have been considered noteworthy. I interpret the evidence as the remains of a simple, square fortification. However, an alternative possibility is that the palisaded trench represents a large bastion at one end of an extremely large palisaded fort. Fortifications with only two bastions, built in the shape of a diamond (or square), are known from contemporary accounts of Dutch colonial sites on Delaware Bay (Becker 2001; Bonine 1956:Plates 1, 3; Bonine 1964). Some external posts or supports seen at Fort New Gothenburg may have served either to support a small tower or possibly a protected entryway.

During excavation of the palisade trench, each of the post molds was mapped in place, and sections were made through several examples to recover information about how they had been set and how this fortification had been constructed. The individual pales averaged only 10 to 12 cm in diameter. Those few pales that were formed from trees greater than 20 cm in diameter had been split before being added to the palisade line (Becker 1997). This suggests that an individual or a two-person team could rapidly fell and transport single pales for rapid construction. The ditch itself also is interesting since the construction began with the digging of a very regular trench, typical of European palisade construction, but quite different from any known Native American examples. Examination of the base of each sectioned post in the fortification palisade showed that the ends placed in the ground had been pointed with an ax or similar tool. The depths of these pointed tips extend slightly below the actual floor or bottom of the ditch. Quite clearly the poles were thrust into position in order to sink them well into the ground. The walls of the trench that had been dug for the palisade are still quite vertical, indicating that the earth packed into the ditch had been tightly tamped into place to hold the posts securely upright. The only historic artifact recovered from the excavations to reveal this trench was a brass button, supporting our conclusion that the feature was an early

European construction. No Native artifacts, not even stone chips, were recovered.

For pre-contact archaeological research in this region, the most important discovery in 1986 was the evidence for a Native *wikiup*, or simple shelter, often called a wigwam (Becker 1993). Far smaller than the well-known long houses of the Susquehannock and Five Nations (Iroquois), a wikiup leaves few traces for archaeologists to recover (see Custer et al. 1998: 18). The few small post holes left from these shelters, which probably were used for only one season, are easily obliterated by any kind of disturbance. The "Corinthian wikiup," which actually includes portions of two sequentially built structures on the same location, is roughly circular, measuring about 4.0 to 4.2 m across, with each of the many poles used in the construction averaging about 4 cm in diameter. These structures appear remarkably similar to an example reported from site 7NC-E-60 in nearby New Castle County, Delaware (Custer et al. 1998:16–18). The Delaware site also lies within the realm of the historically known Lenape. Similarities are noted in the overall size of these structures, the intervals between posts and possible placements of fire pits close to the margins rather in the center as might be expected. Diagnostic artifacts are not available in either of these locations, but a sequence of superimposed wikiup patterns of oval shape, measuring 4 by 5 m, from Pig Point in Maryland have been 14C dated to 210, 520, and 1200 CE (Roylance 2010). The people at Pig Point, however, belonged to a culture quite distinct from that of the Lenape (Becker 2018).

An additional discovery during the 1986 season was a ditch a short distance to the west-northwest of the foundations of the house, that had been filled with an undisturbed deposit of charred remains apparently dumped there after the Printzhof fire in November of 1645. This find from the Printzhof reveals that this process of leveling the landscape had begun as soon as Europeans first settled in a forested land characterized by nature's irregular terrain. Not only were the depressions and gullies of the normal landscape a problem to colonists who were interested in house construction and farming, but these hidden rills provided potential cover for attackers. The filling of these low places was an ongoing concern in the management of the colonial landscape.

It is interesting that the filling of this particular feature seems to have taken place quickly, with no effort seemly expended to salvage metal spikes and nails for reuse or trade. The need to erect a new residence during this winter period apparently absorbed all the human resources available.

Modern excavation of this deposit recovered iron artifacts along with burned sherds of European pottery, clay tobacco pipes, drinking glasses, and yellow bricks. Of particular interest among the fragments of European material culture were the glass rim fragments and prunts (decorative knobs) from one or more roemer drinking glasses, all of a form typical of the 1640–1650 period (Theuerkauff 1968, 1969; see Figure 6).

In addition to the significant evidence for a colonial governor's lifestyle in the middle of the seventeenth century, the excavations at Fort New Gothenburg provide considerable evidence to support our belief that Printz was collecting examples of Native trophies and tools to send home. The practice of collecting "trophies" from the people native to places where military officers were stationed is documented throughout Europe. These collections provide us with some of the best documented and finest examples of early Native artifacts (Becker 1990a). Some examples are believed to be of Susquehannock origin (see Becker 1980, 1990b; Johnson 1930:117, 140), a subject elaborated in an earlier paper (Becker 2011a:16–21).

CONCLUSION

The importance of the excavations of the palisade of Fort New Gothenburg lies in much more than allowing a better understanding of the processes by which this site was formed in 1643. The development of the Swedish residential complex "behind" the fort helps us to interpret this early colonial defensive strategy and apply this information to our understanding sites elsewhere in North America (Becker 2000). Although other archaeological excavations at Dutch or suspected Swedish outposts in this region often mention, by inference, what we might suggest represents the presence of a palisade (e.g. Heite and Heite 1989:46), not one example of a fortification has been identified at any other early colonial site in the Delaware Valley. The archaeological record from the Printzhof excavations offers clues to colonial and Native lifestyles and the interactions of the several groups within each of these "cultural" spheres during the early period of European contact. What we describe here took place in the earliest period of trade, before English colonial expansion and significant Native interactions had compounded the already complex social dynamics from the Middle Atlantic region (see Becker 1998, 2011). This period covers a time when cultures were in contact along a fluid but very thin frontier situated directly along the Atlantic Ocean and along a few of the major waterways that flowed into it. We now have direct archaeological evidence to complement an abundant documentary record dating from the important 40 years of Dutch and Swedish activities that preceded the English takeover of the Delaware drainage in 1664. The archaeological finds from the site on Tinicum Island identified as 36DE3 provide direct evidence for the Swedish presence on the Delaware River and their interactions with Native and Europeans along the river.

IV

Artifact Studies

12

By Any Other Name

Kookpotten or Grapen? Little Pots, Big Stories

Meta F. Janowitz and Richard G. Schaefer

As Charles Gehring notes in the beginning of this volume: "Evidence of the existence of New Netherland didn't vanish with the arrival of the English. Most of the inhabitants didn't just pack up and return to Europe. They had large families and were for the most part firmly rooted in the New World. Their language and customs survived for generations." Families must be fed, and the customs of how they are fed are the focus of the study of "foodways"—a term encompassing not only the specific foods people eat but also how these foods are processed and what artifacts are used to prepare, cook, and consume them. Archaeologists reconstruct historical foodways using images, recipes from printed cookbooks and handwritten family documents, faunal and floral remains, and excavated artifacts, although some of the artifacts used to prepare, cook, and eat food are not preserved and cannot be excavated and examined. Wooden artifacts decay rapidly in the ground unless they were disposed of in oxygen-free environments, and metal from vessels was commonly recycled rather than thrown away. Ceramic and glass artifacts fare better, especially ceramics. Objects made of earthenware, stoneware, or porcelain clays can last indefinitely after discard and are central to the reconstruction of foodways. Ceramic vessels also serve as evidence of cultural persistence, adaptation, and trading networks. This chapter is about some unpretentious earthenware cooking vessels used in everyday foodways and what their presence can reveal about Dutch trade along the mid-Atlantic coast outside New Netherland and the persistence of Dutch American foodways.

The great variety of food-related earthenware vessels made in the Netherlands during the seventeenth century has already received scholarly attention, both in the United States and in the Netherlands (see, e.g., Gawronski 2012; Schaefer 1998). This assortment of vessels includes cooking pots, skillets, pans, and colanders made of red- or buff-firing earthenware clays coated with lead glazes (Figure 12.1). Among this variety, one group of homely objects stands out, small- to medium-sized three-legged cooking pots with distinctive rims and handles that are frequently found on New Netherland archaeological sites (Wilcoxen 1985, 1987).

First, a few words about what to call these vessels. When American historical archaeologists working in areas that had been New Netherland began to establish contacts with Dutch archaeologists and material culture experts during the latter half of the twentieth century, the Netherlanders already had an established typological vocabulary. At the time of first contact between archaeologists from both sides of the Atlantic, Dutch archaeologists tended to use the term *grape* (CHRAH-peh), probably borrowed from German archaeologists, to refer to this ubiquitous tripodal earthen cooking pot (Baart et al. 1977:passim; Kleyn 1965:plate 6A, 6C, 9A; Renaud 1948:73–80). "Grape" was and is a useful term, since it clearly denotes a certain type of globular cooking pot, usually of undecorated lead-glazed red earthenware, but also found in white earthenware and in metal. In reviewing seventeenth-century Amsterdam assemblages, Schaefer found 173 grapen. Of these, 122 (70.5%) were lead-glazed red earthenware, 26 (15.0%) were lead-glazed buff/white earthenware, and 25 (14.5%) were lead-glazed red earthenware decorated with white slip (Schaefer 1998: 22). Two main attributes define *grapen* (the plural of "grape"): (1) three stubby legs, called *poten* (feet, or the diminutive, *pootjes* [little feet]), attached to the pot's bottom—a popular twentieth-century term for this vessel was *driebeen* or "three legs" (Renaud 1948:73); and (2) one or two vertical ear handles (one *oor* or two *oren*), attached at the top outside edge of the rim and at the pot's shoulder.

Currently, however, the term used by many Dutch archaeologists and material culture specialists to refer to these vessels is *kookpotten* (cooking pots, singular *kookpot*). This evolution in nomenclature is grounded in historical documents, which refer to kookpotten or simply *potten*, but in which "grape" is nowhere to be found (e.g., Roodenburg 1993:91n3; Schaefer 1998:21–22; Slootmans 1970:28). Numerous Dutch scholars have been quite pointed in their denunciation of "grape" (Kicken et al. 2000:98). To

Figure 12.1. Nicolaes Maes, *Interior with a Sleeping Maid and Her Mistress* (*The Idle Servant*), ca. 1655. National Gallery, London. *On the floor, left to right:* a pewter plate, an earthenware kookpot, a tin-glazed lobed dish, a metal kookpot, a metal strainer, large and small pewter plates, an earthenware kookpot, a large wooden spoon, two tin-glazed plates, a metal kookpot, and an earthenware colander.

give them their due, some Dutch antiquarians seemed to be uneasy with the term quite early, using "grape," "kookpot," and "driebeen" interchangeably (Renaud 1948), while on the other hand, the Deventer System, the dominant typological system in Dutch historical archaeology, still codes these pots with the letters *gra* (e.g., Gawronski 2012:321, artifacts 591–602). It may be the clarity of "grape" and the extreme vagueness of "kookpot" that has driven scholars to the barricades. Although we archaeologists of New Netherland may continue to use "grape" in our unguarded moments, in order to study seventeenth-century foodways through the contemporary written or printed word, it is necessary to employ the correct nomenclature to avoid confusion. Thus, this article will use the term "kookpot," even though the authors have previously used the older, anachronistic terminology (Janowitz 1993; Janowitz et al. 1985; Schaefer 1998).

Before closing the discussion of nomenclature and moving on to the kookpotten themselves, a further caveat is necessary. Based on size, material, decoration, and other attributes, vessels of kookpot form were used for a range of different activities (even as musical instruments! see Schaefer 1998:99), although their major foodways-related tasks were cooking and eating, and sometimes both. Dutch archaeologists have tended to distinguish between these functions by applying the term "kookpotten" most frequently to the two-eared pots, which tend to be larger and used for cooking, based on the evidence of burning commonly found on archaeological specimens. The smaller, one-eared pots, however, are found unburned more often than their larger cousins, indicating that, in addition to their cooking tasks, they were also or even exclusively used as serving and dining vessels. Muddying the waters somewhat, many of the Dutch employ the term "kookkan" (literally "cooking pitcher" or "cooking jug" in British terminology) for the one-handled form, perhaps taking their cue from the pouring lip that sometimes appears opposite a single ear handle (Clevis and Kottman 1989:28; Groeneweg 1982:66, 89; Museum Boijmans van Beuningen 2018). The current authors have not encountered "kookkan" in historical documents and so are cautious about employing the term and do not do so here. The corresponding English form in both size and usage for these small pots would be called a "pipkin"; the authors purposely do not use "pipkin" here and elsewhere, to avoid confusing Dutch and English vessel forms.

Description

Red earthenware cooking pots were first introduced in the Netherlands during the early thirteenth century, and the stubby poten, or legs, appeared between 1250 and 1300, possibly because the tripodal base gave a firmer footing to the pots than rounded bases, particularly on the brick or stone hearths that replaced dirt hearths about that time (Hurst et al. 1986:130). The most common shape for cooking pots until circa 1700 was a spherical or globular body with a constricted neck and a flaring rim (Figure 12.2a, c, e). This shape was especially common among the potters in the ceramic manufacturing center at Bergen op Zoom and those who copied their style (Schaefer 1998:22). The pots' common size range is from 10 cm (3.9 in) in height with a rim diameter of about 10 cm, to 24 cm (9.4 in) height and a 24 cm rim diameter, with some large vessels having rim diameters as large as 40 cm (15.7 in).

Another shape for cooking pots was more similar to metal cooking pots, and is sometimes called bullet- or kettle-shaped (Carmiggelt et al. 1987:26) or egg-shaped (Groeneweg 1982:89) (Figure 12.2b, d).This form was already in widespread use by the sixteenth century, and vessels in this style were manufactured throughout the seventeenth century. The bullet form is generally narrower in proportion to its height than the spherical versions and was not made in sizes as large as the first form. Common sizes range from a height of approximately 9.5 cm (3.7 in) with a rim diameter of approximately 7 cm (2.8 in), to a height of approximately 17.5 cm (6.9 in) and a rim diameter of approximately 17.2 cm (6.8 in). With both body forms, one or two vertical ear handles were attached at the top outside edge of the rim and at the shoulder. Larger pots generally have two handles.

During the seventeenth century, oren (ears) were the usual form of kookpot handle in the Netherlands (Figure 12.3), while potters in nearby northern Germany and England overwhelmingly favored rod handles on their small earthenware cooking pots. Two basic kinds of oren were used for both red and white earthenware kookpotten. The prevalent oor used is described as *worst-formig*, meaning wurst-form or sausage-shaped, because it maintains a more or less round cross-section with little distortion in diameter except where it is attached to the pot's rim and shoulder (Figure 12.3a). Pinching done when the ear was joined to the rim created a ridge (the top of the "ear") where the handle angles upward. This type of handle was easy to form and attach and could be done by apprentices or unskilled workers (Schaefer 1998:13–14). Aside from streamlining the production

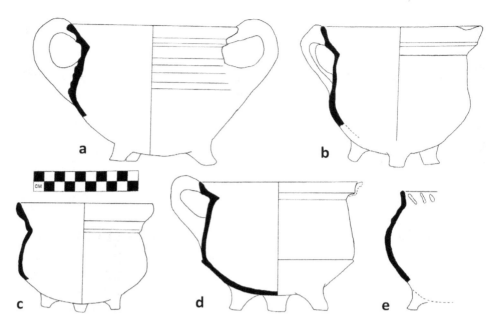

Figure 12.2. Kookpot shapes: (*a*) Red earthenware kookpot with worst-formig oren (wurst- or sausage-form ear handle) (Schaefer 1998:Figure 10.3); (*b*) red earthenware kookpot, bullet/kettle form, strap-form oor with pouring lip opposite (Schaefer 1998:Figure 13.3); (*c*) red earthenware kookpot with worst-formig oor (Schaefer 1998:Figure 10.2); (*d*) red earthenware kookpot, bullet/kettle form, strap-form oor with pouring lip opposite, (Schaefer 1998:Figure 12.1); and (*e*) red earthenware kookpot, trailed "North Holland Slip" decoration on shoulder: "ANNO 1663" (Schaefer 1998:Figure 13.1).

process for master potters, the thick ears were strong and can be found on all large pots, as well as other kinds of vessels, such as chamber pots. Over the course of the seventeenth century oren grew in size in relation to the pot (Hurst et al. 1986:130), possibly because larger oren were effective in minimizing contact between vessels during kiln loading. The other form of oor has been called strap form (Schaefer 1998:112) because in cross-section it is generally much wider than it is thick (Figure 12.3b). During the process of joining it to the exterior of the rim, the two sides of the handle were usually pinched together, leaving a distinctive conical hollow on the top of the oor. This form is rare on vessels made in Bergen, but was used widely on vessels made in other areas, such as the city of Gouda in western Holland.

The common seventeenth-century Dutch kookpot rim form, employed throughout the United Provinces and found on all forms of kookpotten,

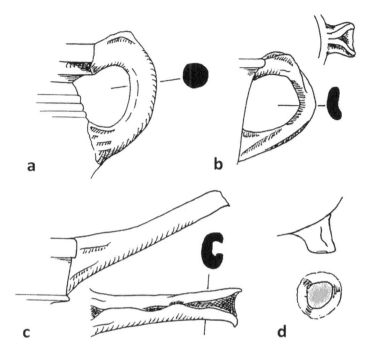

Figure 12.3. Handle and foot shapes (artist's rendering, not to scale): (*a*) Worst-formig oor (wurst- or sausage-form ear handle); (*b*) strap-form oor, view from the side and from above; (*c*) celery rod handle, used on earthenware skillets, view from side and from above; and (*d*) *poot* (foot), view from the side and from below (Schaefer 1998:Figure 9).

had already developed by the sixteenth century (Figure 12.4h–t). Naturally, due to its widespread fabrication by individual potters throughout the country, it appears in many versions. The rim flares with a thickening at the edge, and an exterior bead runs midway between this edge and the neck. The interior is smooth and slopes inward. It is often concave. The bead can range from an almost invisible bump to a sharply pointed ridge. Some rims were probably formed using a template and others using fingers or a tool, such as a rib. This common rim form can be tilted at various angles and sometimes stands almost vertically. If the section between the brim and a prominent bead is not strongly indented, the exterior face of the rim appears to form a collar. This latter rim type has been distinguished from the common rim by the label "everted collared rim" (Hurst et al. 1986:132), but only the most extreme types are truly distinct, meriting a different category.

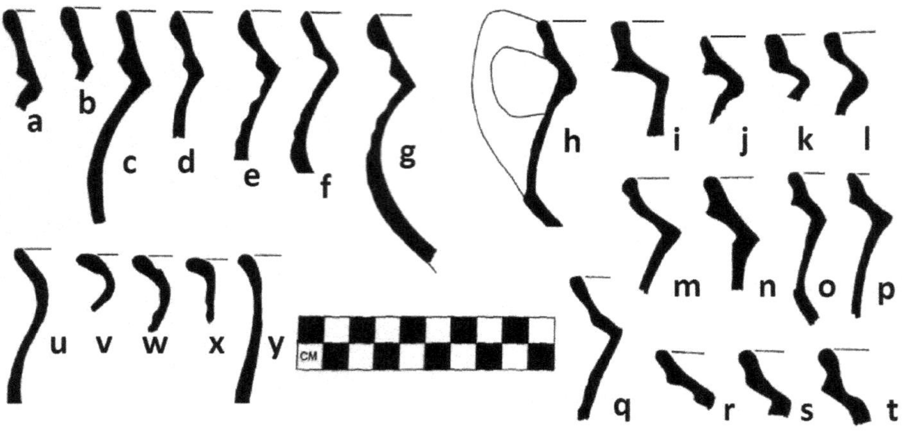

Figure 12.4. Dutch seventeenth-century kookpot rim forms: (a–g) everted bead or ogee rims, red-bodied earthenware wasters from the Croonenburgh pottery in Bergen op Zoom; (h–n) common rims, red-bodied kookpotten from Amsterdam Taanstraat cesspits; (o–t) common rims, buff- or white-bodied kookpotten from Amsterdam Taanstraat cesspits; (u–y) smooth flaring plain rims from red-bodied kookpotten from Amsterdam cesspits (Schaefer 1998:Figures 12, 13).

In these more extreme types the exterior of the collared rim is relatively smooth and vertical and overhangs the neck, looking almost hammer-headed in cross-section.

Bergen op Zoom potters evolved a distinctive kookpot rim form by which their products can be identified in contemporary paintings (Sloot-mans 1970:xxi) and archaeological assemblages (Rothschild and Pickman 1990). It is related to the common rim but is much more massive (Figure 12.4 a–g). In the literature, this rim is referred to as an "everted bead rim" (Hurst et al. 1986:131, Figure 59.187, 133, plate 21) or as an "ogee rim," nei-ther of which do justice to the shape. Too complicated to be formed using fingers alone, this rim was made using a template pressed against the pot as it spun on the potter's wheel. The interior of the rim is smooth and slightly indented as a result of the finger pressure used to support the rim as it was pressed against the template. Despite the use of templates, Bergen kookpot-ten rims still display a great deal of variation (Schaefer 1998:113–114). The heavy ridge or beading would have added strength to the rim, necessary both before and after drying, especially since the upper oor attachment was on the rim itself.

The three feet, poten, on kookpotten were stubby by the seventeenth century, having about the same width as height, and roughly triangular in cross-section (Figure 12.3d). On vessels with a single handle, there is always a *pootje* directly beneath the handle, giving the pot sturdy footing when it is set down and making it possible to pour liquid from the vessel by tilting it and resting it on the two front legs instead of picking it up.

Most kookpotten were completely lead glazed on the inside and to somewhere between the neck and the waist on the exterior by the start of the seventeenth century. One-eared kookpotten usually also have an exterior "bib" of glaze beneath the pouring lip. It has been suggested that if the bottom of the pot were glazed it would burst when placed on a fire (Erftemeyer et al. 1987: 44). Whether or not this is accurate, it is certainly true that the great majority of coarse earthenware cooking vessels are unglazed on the surface that comes into direct contact with flames; for example, British-made buff-bodied slipware dishes and Pennsylvania-made redware pans and dishes, with very few exceptions, have unglazed exteriors. These pans and dishes were made to be used in open-hearth cooking. Glaze on pot interiors and around the upper parts of their exteriors would have prevented cooking liquids and oils from penetrating the porous earthenware body. Porous bodies are difficult to clean and can impart unpleasant odors and flavors to food. (The use of lead glaze did not fall out of favor with coarse earthenware potters and consumers until well into the nineteenth century [Janowitz 2013]). Some small kookpotten have white slip on their interiors under a yellow-appearing lead glaze or a green glaze, if the lead glaze is colored with copper oxide (see Wilcoxen 1987:plate 13).

Other forms may display one or more typical grapen attributes, but since their use was not for food preparation, telltale evidence of wear and glazing indicate that they are not kookpotten. Poten and single ear handles are found on seventeenth-century braziers (*testen*), although the upper walls and rims of these vessels are practically vertical, and the evidence of burning is found on the *inside*. There was no concern about grease and oils contacting the brazier, so the extent of glazing is relatively modest or omitted altogether. Likewise, chamber pots, although they tend to have the rounded bodies of larger kookpotten, are rarely burned, have distinctive flattened rims, and have foot-ring bases rather than poten.

How Kookpotten Were Used: Paintings, Documents, and Use Wear

Scenes of food preparation and consumption were among the popular themes depicted by Dutch seventeenth-century artists. Food-preparation scenes, for the most part, show middle- and upper-class women or their servants working indoors, usually in multipurpose rooms, infrequently in separate kitchens (for example, Nicholas Maes, *Woman Plucking a Duck*, Philadelphia Museum of Art) or occasionally outdoors, if the activity is messy, as in Pieter de Hooch's *Woman and her Maid in a Courtyard*, in which the maid is cleaning a fish. When men are shown as cooks, it is either in elite kitchens or at peasant hearths (Adriaen Brouwer, *The Pancake Baker*, Philadelphia Museum of Art). Eating food is a more common subject than cooking food. Scenes of food consumption include solitary meals, family dinners, and elaborate banquets (Jan Steen, *A Twelfth Night Feast*, private collection). Kookpotten with one or two handles were used as props in depictions of solitary and family meals where people are shown eating directly from kookpotten, both small- and large-sized, without transferring the contents to other dishes after heating. For the most part, one-handled vessels, often holding spoons, are shown sitting on tabletops, either permanent or impromptu (such as overturned barrels used as small tables); these almost certainly would have held soup or grain porridge for individual consumption. In *An Old Woman Praying* by Nicholas Maes (Rijksmuseum), a small one-handled kookpot with a small pushed-out pouring lip has been set on a wooden disk, which, in turn, sits on a linen tablecloth, thus protecting the cloth from the presumably sooty poten, evidence that the pot's contents were warmed in the hearth. In the foreground of some of his paintings, Jan Steen, the artist known for his rowdy family scenes, placed a small one-eared kookpot on the floor, lying on its side and empty, as in one of his "merry family" scenes at the Amsterdam Rijksmuseum. Steen included two-handled kookpotten in at least two versions of his treatments of *The Lean Kitchen* theme, depicting poor households and their meager victuals. In the version in the Cheltenham Art Gallery and Museum, a girl crouching on the floor is defending a large kookpot and the dregs of its contents against a boy brandishing a long wooden spoon, as he attempts to take control of the vessel. The girl is scooping out the remains from the pot with her hands while holding it sideways. In the version at the National Gallery of Canada, a boy with a wooden spoon is in sole possession of a kookpot as he sits on the floor. He too holds the pot on its side, the better to reach into it and scrape out the contents. The woman in Gerard Dou's *Woman Eating Porridge* holds her large kookpot in the same sideways position, but she sits on an overturned basket and rests the pot in her lap with a coarse cloth under it to protect her clothing. Perhaps the most famous kookpot used as a prop is the large two-handled vessel into which a woman is pouring milk in Johannes Vermeer's *The Milkmaid*. This painting is unusual because it shows a kookpot used in food preparation rather than consumption, albeit at an early stage of preparation, before the pot goes to the hearth.

Lambertus Burema's survey of food in the Netherlands from the Middle Ages to the mid-twentieth century used documents and personal recollections to reconstruct foodways. The author's reconstruction of the common seventeenth-century Dutch diet was three meals a day with extras, especially afternoon snacks. Breakfast (*ontbijt*) was a simple meal: bread with butter or cheese, and water, milk, mead, or small beer to drink (Burema 1953:89). Wealthy households might also have meat for breakfast. In rural areas summertime breakfasts might include sweet and sour cream with cherries, strawberries, and rusks in addition to the usual bread, butter, and cheese.

The midday meal (*middagmaal*) was the largest meal of the day. It could include bread, meat, and side dishes of vegetables, fish, mussels or other shellfish, and fruit or salad (Burema 1953:96–97). Typical dishes were peas with butter and vinegar; fresh or dried beans with prunes, butter, ginger, and sage; wheat bread sopped in meat or chicken broth; stewed sweet roots with fish; cold cooked vegetables; carrots stewed with potherbs and vinegar; or *hutspot* (a stew of meats and vegetables). Fresh meat was eaten in the summer, salt meat in the winter. The last foods to be served at the midday meal were fruits, salads (greens dressed with oil or melted butter and vinegar, and sometimes with salt, cheese, and various herbs), vegetable mashes (especially cabbage cooked with bacon and milk), cookies, cakes, and—for the well-to-do more than for the common people—tarts (Burema 1953:97). Burema (1953:95) quoted an eighteenth-century writer who recalled three examples of midday meals from his youth: the first was dishes of groats (boiled crushed grains), porridge, buckwheat cakes, and water; the second was broth, beans with sausage, gray peas, roasted veal, and beef; the third was pheasant, partridge, or other costly wild bird, fancy cakes, and confections with all sorts of wine. Although it was not stated as such in the text, it is clear from the context that these three examples represent typical midday meals in poor, middling, and rich households.

The evening meal (*avondmaal*) was simple and could consist of bread with butter or cheese (again), or could be various gruels or porridges, or leftover dishes from the midday meal (Burema 1953:106). Kookpotten would have been used to cook the gruels, porridges, groats, stews, broths, and vegetable mashes that made up a large part of the Dutch diet, and as a result kookpotten made of metal or earthenware were the most important cooking utensils in the Dutch kitchen.

During the seventeenth century many of the books written and published in the Netherlands were moral treatises, books intended for teaching people how to lead virtuous lives. The cookbook *De Verstandige Kock* was in this literary tradition; it was part of a household manual that contained information on, among other subjects, gardening, medicine, housekeeping, brewing, and how to lead an orderly and moral life (Schama 1987:158). *De Verstandige Kock of Sorghvuldige Huys-houdster* (The wise [or intelligent or sensible] cook or careful householder) was first published in 1668 and was republished often until the early nineteenth century (Rose 1989:4). A few cookbooks had already been published in Dutch during the previous century and a half (Winter 1976:141, 148), but *De Verstandige Kock* became "the standard cookery book designed for households of the middling sort" (Schama 1987:158).

Most cookbooks published before the mid-nineteenth century were not precise in their measurements or in their specifications of cooking utensils, and *De Verstandige Kock* follows this pattern. For example, *aerde* pots (earthen pots) were specified in only one meat and several fruit recipes. The authors of *De Verstandige Kock* perhaps assumed that most cooking would be done in metal pots or thought that the material did not matter, *except* in those recipes that specifically called for earthen pots. The recipe "Om Olypodrigo te maken die goet is" (How to make a good stew) says to take a hen, a piece of mutton, a piece of pork, and some veal, and put them in an earthen pot with water. The pot was then set "op" the fire. *Op* can be translated as "on," "upon," "at," or "in" depending on the dictionary used (Jockin-la Bastide and Van Kooten 1980:392). After the meats had cooked for a while, other ingredients were added (a pigeon, chopped veal, sausage, endive, cauliflower, mace, and pepper), and the mixture was again set "op" the fire. One thing is clear from this recipe—the earthen pot must have been quite large to accommodate all of these ingredients.

The decision to use an earthen or a metal pot for cooking is based on several important factors. The first is cost. In the seventeenth-century Netherlands, where a skilled worker earned 2.80 guilders weekly and a schoolmaster (*predikant*) less than 4.00 guilders (Schama 1987:617), the prospect of spending 2.75 guilders for a copper pot and 0.80 and 1.25 guilders, respectively, for two iron pots with lids, as recorded in a 1636 probate inventory from the town of Medemblik, would have been a major outlay. This inventory also listed "some" earthenware for 0.20 guilders. A 1678 inventory from the same town records the value of two "big earthen" pots at 0.95 guilders (Schaefer 1998:21).

Unfortunately, price comparisons in the New World are more difficult to make because inventories from New Netherland are not plentiful and were often not complete accounts of household goods, especially for earthenwares (Wilcoxen 1985:121–122). For example, the inventory of a woman who died at Pavonia (New Jersey) in 1641 listed an extensive collection of pewter tablewares, an iron gridiron and pan, and seven copper "store" kettles. (At least some of these kettles were probably intended for trade rather than the needs of the household, because one of them is listed as "partly old," which implies that the others were unused.) No earthenwares of any kind were listed in this inventory (Van Laer 1974a:325). The 1651 inventory of Jan Jansen Damen, who had a large farm and brewery just north of New Amsterdam's wall (modern Wall Street), included many metal artifacts; he also had five wooden dinner plates and nine "earthen dishes" (the term "dish" is ambiguous) and an "earthen bowl" (Van Laer 1974b:270–273). Even when earthenwares are listed in inventories, they are often lumped with other goods, so their price cannot be determined. In the inventory of Tryntie Janssen, taken in 1665, iron and copper pots, kettles, and pans are evaluated on the same line as earthen pots and earthen and "tin" (pewter) plates (Pearson 1869:70). Contemporary auction records regularly list earthenwares among household goods sold, but, again, they are not usually distinguished as unique items with discrete prices (Pearson 1869: 68, 206, 350). The ubiquity of large iron or copper cooking pots in inventories and the relative absence of earthenware pots in these records could be due, in at least some cases, to the enumerator's omissions: earthenware vessels were not worth as much as metal vessels so were not noted separately.

Iron and copper would have been preferred materials for large pots, kettles, or cauldrons as opposed to ceramics for several reasons: they were less likely to break, they transferred heat more rapidly, and they could be made with handles for suspension over the fire. Metal pots could be repaired, but earthenware pots, when broken, were useless for cooking, unless the damage was minor. Earthenware pots may have their shortcomings, but they also have their advantages, particularly the even distribution and retention of heat. A modern food writer stated: "Earthenware pots have a wonderful

214 · Meta F. Janowitz and Richard G. Schaefer

ability to coddle food, bringing out bright natural flavors and aromas and producing an unctuous tenderness" (Wolfert 2009:xiii). In other words, compared to metal pots, earthen pots cook food more evenly and meld flavors better.

Pots with minimal damage could still be functional, as can be seen in both Dou's *Woman Eating Porridge* and Maes's *Old Woman Praying*, where both women use pots with chips at their rims. Broken off sections of the rim did not prevent use as cooking containers, or mixing or batter bowls (See Donck, *Pancake Baker*; Jan Molenaer or Pieter Quast, *Peasant Interior*). Even when kookpotten could no longer hold liquids to their full capacities, they still had potential for reuse. The evidence for this comes mainly from paintings that show kookpotten used as pipe braziers, drip catchers beneath spigots and butchered carcasses (Frans van Mieris, *The Peasant Inn*, De Lakenhal) and even as a tax collector's coin holder in Frans Hals II's painting *Peasants and Tax Collector*.

How earthenware kookpotten were used can be seen not only in contemporary paintings, but also in the marks left on the vessels themselves. The presence of carbon deposits are a kookpot's chief usage mark. Carbon deposits are usually found only on the unglazed parts of the vessel, since any buildup on the glazed sections would flake off or could be cleaned off. One-eared kookpotten glazed only down to the exterior shoulder generally show heavy burning on their bottoms and the pouring-lip side, opposite the handle. (This commonsense positioning of the pouring lip and handle kept the cook's fingers out of the fire and the oor relatively cool for removal of the pot from the flame.) However, a vessel with no carbon deposits does not necessarily mean it was not used for cooking. Steaming food in pots placed in larger cooking vessels would have left the pot soot-free (McCarthy and Brooks 1988:105). Pots could also have been placed in bake ovens alongside bread or other dishes. Bake ovens cook with heat reflected from their surfaces after fuel has been burned in them; the burned residues are swept out before food is placed inside, leaving no charcoal to mark vessels.

The fact that many kookpotten do not exhibit abrasive wear marks on their interiors suggests the shortness of the average pot's life. If a kookpot survived the perils facing earthenware cooking pots for any length of time, it should show definite signs of wear on the interior, particularly horizontal scratches on the sides and near the bottom from stirring and scraping the contents, although it is likely that the use of wooden spoons rather than metal utensils would reduce wear marks. On the interior of some kookpotten the lead glaze is worn off the projecting ring around the interior of the rim, where the neck reaches its narrowest point. This ring would encounter friction whenever anything was added to or taken from the kookpot, especially during stirring. Kookpotten can also show wear on their unglazed feet from contact with hard surfaces.

ARCHAEOLOGY

New York City

The kookpotten that have been recovered during archaeological excavations in New Netherland are both one- and two-handled types (Diamond 2004; Fayden 1993; Grossman 1985; Huey 1988a; Rothschild and Pickman 1990; Rothschild et al. 1987; Schaefer 2012, 2015). In New York City, archaeological projects along the East River have recovered seventeenth- and early eighteenth-century artifacts, including kookpot sherds, from both fast land and landfill sites. Lower Manhattan's East River shoreline today is not where it was when the Dutch first came to the island. New Amsterdammers began to modify the shoreline in the 1650s with the construction of a seawall that, by circa 1660, extended from the tip of Manhattan to the wall at Wall Street. In 1680, under an English government, a new city charter granted the municipality the right to sell "water lots," which extended into the river between high- and low-water marks (Burrows and Wallace 1999:110, Cantwell and Wall 2001:110, 325). Purchasers had the right to erect retaining walls to restrain the river and were expected to fill in their lots with whatever materials they could find. Merchants' establishments and domestic structures were built on the "made land." Made land along the East River in Lower Manhattan was first created between Pearl Street and Water Street in the late seventeenth century, extended from Water Street to Front Street during the mid-eighteenth century, then to South Street at the end of that century.

At the 7 Hanover Square site, filled during the 1680s and early 1690s, archaeologists found that the foundations for houses built along the Pearl Street (inland) side of the water lots had been constructed on the natural shoreline, not on the landfill (Cantwell and Wall 2001:236–237). Landfill surrounded the walls, but their basal support was the natural shore; the house foundations were part of the landfill-retaining structure. The first buildings on the Pearl Street side of the block were six narrow Dutch-style houses whose gable ends faced the street and a larger square Georgian-style house built for William Kidd, the privateer, on the corner. The basements

Figure 12.5. Small red earthenware and large buff earthenware kookpotten with lead glaze from the 7 Hanover Square site, New York City. By permission of the Archaeological Repository of the New York City Landmarks Preservation Commission.

of each of these houses were excavated. In one, located on lot 13, a mortar surface lying atop the landfill was identified and sampled with six excavation units (Rothschild and Pickman 1990:195–197). Sherds from three kookpotten and other ceramics were found on the mortar surface itself, not in the landfill. The mortar surface could have been a floor designed to cap the landfill or a casual deposit associated with the construction of the first building on the site. The deposit on the mortar surface was dated circa 1690–1700. If the surface were a mortar floor laid to keep out dampness from the landfill, the artifacts lying on it could be a domestic deposit associated with the first occupants of the house; however, it is possible that the artifacts were deposited during construction of the house and thus cannot be associated with a particular household. In either case, the deposit dates to well after the 1664 acquisition of New Netherland by the English.

The ceramics from this deposit came from at least 22 vessels, including 28 sherds that mended to form approximately one-third of a large two-handled kookpot made of coarse buff earthenware with a thin yellow lead glaze, and 11 sherds from two small red-bodied kookpotten (Figure 12.5). These kookpotten are evidence of the persistence of Dutch-influenced foodways more than two generations after 1664 (Janowitz 1993). No British-made food-preparation vessels were part of this deposit.

Another deposit at the 7 Hanover Square site, found on the original riverbed beneath the landfill, was made up of more than 300 sherds from kookpotten and other red earthenware vessels, including dishes and colanders (Janowitz et al. 1985: 44). The vessels were probably discarded in the river because they broke in transit, a not-uncommon event that has been documented in several archaeological deposits in Manhattan. (In the fill of Whitehall Slip circa 1801–1809, for example, an extensive deposit of broken pearlware vessels—approximately 30 ft long and 2 ft thick—was probably dumped directly into the slip from the ship that had carried them from England [AKRF et al. 2012:6-53–6-57; Janowitz and Wall 2017:175–176]). The river-bottom sherds from Hanover Square have distinctive dark red, somewhat sandy bodies and dark green or brown lead glazes. Based on their pastes and rim profiles, the vessels from which the sherds came might have been made by Bergen op Zoom potters, purchased by the Dutch West India Company for its colonial employees or for trade. The Bergen potters did not usually sell directly to consumers, but instead sold to distributors who had their own shops or who offered goods in public markets. Amsterdam was one of the major markets for Bergen pottery during the time that the Amsterdam Chamber of the WIC was supplying its New Netherland settlements (Schaefer 1998:10), and it is quite likely that the directors bought Bergen pots in bulk to send to New Amsterdam.

The Chesapeake

The Compton Site, a seventeenth-century site from outside the borders of New Netherland, included a variety of Dutch food-preparation earthenware vessels along with other European ceramics. The Compton Site (18CV279) was a small tobacco plantation near the mouth of the Patuxent River at Solomons Island in Calvert County, Maryland. The assemblage included faience and majolica, German stoneware, North Devon earthenware, and Italian slipware (Louis Berger and Associates 1989:76). The presence of Dutch vessels in English territory can be explained in at least two ways: the European occupants came from New Netherland or directly from the Netherlands, or they traded with Dutch merchant sailors who came to Maryland for tobacco, obtaining earthenware vessels either for their own use or for later trade with others. Dutch merchants carried on an extensive trade with Maryland, especially in the 1640s when stresses caused by the English Civil War created shortages of imported goods in the British colonies. Maryland's trade with the Netherlands was greater than that of any other non-Dutch colony (Wilcoxen 1987:23–25). Dutch traders were an essential part of "the often invisible network of personal communications necessary to conduct trade in the Chesapeake (an area without central ports). . . . Dutch merchants living in the Chesapeake, such as [Augustine] Hermann, connected English colonists to New Netherland and Dutch markets to which they may not otherwise have had access" (Hatfield 2005:213). Archaeological investigations make these networks visible, at least in part.

The European occupation of 18CV279 began in 1651 when William and Magdalen Stevens acquired the land; they are thought to have come to Maryland from Virginia (Jefferson Patterson Park and Museum 2018), making it unlikely that they obtained their household goods directly in New Netherland or the Netherlands. They lived at the site until about 1665, after which tenants of unknown name and ethnicity occupied the land until about 1685. The features excavated at the site could not be separated definitively between the two occupations, so the Dutch earthenware cannot be firmly associated with a specific household, although dates derived from clay pipes suggest that the feature fill from which the majority of the Dutch earthenware cooking vessels was recovered (Feature 8, probably a borrow pit filled in with refuse) was among the earliest deposits at the site (Louis Berger and Associates 1989:87, 116), supporting the supposition that the vessels were associated with the extensive midcentury tobacco trade between the Netherlands and Chesapeake plantations.

The Dutch red earthenware vessel forms in the archaeological assemblage (Figures 12.6 and 12.7) are kookpotten, skillets, porringers, and bowls (Louis Berger and Associates 1989:59–69). Some of the vessels, those with red-orange sandy pastes and light brown or greenish-brown glazes, are probably Bergen op Zoom products. Two of the vessels identified as bowls have green glaze over white slip on their interiors. A pitcher with a handle that has a typical pinched strap-form oor attachment has a buff body with yellow glaze on the interior and green glaze on its exterior. The six vessels identified as skillets have mustard-yellow to light orange glazes and distinctive "celery-shaped" handles (Figure 12.3c). Some have flat bases, but others have slightly rounded bases and, possibly, three poten, although these sections of their bases are missing. The kookpotten sherds come from at least nine vessels. The most complete probably had one oor, based on the wear patterns on its poten, which are all worn down in the same direction opposite the side with the handle, most likely from repeatedly pulling the vessel over a stone or brick hearth. The handle present is worst-form, and there is light charring on the vessel's exterior. The lack of stir marks on its

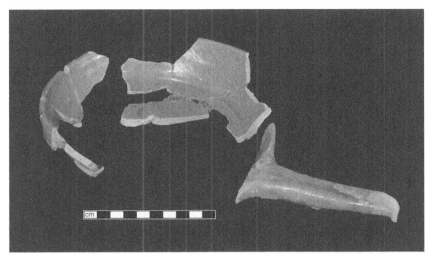

Figure 12.6. Skillet from the Compton site, Calvert County, Maryland. By permission of Jefferson Patterson Park & Museum, Maryland State Museum of Archaeology.

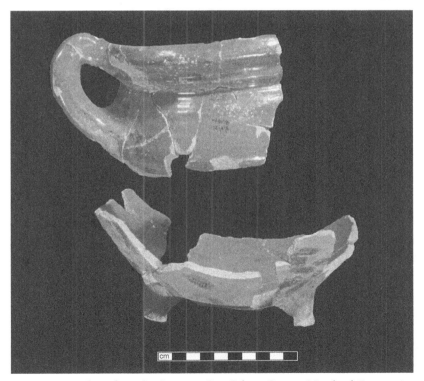

Figure 12.7. Kookpot from the Compton Site, Calvert County, Maryland. By permission of Jefferson Patterson Park & Museum, Maryland State Museum of Archaeology.

interior is probably because wooden rather than metal spoons were used while cooking.

The quantity of Dutch vessels in this assemblage is unusual for a site of this size and location. Some of the nine kookpotten, six skillets, and other vessels might have been destined for trade with other European colonists or Native Americans. Dutch food-preparation vessels have been found on Indian sites within the former New Netherland (Wilcoxen 1987:92), so it is possible that the inhabitants of the Compton Site kept ceramics for trade as well as for their own use.

SUMMARY AND SUGGESTIONS FOR FUTURE RESEARCH

Tripodal earthenware cooking pots, by any name, have been essential components of food preparation for hundreds of years. The presence of Dutch-style kookpotten in archaeological assemblages from within and outside New Netherland is evidence of Dutch foodways and of Dutch trade. Vessels from a late seventeenth-century context in New York City are indicative of Dutch-derived foodways 30 years after 1664. The Dutch vessels at the Maryland Compton Site are testimony to Dutch trade and trading connections between New Netherland and the Chesapeake.

At least two areas of future research concerning kookpotten could prove interesting. The New York City river-bottom deposit of Bergen-made vessels, which may date as early as the 1620s or as late as the 1660s, and the assemblage of Dutch-style earthenware from the midcentury Maryland site both include a greater variety of forms than were found in the late-century basement deposit from 7 Hanover Square. This could be simply a matter of sample size, but it might be due to differential replacement: kookpotten, vessels used to prepare many basic foods, might have continued in use, while other more specialized vessels, such as earthenware skillets and colanders, were replaced by metal or other types of earthenware vessels—either British or American made. A much larger sample of late seventeenth-century ceramic assemblages is needed to see whether the persistence of kookpotten and the loss of other forms seen at the 7 Hanover Square site is a pattern or an anomaly.

It would also be informative to catalogue the distribution of kookpotten on seventeenth- and early eighteenth-century sites along the East Coast, from Quebec through the Middle Atlantic, and to note what other Dutch-form earthenwares have been found with them. Were Dutch earthenwares widely available to Dutch and English settlers? If so, did they choose to obtain and use kookpotten because the pots were superior cooking vessels or because there was no other choice? These questions might be answered by comparing the forms of cooking pots and their origins at sites with well-dated primary deposits.

Another area for future research is determining the places of manufacture of red earthenware kookpotten. Were some or all the Dutch-style red-bodied vessels found in mid- and late seventeenth-century East Coast archaeological assemblages made locally in New York rather than the Netherlands? Dutch earthenware potters were working in New York City by midcentury at the latest. Dirck Claesen, from Leeuwaarden in Friesland, lived and worked in New Amsterdam/New York City from before 1655 to 1686; his stepsons, Jan Euwatse (also recorded as John Ewouts) and Ewout Euwatse, worked in Brooklyn before establishing themselves in Manhattan in 1695 and 1716, respectively (Ketchum 1987:35–38). Two analytical tools, portable X-ray fluorescence (pXRF) and inductively coupled plasma-emission spectroscopy (ICP) should be useful in determining sources of clay and, by inference, places of manufacture for red earthenware vessels. To the authors' knowledge, systemic pXRF studies have not yet been applied to American-excavated kookpotten. A sample of late seventeenth-century earthenware vessels has been studied using ICP analysis, however, including jugs from the circa 1670–1706 Kings Tavern, a block away from the 7 Hanover Square site (Fayden 1993). The ICP analysis of these jugs and the approximately 500 samples from other red earthenware vessels excavated in New York and New Jersey identified distinct groups based on the minerals in their clay bodies: a European-made group clustered around a kiln waster from Bergen op Zoom, and an American-made group centered on a group of redware dishes attributed to New Jersey potters. Three other groups were close to these two: one group was close to the New Jersey cluster and two others were close to the Bergen group; but one group, which included the tavern jugs, was separate from either. This latter group had characteristics similar to a group of seventeenth-century pantiles from the Broad Financial Center site in Lower Manhattan and the Fort Orange site in Albany (Gilbert and Janowitz 1990). The origin of the clays used in this pantile group has not yet been determined, although pantiles were made in New York City during the late eighteenth century from clays dug on Manhattan from the common near the Collect Pond (Ketchum 1987:43), and tiles possibly were made in Brooklyn, using local clays, as early as 1639 (Ketchum 1987:69). ICP research on red earthenware clays is ongoing and likely will be paired with pXRF analysis in efforts to identify clay sources.

To return to Gehring's chapter in this volume, the past is indeed elusive. But archaeologists are privileged to be able to touch fragments of the past that have the potential to make the everyday life of former times tangible. Kookpotten are humble everyday objects that people took for granted when they were in use but that archaeologists can now study to make the past come alive.

13

Marbles in Dutch Colonial New Netherland

Paul R. Huey

Marbles are an ancient artifact type, found in Egypt, Greece, and Rome. Fired clay pellets and larger, roughly formed clay balls also have been excavated at prehistoric sites in Europe and in North America (Luff 2000:518; Walthall 1990:85–86). Spherical "game balls" of fired clay and stone varying in size from less than 1.5 in diameter have been excavated at prehistoric Native American sites, but it is not known if they were used in a game (Murphy and Murphy 2011). Ovid and other classical writers described games played with round nuts or cherry pits, which evolved into the small round balls made of fired clay or stone, usually less than an inch in diameter. Nuts and cherry pits continued to be used for games and entertainment long after spherical marbles were developed for games apparently in the fourteenth century. In Shakespeare's *Twelfth Night* of 1602, for example, Sir Toby Belch proclaimed, "'tis not for gravity to play at cherry-pit with Satan."

Excavations frequently recover clay and stone marbles from sites in New York State dating from the Dutch colonial period. Marbles also are found in eighteenth-century sites in New York, suggesting a pattern that continued through the British colonial period and until 1800. Comparative study of marbles from these sites reveals possible differing uses for marbles and change through time. Some of those marbles have been measured in thousandths of an inch using a micrometer, with multiple measurements revealing that some marbles are precisely spherical while others are irregular. Additionally, it is not always easy or even possible to visually distinguish unglazed marbles made of fired clay earthenware from those that are more highly fired stoneware or from those made of actual stone. Highly fired stoneware marbles are sometimes salt-glazed with the telltale "orange peel" surface. Stone marbles were manufactured by grinding in a mill. The frequency of the recovery of marbles from dated contexts in Amsterdam and other locations in the Netherlands adds an important perspective to their recovery from sites associated with New Netherland and colonial New York.

ARCHAEOLOGICAL EVIDENCE

The archaeological data are organized geographically. First, North American Dutch finds are reviewed, then European data on marbles are presented.

New Netherland and New York

In the winter of 1970 and 1971, excavations by the author at the site of Fort Orange in Albany, New York, resulted in the recovery of 15 marbles from seven separate contexts dating between 1624 and 1664, the period of Dutch occupation (Huey 1988a:783–784). Only a portion of the site, within the fort along the east curtain wall, was excavated. Fort Orange was constructed in 1624 by the Dutch West India Company on the west side of the upper Hudson River in order to profit from the lucrative fur trade with native peoples. It was continuously occupied by the Dutch until the English took the fort in 1664. The English abandoned the fort in 1676. Archaeological contexts were dated by means of documented events in the history of the fort.

The diameters of the marbles ranged from as small as .454 in to as large as .707 in. The marble from the earliest dated context, of circa 1624 to 1640, was made of smooth, hard clay. Only two other clay marbles were found, both from contexts dating between circa 1657 and 1664. The remaining marbles are all of either very hard-fired clay stoneware or stone. Two very hard-fired clay marbles have a dark brown glaze, while another marble appears to be a brown stoneware; all three are from the circa 1657 to 1664 context. From a context dated circa 1651 to 1664 there are seven marbles, all very hard-fired clay or stone. The single marble from a context of circa 1648 to 1657 is made of a dark gray stone that is harder than steel. The distribution of the marbles suggests two areas of concentration. One cluster of six marbles in various contexts of between circa 1648 and 1664 was around the path leading east to the fort entrance, where there was also a considerable concentration of glass trade beads. The other cluster of five marbles was in the fort at the site of the Hendrick Andriessen van Doesburgh house near the southeast bastion, a context of circa 1651 to 1664.

Hartgen Archeological Associates, Inc., excavated a seventeenth-century colonial Dutch house site near Quackenbush Square in Albany, located two-thirds of a mile north of Fort Orange, in the winter of 2000 and 2001. It stood near the site of the Rensselaerswijck brickyard of 1651. While the house may have predated 1651, it was rebuilt in 1654 to serve as the home of the brickmaker. Four marbles were recovered from strata representing occupation from 1654 to 1686, and eight additional "finely made marbles of stone, stoneware, or redware" were excavated from the pre-1654 strata. Eleven of the 12 marbles were recovered from strata within the house (Moody 2005: 93, 130, 149).

South of Fort Orange and across the Hudson River, another early Rensselaerswijck site is located near the north end of Papscanee Island. Believed to be the location of the farmhouse of Cornelis Maessen van Buren, built in 1639, the site was occupied probably until the 1690s (Huey 1984:71). The seventeenth-century Dutch artifacts from the site unfortunately are from mixed contexts including much later artifacts. There are, however, numerous marbles from the site, and most of them are stone or hard-fired clay stoneware marbles. Of six smooth stone or hard-fired clay marbles, reddish brown to dark brown in color, one appears to have a dark brown glaze. The other five all have small pits, chips, cuts, scratches, or scars on one side. The total sample of nine marbles from the site includes three softer, white, fired clay marbles. The diameters of the marbles vary from the smallest, at .485 in, to the largest at .678 in.

Other seventeenth-century marbles have been recovered in Kingston, New York, originally the Dutch town of Wiltwijck established in 1658 near the Hudson River between Fort Orange and New Amsterdam. Excavations by Joe Diamond at the site of the house of surgeon Gijsbert van Imbroch revealed the remains of the adjacent town stockade predating a layer of charcoal and debris from the burning of Kingston by Native Americans on June 7, 1663. Two stoneware marbles were recovered from pre-1663 deposits, and one glazed clay marble was found in a later seventeenth-century context (Diamond 2004:48–49, 51).

In New York City, which was New Amsterdam until 1664, excavations on Broad Street by Joel Grossman recovered seventeenth-century Dutch artifacts from a number of discrete contexts. One feature uncovered there has been the subject of considerable interest. It appeared at first to be a basket but was found actually to be a wooden barrel reinforced with coils of rope. The bottom was perforated with 45 small holes, and the barrel was buried in the ground in the backyard of Cornelis van Tienhoven's residence. It originally served as a drain. Excavations in Amsterdam, the Netherlands, in 2004 and 2005 uncovered a similar barrel used for drainage. On Oude Turfmarkt a cellar with a clay tile floor had a wooden barrel buried in one corner. The upper edge of barrel was even with the floor level. The bottom of the barrel was pierced with eight holes, and water swept into the barrel from scrubbing the cellar floor would slowly drain through the holes into the ground. Such a feature was called a "scrubbing well," or *schrobputje*. The barrel was inscribed with the date 1624 and was used for this purpose until circa 1675 (Gawronski et al. 2010: 22).

Van Tienhoven disappeared in 1656, but his widow, and later his son, continued to live there until 1679. The contents of the barrel consisted of a surprising variety of objects: a large portion of a Dutch tin-glazed (Delftware) plate with blue Wan Li decoration, a Delft tile fragment, wine glass fragments, an iron key, shell wampum beads, glass beads, food refuse bones, small lead shot, nails, window lead, clay pipe stems, and 17 marbles, besides other small items (Figure 13.1). The dating of the artifacts is a matter of conjecture. The Delftware plate is considered by some to date between 1640 and 1660, but it can be argued stylistically that it may date from after 1670, especially also because of its association with post-1676 lead glass goblet fragments (Cantwell and Wall 2015:38, 40; Dallal 1996:218–221; Grossman 2011:80–81, 96).

Three of the 17 marbles from the Van Tienhoven feature are very large. They appear to be dark-brown-glazed hard-fired clay stoneware. The largest has a maximum diameter of 1.375 in. Maximum diameters of the others are 1.275 and 1.185 in. The other 14 marbles are either stone or hard-fired clay stoneware and vary in diameter from .454 to .627 in. The colors range between gray, tan, brown, reddish brown, and orange-tan. One brown marble has orange veins, and a gray marble has a yellow vein, suggesting they are very hard-fired clay. The orange-tan marble seems to be unevenly fired. One gray marble appears to be salt-glazed, and another definitely is. Ten of the marbles have a flaw on one side: a small dimple or chip, a pin hole, a pimple-shaped bump, a deep pit, scratches, or grooves.

The unusual contents of this barrel indicate that after it had served as a drain it was filled with small items by enslaved Africans to serve as a "divination basket," or *ngombo*. Divination baskets were used by diviners in Zambia, Angola, and the Congo. Called *chuma* in many Bantu languages, a revelatory treasure was assembled in a basket including small items such as cowrie shells, feathers, metal bracelets, wood carvings, beads, claws, bits of glass, teeth, seeds, and other miscellaneous items. When the contents of

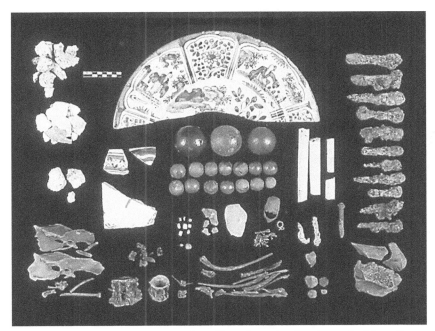

Figure 13.1. Contents of the rope-reinforced barrel excavated in the yard of Cornelis van Tienhoven's residence in Broad Street, New York City, dating from ca. 1650 to 1680. Courtesy of the New York State Museum, Albany.

such a basket are shaken by a diviner, how they fall is considered to have significance (Werbner 2015:290).

Rescue excavations elsewhere in New York City have produced numerous marbles. Six stoneware marbles were found in pre-landfill river-bottom clay deposits, dating from circa 1687 to 1700, at 64 Pearl Street. Their diameters range from .551 in to .630 in. A nearly spherical, smooth stone ball was also found with a diameter of .945 in (Pickman and Rothschild 1981:14, 46, 70). At the Stadt Huys site, a well filled between circa 1690 and 1720 and associated with the household of Louis Carré, a Huguenot immigrant, contained a marble. At 7 Hanover Square the circa 1710 to 1720 basement midden of the home and workshop of Simeon Soumaine, also a Huguenot, contained seven marbles. Of these eight marbles, six are of stone, and two are of clay (Maghrak 2013:47–49, 50–51, 58–59, 76).

Marbles also are found in eighteenth-century contexts at sites associated with Dutch families, and at other sites, in the Hudson and lower Mohawk Valleys, the original heart of New Netherland north of New York City. Three clay marbles were recovered from pre-1760 contexts at Crailo State Historic

Site, originally a Van Rensselaer family home, in the city of Rensselaer, across the Hudson River from Albany (Feister and Huey 2012:260–261, 282; Feister and Sopko 2003:19). Along the Albany waterfront, a stone marble was excavated from riverfront landfill of the late 1760s, and a marble was also found in the builder's wall trench of the house of Stewart Dean, built in the 1760s (Hartgen 2002:7, 27, 32). Dean was a sloop captain who moved from Maryland to Albany and married an Albany Dutch wife.

The Schuyler Flatts site, located about four miles north of Albany, was the valuable Schuyler family farm owned by the wealthy and socially prominent "Aunt" Margarita Schuyler until her death in 1782. She was a widow after 1758, loved children, and raised many children not her own (Wilson 1903:I.201–202). The Schuyler house at the Flatts was built about 1672; it burned in 1759 but was rebuilt. Excavations by the author in the backyard area revealed strata probably associated with the destructive fire of 1759 and representative of occupation until about 1780 or 1785. Preliminary study of a sample of 25 marbles from these contexts reveals that most of them are of stone or stoneware. Only four appear to be clay, fired less hard than stoneware. The smallest marble diameter measured is .399 in, while the largest is .745 in. Among these marbles are three smooth, nearly spherical stone pebbles which probably served as marbles. One stoneware marble has what appears to be the trace of a sprue, suggesting that some marbles were perhaps cast of clay in bullet molds. The circumference of this marble varies from .496 to .512 in. Three of the 18 stone or stoneware marbles are chipped or pitted, one is broken, and one has a dimple on one side. Otherwise most of the surfaces are smooth and polished, while one clay marble is soft and eroded. Two stone marbles have flat surfaces or facets on opposite sides, indicating these marbles were originally small cubes of stone that were incompletely rounded by means of grinding in a mill. Marbles with similar facets were excavated at Place Royale in Quebec (Tremblay and Renaud 1999:72).

Marble diameter measurements reveal which marbles are precisely, or almost precisely, spherical, and which marbles are irregular. Such differences may indicate their value and their suitability for games or other uses. The diameters of marbles recovered from Fort Orange, the Van Buren site, the Van Tienhoven barrel, and the Schuyler Flatts site were measured in thousandths of an inch using a micrometer at various points around each marble. Table 13.1 displays the results from the 15 marbles excavated in pre-1664 contexts at Fort Orange, ranked by amount of variation in each. The

Table 13.1. Diameters of Fort Orange marbles, ca. 1624–1664 (New York State Museum)

CONTEXT	MINIMUM DIAMETER	MAXIMUM DIAMETER	VARIATION	DESCRIPTION
1657–1664	.500	.500	.000	Hard-fired clay, with dark brown glaze
1651–1664	.542	.542	.000	Hard-fired clay or stone
" "	.542	.542	.000	"
" "	.565	.565	.000	"
" "	.569	.569	.000	"
" "	.575	.575	.000	"
" "	.585	.585	.000	"
1657–1664	.585	.585	.000	"
1651–1664	.586	.586	.000	"
1657–1664	.596	.601	.005	"
" "	.507	.515	.008	Clay
1624–1640	.562	.574	.012	Clay
1657–1664	.494	.510	.016	Soft buff clay
1648–1657	.561	.578	.017	Stone
1657–1664	.630	.707	.117	Brown stoneware

two stratigraphically earliest marbles are slightly less spherical than most of those from later contexts. The clay marbles tend be less precisely round than the stone or stoneware marbles, but most of the marbles from Fort Orange from before 1664 are remarkably exactly round.

The sample of marbles from the Van Buren site, occupied as a Dutch farm beginning about 1639, is from multiple contexts, and the marbles are remarkably spherical but less so than those from Fort Orange. Curiously, unlike the marbles from Fort Orange, the softer unglazed white clay marbles are more exactly round than most of the stone or stoneware marbles (Table 13.2).

The marbles, all hard-fired clay stoneware or stone, from the Van Tienhoven barrel varied from being precisely spherical with 16 of the 17 marbles falling neatly within the range of variation of all but one of the Van Buren site marbles (Table 13.3).

The sample of marbles from before circa 1785 at the Schuyler Flatts site is probably a mixture from the seventeenth and eighteenth centuries. The earlier marbles, if any, would likely include those deposited during or after

Table 13.2. Diameters of Van Buren site marbles, ca. 1639–1690 (New York State Office of Parks, Recreation and Historic Preservation)

CATALOGUE NUMBER	MINIMUM DIAMETER	MAXIMUM DIAMETER	VARIATION	DESCRIPTION
A.PX.1986.39	.568	.572	.004	Hard-fired clay, glazed dark brown
A.PX.1986.37	.627	.631	.004	Soft white clay, unglazed
A.PX.1986.39	.608	.613	.005	"
A.PX.1987.41	.638	.644	.006	"
A.PX.1992.59	.582	.592	.010	Hard-fired clay or stone, possibly glazed
A.PX.1987.41	.621	.634	.013	Stone, light brown, possibly glazed
A.PX.1986.39	.485	.501	.016	Hard-fired clay or stone, glazed dark brown
A.PX.1993.64	.537	.565	.028	Hard-fired reddish brown to gray clay or stone, unglazed
A.PX.1986.37	.575	.678	.103	Hard-fired medium brown clay or stone, unglazed

the fire of 1759. As at Fort Orange, the stone or hard-fired clay stoneware marbles at the Flatts tend to be more precisely spherical than the clay marbles. They consistently vary in circumference by .006 in or less, with few exceptions (Table 13.4). At the Van Buren site and in the Van Tienhoven barrel, however, the variation in circumference of most of the marbles is considerably greater than .006 in. One must conclude that the marbles at Fort Orange and the Schuyler Flatts were of a better quality and more expensive.

The Netherlands and Germany

Marbles are recovered frequently in excavations at post-medieval sites in the Netherlands. "They are found very often" (Bartels 2017). Excavations in Amsterdam have produced hundreds of marbles about which reports had yet to be published as of the late 1990s (Gartley and Carskadden 1998:20). In Brussels, Belgium, an excavation at the site of the Arme Klarenklooster uncovered 17 marbles dating from the 1450 to 1550 period, while excavations

Table 13.3. Diameters of Van Tienhoven barrel marbles, ca. 1650–1680 (New York State Museum)

CATALOGUE NUMBER	MINIMUM DIAMETER	MAXIMUM DIAMETER	VARIATION	DESCRIPTION
2.5	.614	.618	.004	Stone
2.13	.563	.569	.006	Hard-fired orange-brown clay
2.1	.566	.573	.007	Hard-fired gray clay, salt-glazed
2.10	.454	.463	.009	Unevenly hard-fired brown-tan clay
2.17	.614	.624	.010	Hard-fired brown clay
2.15	.610	.622	.012	Hard-fired gray-tan clay or stone
2.24	.569	.581	.012	Brown stone
2.9	.613	.627	.014	Hard-fired gray-tan clay or stone
2.3	.613	.627	.014	Hard-fired clay or stone, gray with yellow vein
2.12	.587	.603	.016	Reddish brown stone
2.8	1.167	1.185	.018	Hard-fired clay or stone, glazed dark brown
2.6	.567	.586	.019	Hard-fired gray clay, salt-glazed
2.17	.568	.589	.021	Hard-fired gray-tan clay or stone
2.11	.589	.610	.021	Hard-fired brown clay or stone
2.2	1.350	1.375	.025	Dark brown clay, glazed
2.7	1.250	1.275	.025	Hard-fired dark brown-tan clay
2.14	.500	.576	.076	Hard-fired gray-tan clay or stone

elsewhere in Brussels have recovered marbles from the seventeenth century (Van Bellingen 2013:80).

Excavation of the Latin school privy in Groningen, dating from about 1500 to 1550, revealed numerous marbles and other toys such as tops, knucklebones, a ball, and wooden blowguns (Willemsen 2003:13–14; Willemsen 2008:8). To the southeast of Groningen, in the small village of Oudeschans (Old Fort) in Bellingwedde, two marbles were recovered from within the fort from a deposit dating from 1593 to 1625, or perhaps as late

Table 13.4. Diameters of Schuyler Flatts site marbles, ca. 1672–1785 (New York State Museum)

CATALOGUE NUMBER	MINIMUM DIAMETER	MAXIMUM DIAMETER	VARIATION	DESCRIPTION
A.SF.1971.699	.629	.630	.001	Stone, smooth
A.SF.1971.66	.650	.651	.001	Stone, chipped
A.SF.1971.72	.548	.549	.001	Stone, broken
A.SF.1971.124	.627	.628	.001	Stone, pitted
A.SF.1971.229	.579	.580	.001	Stone, with dimple
A.SF.1971.425	.681	.683	.002	Stone
A.SF.1971.289	.628	.630	.002	Stone, with 2 flat sides
A.SF.1971.769	.543	.546	.003	Stone, smooth
A.SF.1971.448	.519	.522	.003	Stone, smooth
A.SF.1971.308	.593	.597	.004	Stone, with flat facets
A.SF.1971.411	.625	.629	.004	Stone, polished smooth
A.SF.1971.55	.607	.611	.004	Stone
A.SF.1971.761	.622	.628	.006	Stone, smooth
A.SF.1971.172	.739	.745	.006	Stone, pitted
A.SF.1971.172	.512	.519	.007	Clay, pitted
A.SF.1971.735	.399	.410	.011	Stone, smooth
A.SF.1971.198	.496	.512	.016	Stoneware, with sprue
A.SF.1971.274	.510	.528	.018	Clay, smooth
A.SF.1971.769	.429	.462	.033	Natural stone pebble
A.SF.1971.761	.493	.533	.040	Clay, smooth, reddish brown
A.SF.1971.376	.499	.564	.065	Natural stone pebble
A.SF.1971.429	.429	.500	.071	Stone
A.SF.1971.469	.486	.563	.077	Soft clay, eroded
A.SF.1971.272	.515	.613	.098	Natural stone pebble
A.SF.1971.189	.552	.654	.102	Stone

as 1640, when the ditches were filled (de Wit 2009:26, 30, 34). To the east of Groningen, in Leeuwarden, Friesland, excavation of a well dating from the first half of the seventeenth century produced six marbles of about 1.5 cm (.591 in) diameter (Elzinga and Korf 1978:11–12). Clay marbles of exactly that size were excavated at Smeerenburg, the site of a Dutch whaling station on Spitsbergen occupied from 1619 to 1660 (Hacquebord and Vroom 1988:190). In the Zuiderzee, the vast, shallow bay extending into the Netherlands from the North Sea, artifacts from the sunken wreck of a flat-bottomed freight barge dating from the first quarter of the seventeenth century include white and brown ceramic marbles, now in the archaeological collections of the Rijksdienst voor Cultureel Erfgoed in Lelystad.

Many seventeenth-century artifacts, including marbles, have been found in the dredge spoils from canals outside Amsterdam, and archaeologists working in Amsterdam have noted that two common sizes of marbles are .551 to .591 in and 1.024 to 1.181 in (Jayasena 2017; Van der Sleen 1973:110). The excavation of a privy in the inner courtyard of the Rembrandt House in Amsterdam produced at least two marbles from the period when Rembrandt lived there. Rescue archaeology at Elandsstraat 101 in Amsterdam resulted in recovery of two marbles in association with a toy ceramic vessel from a privy dating circa 1650 to 1700. A privy at Herengracht 12 in the Amsterdam Grachtengordel district produced nine marbles also associated with toy ceramic vessels, and this privy dated from circa 1675 to 1750 (Gawronski et al. 2012:34; Gawronski and Jayasena 2013:16–17, 50).

On the Amsterdam waterfront, at Oostenburgermiddenstraat 26, not far from the East India Company shipyards, fired clay stoneware and stone marbles were unearthed along with knucklebones and other objects from a privy dating circa 1738 to 1805 (Baart et al. 1986:92, 137–138, 150). Marbles also found their way onto East India Company ships. Artifacts from the wreck of the *Amsterdam*, sunk in 1749 on the coast of England, include both stone and brown salt-glazed stoneware marbles. Marbles were found on a lower deck where the crew lived (Gartley and Carskadden 1998: 41; Marsden 1975: 46–47, 180). A privy at Oudezijds Armsteed 20 in Amsterdam held seven stoneware marbles, together with an unusual number of toys. It dated from circa 1750 to 1800. The same privy contained a "Rhode Island Ship Token," which depicted an American defeat at the hands of the British in Rhode Island in 1778. The token was produced in England in 1779 and circulated in the Netherlands as anti-American propaganda (Gawronski and Jayasena 2011: 42, 71; Jayasena 2011: 126–127). Still another privy, this one dating circa 1750 to 1825 at Derde Weteringdwarsstraat 1 in Amsterdam, held seven stoneware marbles (Gawronski and Jayasena 2008: 7–9).

It is likely the stoneware marbles recovered from Amsterdam privies and at other sites were produced in the Westerwald and elsewhere within Germany (Gartley and Carskadden 1998:x). At Mansfeld in Saxony-Anhalt, Germany, excavations conducted at the boyhood home of Martin Luther, where he lived from 1484 until 1496, revealed not only fired clay and stoneware marbles but also knucklebones, a part from a very small crossbow, and garbage bones. Seven marbles were recovered, but not all of them were exactly round, and it has been suggested that some of the marbles may have been made by the children in the household and were fired in the kitchen. The sizes of the marbles vary from .433 to .591 in. The bones include those of fish, pigs, cows, and geese, but it may be significant that there were also bones of partridges and songbirds, especially robins (Schlenker 2007:72; Schlenker 2016).

Northwest of Mansfeld at a sixteenth-century pottery site at Lüneburg, in northern Germany, numerous clay miniatures and toys as well as 90 marbles have been recovered. The marbles vary in size, with diameters ranging from .394 to .945 in but mostly from .591 to .709 in. The gray marbles all have a diameter of .472 in. Some were perfectly round with a post-firing grinding and polishing, while others had rough surfaces or were not perfectly round (Ring 2012:274, 276). Marbles also have been excavated from early seventeenth-century trash pits in central Germany (Gartley and Carskadden 1998:31).

DOCUMENTARY EVIDENCE

Documentary evidence provides context to support the interpretation of marble finds. The evidence suggests that they functioned not exclusively as toys.

Marbles as a Game

Suetonius, a Roman historian writing in 121 AD, recorded that in the first century BC Casear Augustus for his amusement would sometimes "angle, or play with dice, pebbles, or nuts" (Thomson 1896:132). Charles IV, king of France, in 1319 forbade "games of dice, tables or trictrac, quills, palms, balls, marbles [billes], and generally all other games, which do not exert men to war and to handle arms" (Ganeau and Plaignard 1707:1074). This ordinance was renewed by King Charles V in 1369 and evidently referred to actual marbles rather than pebbles, nuts, or billiard balls.

The painting by Dutch artist Hieronymous Bosch about 1475 or 1480 of *The Conjurer* depicts marbles in association with trickery and thievery. A game of cups and marbles is played, while the victim is being robbed and tricked by the evil conjurer. Marbles are established as a children's game, however, about 1500 in a breviary from Ghent and Brugge, Belgium. The breviary has a calendar of months matching children's games to times of the year. There is sledding and throwing snowballs in January, marbles in September, and playing with knucklebones in November at the time of slaughter (Willemsen 2003:17). Later, the famous Netherlandish painting

Children's Games of 1560 by Pieter Breughel the Elder shows at least three different games of marbles with both boys and girls. In the upper right portion of this painting, boys are shown playing with marbles, while nearby boys and girls aim marbles at knucklebones set up along a wall.

The Dutch social satire of 1617, *Spaanschen Brabander* by G. A. Bredero, while describing boys competing for marbles, also presented a negative view. "'Tis sure 'tis foolish to give alms to those who, come Sunday morning, will gamble it away before the gates, dicing with cutthroats and snatch-purses, playing among themselves at cards and skittles, lobbing marbles, flipping coins, guessing heads or tails" (Brumble 1982:55, 61, 86, 128–130). Numerous Dutch paintings and drawings of the late sixteenth and the seventeenth centuries nevertheless depict children playing marbles. At the same time, ball games such as skittles (bowling), golf, and billiards also grew in popularity. As early as 1618, Dutch paintings of church interiors frequently included children quietly playing marbles near a massive column, as if to symbolize the triviality of human behavior (Nash 1972:78). Between 1650 and 1660 Dutch paintings of church interiors depicting children playing marbles were especially popular. There is one example as late as 1765 (Broos 1989:47; Liedtke 2001:107, 110, 411, 413; Pluis 1979:18). Jacob Cats, the Dutch writer famous for his moralistic emblem books, in 1655 wrote about a boy who was determined to retrieve a marble lost under a propped-up tombstone in a church (Cats 1655:49; Pluis 1979:17). The flat stone-paved floor of a church served as an ideal place on which to roll marbles (Figure 13.2; Barnes and Rose 2012:94).

Gaming regulations focused on preventing public officials, soldiers, the clergy, and individuals who provided necessary services from spending their time on such activities. There were restrictions on playing with dice and playing other games in Leiden as early as 1406, and in 1472 the city issued an order prohibiting the judges and other members of the bench from playing any of the forbidden games. Any justices found or reported to be gambling were to be fined double (Hamaker 1873:117–118, 262–263). Soldiers in Flanders were not allowed to play games by an edict in 1596. In 1663 it was forbidden to play or engage in any games or songs "that might cause scandal or other bad examples" unless approved in writing by local officials (Wulf 1766:565). Beer carriers in Amsterdam in 1650 were not allowed to dice or play games, and in 1667 there were regulations against gaming, playing dice, drinking, or swearing by the regents of a colonial leprosy hospital (Commelin 1726:637; Van der Chijs 1886:431–432). A statute in Flanders in 1699 outlawed playing with cards or dice "under penalty of Dishonor for

Figure 13.2. Drawing by Johannes Monnickxs used as a plate in *Invallende gedachten* (Random thoughts) by Jacob Cats published in 1655 (Christie's 1996:lot 115).

the Offenders and removal from their Offices," with impoundment of four times their profit or loss (Wulf 1766:565).

Dozens of Dutch paintings and engravings from the sixteenth through the seventeenth centuries illustrate the popularity of gaming, specifically backgammon and trictrac, in the Netherlands. The Dutch artist Jacques de Gheyn II in his engraving *Vanity* of 1595 depicted a young woman seated by a table on which there is a backgammon game, playing cards, and some marbles. Paintings by Dirck Hals, Theodor Rombouts, Jan Steen, Jacob Ochtervelt, and many others depict well-dressed men and women playing games or observing. A painting in the York Art Gallery by Dirck van Baburen from the 1620s of backgammon players is inscribed "A dicer and gamer is a wretch, he drinks and squanders his money and beats his wife." Other artists, such as Adriaen Brouwer, David Teniers II, Adriaen van Ostade, and Cornelis Dusart, portrayed tavern scenes with lowly peasants playing backgammon and trictrac from the 1630s through the remainder of the century. As in literature, the paintings convey double meanings of harmless diversions or of admonitions against idleness and wasted time (Sutton 1992:144).

Permitted games could not be played in Flanders "during the Divine Service on Sundays and Holy Days" under a regulation in 1601, and in 1622 this prohibition was extended in Ghent, Belgium, "for the eleven hours before noon, and from one to three hours after the Vespers." Offenders were heavily fined (Wulf 1766:565). In 1656 the director general and council of New Netherland passed an ordinance making illegal any "Dancing, playing Ball, Cards, Tricktrack, Tennis, Cricket or Ninepins" on Sundays. Two months later the City of Amsterdam issued an order prohibiting "any dice, cards, or any other implements of gaming" on any ship carrying servants or colonists to New Netherland, unless permitted by the skipper (Gehring 1991:71; O'Callaghan 1868:259, 282). In the Netherlands, the city of Leiden in 1658 passed an ordinance prohibiting swimming and ball games including golf, knucklebones, and apparently marbles anywhere within the city (Pluis 1979:17). The City of Amsterdam in 1659 enacted a statute regulating activity at the stock exchange there. No beggars nor children playing with marbles or other playthings were allowed in the exchange "in order to prevent hindering or annoying the traders in their business during the Exchange hours, neither before nor after Exchange hours, on pain of twelve stuyvers" (Commelin 1726:620).

In New Netherland in 1662, "graceless and idle loafers" who spent every day, even Sunday, in "an ungodly manner, Drinking, Card playing, and other such like disorders," just waiting for the arrival of Native Americans to trade for furs, were considered a reason for the "ruined Trade." A year later an ordinance was passed, again making gaming illegal on Sundays. In 1673 at Willemstadt (formerly Beverwijck, presently Albany) and in Rensselaerswijck, the Dutch court ordered measures to be taken to remove "all mobs, gamblers, whore-houses and such like impurities" (O'Callaghan 1868:426–427, 448, 487). Under the English, the city of New York in 1676 again issued a regulation that prohibited "Playing att Cards Dice Tables or any other Vnlawful Games whatsoever" on Sundays (Anonymous 1905a:27). This was seconded by a proclamation passed by the commissaries of Albany, Rensselaerswijck, and Schenectady in 1679 that specifically mentioned marbles, or *knikkers*. Activities that were prohibited on Sundays were listed, and they included "Playing at cardes, Trap ball & nickers." The commissaries found it necessary to renew this regulation in 1682 against "Trapball, drinkeing in Tavernes, Cards or nickers, or any other Exercises, which is Tolerated on oyr days" (Van Laer 1928:402; Van Laer 1932b:205).

The New York provincial legislature in 1695 passed a law against "Profanation of the Lord's Day, called Sunday," outlawing on that day "shooting, fishing, sporting, playing, Horse-racing," or "any other unlawful Exercises or Pastimes" (Anonymous 1894:356–357; Stokes 1922:391).

In 1722 and in 1731 laws in New York City prohibited all enslaved Africans and Native Americans, "or any Other Negroe or Indian" within the city, from any "Gaming or Playing" using any sort of coinage or paper money (Anonymous 1905b:227–228; Anonymous 1905c:87–88). Perhaps this encouraged slaves to gamble with marbles. In the trials for the New York Conspiracy of 1741, a slave named Adam testified on behalf of Quack, a slave owned by John Walters. Quack was found guilty and hanged, but Adam said he had known Quack "from their childhood," when they "used to play marbles together." Quack and other slaves implicated in the revolt had also spent time "gaming together" (Davis 1971:232, 258, 301).

Dutch art through the eighteenth century shows children playing games of marbles (Barnes and Rose 2012:93; Pluis 1979:18). A large sandstone sculpture of *Spring*, represented as a young woman and carved in the early 1760s for the palace gardens at Bruchsal, Germany, has a small child playing with marbles at her feet (Kuhn 1965:137, pl. 780). In the Netherlands, while children played with marbles, marbles could also be used in gambling and games of chance by adults. The play *De Ingebeelde Edelman, Blyspel* by Abraham de Wit the younger, published in 1700, in one scene has the sister of the pretentious nobleman go into a garden to play marbles with her suitor, after which the brother mockingly asks her how much she had won with the marbles (de Wit 1700:49–51). The Fourth Earl of Chesterfield later recalled that when he arrived from England at The Hague in 1714, he found that "gaming was much in fashion" there (Stanhope 1853:222). The city of Rotterdam in 1718 prohibited tavernkeepers from allowing high-stakes gambling or gaming in their houses. Offenders were heavily punished (Anonymous 1718:1–2). A book on games as "innocent diversions" written in French but published in Amsterdam in 1728 explained how to play with dice and "permitted card games." The author noted that "not all kinds of entertainment are prohibited. It is a necessity attached to human weakness to sometimes relax from the works to which sin has subjected man; and as inaction is a fatigue for him, Games were invented to occupy him pleasantly without tiring him. I thought it would not hurt to make a collection of the Rules of those which are very innocent" (Anonymous 1728:iii). The games included chess and billiards, but not marbles.

A Dutch print published in Amsterdam in 1742 clearly depicts marbles associated with playing cards and dice. The print is a political spoof, with marbles, cards, and dice scattered on the ground between the figures of Austria and France, perhaps symbolizing the corruption of the two powers (Van Rijn 1901:40). In Denmark, a royal decree in 1753 banned gambling because of the king's "imminent love and fatherly care for our beloved subjects, and to avoid among those fragile, the opportunity to squander what they have acquired." The ordnance absolutely outlawed "Games at Cards and Dice, and in general all that are called Games of Chance; and they will not be permitted at Court but on Drawing-Room-Days." Severe penalties threatened "all who play at these Games, or who suffer them to be played in their Houses" (Anonymous 1753; Linnet 2009:17).

Marbles as a Trade Commodity

The earliest commercial sources or manufacturers of clay or stone marbles are not well documented. Marbles were manufactured at Grossalmerode, in north-central Germany, as early as 1621 (Gartley and Carskadden 1998:31). Thousands of marbles were shipped to the Netherlands, from which the Dutch exported them to other countries. In 1694 alone Britain imported 62,200 and 10 casks of "marbles for boys to play with" from the Netherlands and another 23 tons and 10 barrels of them from Germany. Britain also imported "knickers and bowling-stones" from Germany and the Netherlands. It was proposed in England that "surely a little encouragement would cause them to be made here," and in 1728 a duty of three shillings per thousand was imposed on imported "Marbles for Children" (Cotter 2002:47; Fleming 1741:195, 474; Houghton 1727:29). While retail processes are not well documented, in 1617, a character in the Dutch play *Spaanschen Brabander* by G. A. Bredero advertises, "Who wants to buy marbles? . . . Six for a half cent [*duytje*]!" (Brumble 1982: 61).

Newspaper advertisements record the extensive importation of marbles to the American colonies beginning in 1760, with an advertisement in the *Maryland Gazette* for goods including marbles imported from London (Gartley and Carskadden 1998:19). Marbles "imported in the last Vessels from England" (Curtenius 1765) were likely of German origin. In England, because of the variety among marbles and the beauty of some of the stone marbles, the manufacturing processes used to produce the "common marbles which boys play with" was something of a mystery. It was noted in 1771 that "the invention of them is ingenious; but if we observe their structure, and other circumstances belonging to them, they afford matter for very deep speculation." It was a mystery "how the round form of these bodies was acquired, and whence they derive that exact proportion." Some thought they were "formed in moulds, of paste, and baked, or burned, as the potters do their vessels." Others believed they were turned on a lathe from pieces of alabaster or soft marble (Anonymous 1771:347; Platt 1771). It was finally explained in *The Gentleman's Magazine* in 1773 that "they are brought from Nuremburg (with the best toys, commonly known in England by the name of Dutch toys) to Rotterdam down the Rhine; and from thence dispersed over Europe." The stone marbles were simply pieces of stone that were cut under water in a mill with rotating iron rasps. In 1785 marbles, including even large taw marbles, in Germany were "manufactured in the Saalfeldsche, Koburgsche, Meinungsche, Oettingsche in Baden, Tijrol and Saltsburg, and are transported as entire cargoes to the Netherlands and Holland, from where they are taken as ballast to the Indies, and sold there expensively" (Anonymous 1785:42; Platt 1773).

Marbles as Projectiles

Marbles could serve as projectiles when fired from a stonebow, a special type of crossbow designed to fire small round projectiles, such as small clay balls, or marbles. The stonebow was also called a "clod bow" or "ball cross-bow," a *kluitboog* or *arbalête jalet*, and a French-Flemish dictionary of 1686 defined a *jalet* as a "small earthen ball; a marble [*knikker*] which one puts in a clod bow" (Rouxel and Halma 1686:289). These definitions contin-ued into the eighteenth century. The stonebow was primarily a weapon for hunting small animals, especially birds. Perhaps the Martin Luther family in Mansfeld, Germany, used marbles and a stonebow to hunt the songbirds they ate for food.

It is also possible that clay or stone marbles were used with firearms. In Noord Brabant and elsewhere in the Netherlands brass thimbles, each with a clay marble stuck inside, have been recovered. One theory is that they were intended to be used as bore cleaners, to clean the fouled bores of muzzle-loaded muskets. When a musket was fired, the clay marble would expand the thimble, which would then scrape clean the inside of the fire-arm's barrel. An example (not fired) discovered in the village of Waspik, Noord Brabant, has an overall diameter of 5/8 in for the thimble, or about .63 in (Wagemakers 2017).

CONCLUSIONS

Marbles were more than simple toys or playthings. While commonly used by children, they cannot be assumed to be archaeological evidence of the presence of children. Documents provide evidence the use of marbles also included adult gambling and other uses. In the Netherlands, New Netherland, and colonial New York, marbles are frequently recovered in archaeological excavations, unlike in England and the English American colonies, where marble games may have been considered an unworthy waste of time. For children, critics considered marble playing a bad influence that led to gambling habits.

There are many unanswered questions, and further research on marbles in existing archaeological collections and artifact assemblages is necessary in order to test further these hypotheses. The history of gaming and gambling and the laws and regulations that attempted to control such activities is a complicated subject, but it is a subject of significance in an age where there are multiple opportunities for legal adult gambling. At the same time, the almost universal popularity of marbles as children's toys through the nineteenth and into the twentieth centuries has largely disappeared in favor of modern electronic and digital games.

14

Thank You for Smoking

The Archaeological Legacy of Edward Bird's Tobacco Pipes in New Netherland and Beyond

DAVID A. FURLOW

A mannequin depicting a blue-eyed Swedish aristocrat, wearing knee-high leather cavalry boots, a gold-braided sash of office, and linen shirt can be seen in Sweden's Army Museum in Stockholm. He holds a white clay tobacco pipe in his right hand as he awaits dinner (Figure 14.1). He sits by a window next to a wooden globe that symbolizes the expansion of Sweden's empire across the Atlantic to America. Heavyset, this officer closely resembles Johann Printz, governor of the New Sweden colony that encroached on New Netherland's South River territory along the Delaware from 1638 to 1655.

Gabriel Soares de Sousa (1587:26) described how Europeans like the Swedish aristocrat had recently taken to "drinking" tobacco smoke. "They light this tube at the end filled with petume [tobacco] leaves, and a large amount enters through their nasal passages and throats and is expelled with great force through the nostrils."

Whether at home or abroad, it was commonly understood that "a Hollander without a pipe is a national impossibility, akin to a town without a house, a stage without actors, a spring without flowers" (Schama 1987:198). Tobacco pipes often occupied the center of seventeenth-century Dutch paintings, for example, Pieter Claesz's 1636 *Still Life with Clay Pipes* (State Hermitage Museum, Saint Petersburg) or Jan Jansz van de Velde III's 1650 *Still Life with Stoneware Jug and Pipes* (National Gallery of Art, Washington, DC). Pipes became such an important part of colonial life that Samuel Champlain's colonists in Quebec measured short units of time as *pipes*,

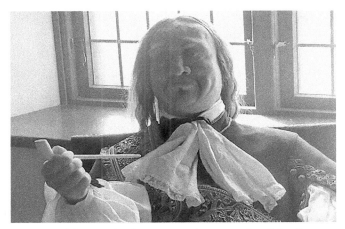

Figure 14.1. Mannequin of a seventeenth-century Swedish officer holding a clay tobacco pipe. Swedish Army Museum in Stockholm. Photo by David A. Furlow.

denoting the time it took to smoke a pipe full of tobacco (Fischer 2008: 634).

The clay pipes that seventeenth-century soldiers, sailors, and settlers used to "drink" tobacco did not long remain unbroken (Walker 1977). Sometimes a pipe broke in the cut and thrust of close combat, but more often it snapped in a back pocket or crumpled in a backpack. Because they were mass-produced and cheap, there was little reason to repair them, so they were often tossed away. Once in the ground or sea, though, their fragments survived, for they had been baked hard as stone. Since they changed with the fads, fashions, and finances of tobacco, each pipe fragment can mark a short passage of time, indicating within a few decades or even a few years the time it was made. Tobacco pipes thus reflect the ebb and flow of commerce, colonialism, and conflict in a measurable series of transitions (Bradley 2000:185; Harrington 2006a:29–35, 2006b:36–40).

This chapter focuses on the pipes produced by Edward Bird, an English exile in Amsterdam, whose tobacco pipes sold in New Sweden, New Netherland, and around the world, reflecting a global trade network.

EDWARD BIRD'S WHITE CLAY "EB" PIPES

Between 1630 and 1660 an English Puritan exile in Amsterdam, Edward Bird, created an Atlantic-wide export business by selling a variety of distinctly different clay tobacco pipes, including some specially made for sale among New Netherland's Native trade partners (Duco 2002 [1981]; De Roever 1987:51–61). Many pipes came to the short-lived New Sweden colony (1638–1655) along the South (Delaware) River, before it was absorbed by New Netherland.

Edward Bird's EB pipes arrived in New Sweden because of a globalizing mid-seventeenth-century tobacco economy (Hochstrasser 2007:171–86). Dutch and Swedish warships dominated the South River, but Anglo-American merchants sailing from New Netherland and New England coasted it frequently and purchased tobacco at fortified trading posts and plantations from Dutch, Swedish, Finnish, German, and English settlers who raised and sold that cash crop (Gehring 1981).

Archaeological sites within the borders of New Netherland, in modern Delaware, Pennsylvania, New Jersey, New York, and Connecticut, preserve a fossilized record of that trans-Atlantic tobacco and tobacco pipe trade network. Many bear Edward Bird's "EB" trademark placed on the heels of the tobacco pipes he manufactured in his Amsterdam home factory.

After clay tobacco pipes left Edward Bird's clay pipe-making factory in Amsterdam, they traveled far and wide in a broad trans-Atlantic arc from Scandinavia to South Africa to Brazil, including Pernambuco, Brazil (DeMello 1983; Hall 1996:131; Huey 1988a); Curacao (Hall 1996); Jamaica (Heidtke 1992; Fox 1999); the Dominican Republic (Hall 1996: 126–134; Huey 2010); French Acadia and English Maine (Faulkner 1980, 1989; Faulkner and Faulkner 1987:173–174, 181; Camp 1993); Plymouth, Massachusetts (Deetz and Deetz 2000 :133–140; Furlow 2008); Maryland (Cox 2002; Cavallo 2004; Huey, 2008); Jamestown, Virginia (Huey 1988b, Furlow 2010), Nominy Plantation in the Northern Neck of Virginia (Hall 1996; Huey 1988b; Mitchell 1976); New Amsterdam (Cantwell and Wall 2001:164, 172, 174), Fort Orange/Albany (Bradley and DeAngelo 1981:111–112; De Roever 1987; Huey 2008:43–45), and other parts of New Netherland (Bradley 2000); Charlestown Harbor, South Carolina (Bradley and DeAngelo 1981; Hall 1996); New Sweden and lands west of it (Cadzow 1936; Davey and Rutter 1981:206–207; Ferguson 1941); and New Sweden governor Johann Printz's Printzhof fort (Becker 2008 and herein). This chapter focuses on that part of the EB arc that ran through New Netherland and New Sweden from the 1630s through the 1660s.

The EB Trademark and a Globe-Spanning Clay Tobacco Pipe Business

English records reflect that one Edward Bird was born around 1610 in Stoke, Surrey, England, near London (De Roever 1987:51–61). At the age of 20, he first appears in Dutch records, when he announced his marriage to a Dutch woman, Aeltje Goverts, then 18 years old (Duco 2002 [1981]). Because he was a minor, he had to obtain his parents' consent to the marriage, but he asserted that both were already dead. Edward and Aeltje married in August 1630 and produced nine children between 1632 and 1658.

Dutch clerks gave this exiled Englishman's name the usual variety of spellings, recording his given name as Edward, Eduard, and a more Netherlandish Evert, while spelling his surname as Bird, Birth, Bord, Bort, Burd, Bjirt, and Bieret. His marriage certificate declared that young Bird was a tobacco pipe maker, employed by an English pipe maker in Amsterdam. In 1635 he began selling the long pipes with the bulbous bowls that first bore his characteristic EB mark impressed in their heel. His sister-in-law married another pipe maker. On August 14, 1638, Bird purchased the Burgher Right that enabled him to establish his own workshop (Duco 2002 [1981]).

As he moved up in the world of pipe-making, he bought a fashionable new residence on the Egelantiersgracht in 1645 as an investment. The next year he made a fortuitous loan to another Englishman, Brian Newton of Herefordshire, who needed to finance his purchase of equipment as the captain of the ship that would transport Petrus Stuyvesant to New Netherlands (Duco 2002 [1981]). That venture with Brian Newton soon brought him into direct contact with New Netherland, where he would make his mark in business and leave traces in the archaeological record.

In 1656, while Oliver Cromwell was in power, Edward became a member of the English church in Amsterdam. His pipes traveled along the coasts of America in the holds of Calvinist merchants, suggesting that he may have seen himself as a part of the internationalist Protestant movement of the time. The expansion of his export pipe business to all corners of the Atlantic world enabled him to pay 3,313 guilders, a modest fortune, on June 24, 1654, to purchase a double townhouse on Amsterdam's prestigious Rozengracht canal, one of the best streets in the city. The lot contained three small houses in the back yard, making it ideal for running a business (Duco 2002 [1981]).

Edward's wife Aeltje died in December of 1658. He buried her in the nearby Westerkerk, the church with the tall tower that dominates the nearby canals. She left him an inheritance that included two houses on the Rozengracht with five smaller houses in their backyards, as well as a sixth one under construction. Half a year later Edward married Anna van der Heijden, a widow (Duco 2002 [1981]).

Edward died in late 1664 or early 1665. Edward's son Evert laid his father to rest in the Westerkerk near Aeltje. The 11-page probate inventory drawn up soon after Edward's death reflects his wealth and the wide scope of his business interests. His Amsterdam home consisted of two rooms facing a prestigious canal, a fireplace in back, a small kitchen in the back used for storage, and an attic (Duco 2002 [1981]).

At his death, Bird was a wealthy pipe manufacturer. He owned two Bibles (one in English), fine tableware including 45 pieces of blue Chinese porcelain, matching blue curtains, oak chairs, a Persian tapestry tablecloth, 15 paintings including 3 family portraits in ebony frames, many linens, and a cabinet filled with silver. The other building housed the business, with front and rear workshops, a clay shed, a storage shed, and a small kitchen with beds, presumably for family members and others who worked there.

Early photographs of Edward's house on the Egelantiersgracht show a typical four-story, brick Amsterdam townhome, with a stylish bell gable and a projecting hoist beam to lift furniture, crates, and other items. His inventory describes the workshop and pipe manufacturing business. Eight benches provided places for the pipe workers. There was a clay shed and privy behind the house. The inventory identifies a stock of some 465,000 pipes, 3,230 gross packed in 134 separate boxes. A contemporaneously specified number of workers permitted twentieth-century researchers to calculate that the workshop produced 160 gross of pipes every week (Duco 2002 [1981]).

The 465,000 pipes at hand when Edward died represented 20 weeks of production. The usual order was for 180 gross, although one client paid for 1,100 gross at once. Edward focused on large orders, where he could employ not only his own workers but independent contractors. Edward tailored his production to his customers' tastes, something he could do with an inventory of 34 separate pipe molds. Pipes available for sale included 66 cases of glossy pipes, each carrying 27 gross; 23 cases of bulbous pipes of 22 gross; 9 cases of short fine pipes each with 25 gross; and 12 ship's cases of 8 gross, apparently designed for sailors and ship's captains (Duco 2002 [1981]). This output suggests that the early onset of the industrial age occurred in Holland, not in England.

Edward did not always demand cash for his pipes. Sometimes he bartered, and thus acquired one and a half hogsheads of sugar designated as "EBX," perhaps short for "Edward Bird Exchange," the result of a sale consummated on the roadstead of Malta. He transacted trans-Atlantic business, too, including sales to Reijnier Rijcke in New Netherland, for which Edward received a consignment of tobacco (Duco 2002 [1981]).

Young Evert assumed control of his father's business and worked with his stepmother to keep that business alive, later renaming it The Rose. He kept exporting the EB pipes his father first sold. Evert did not thrive, however. He first sold the house on the Egelantiersgracht in 1678, then the houses on the Rosengracht in 1683 to pay interest that remained unpaid after an earlier sale. He died sometime after November 26, 1692. Evert's son Evert Bird III left the pipe-making trade to carry on a business in wine (Duco 2002 [1981]).

THE DELAWARE RIVER AND THE MID-SEVENTEENTH-CENTURY ATLANTIC TOBACCO TRADE

Tobacco became an important part of the Delaware River Valley's economy during the seventeenth century. In addition to producing a rich bounty of tobacco and furs, the Delaware River settlements served New Netherland as a buffer zone against England's expanding Chesapeake colonies, particularly Maryland, and as a bulwark against Swedish expansion. To the Swedes and the Finns, the Delaware was a river of dreams, presenting prospects for promoting Swedish profit, power, and prestige in the New World. New Netherland Project Director Charles T. Gehring's (1981) *Delaware Papers* offers the best guide to the tobacco trade that quickly developed along the river the Swedes and Dutch knew as the South River.

Dutchmen were the first Europeans to settle the Delaware River Valley, arriving around 15 years before former New Netherland director Peter Minuit led the Swedish crown to the valley in 1638, erecting Fort Christina at the mouth of the Brandywine in current Wilmington (Hoff 2010). After the founding of New Sweden, Dutch agents Andries Hudde, Willem Beeckman, David Pietersen de Vries, Govert Loockermans, Isaac Allerton, and Augustine Herrman plied the tobacco trade along the Delaware River (Gehring 1981).

New Sweden's new governor, Johan Rising, recorded an illuminating example of the tobacco commerce conducted along New Sweden's South

River when he described Allerton's negotiations for the purchase of tobacco, as follows: "On the 24th, Saturday, an Englishman named Mr. Allerthon [Isaac Allerton] returned from Manaatans [Manhattan] to Fort Christina and brought with him in the ship 60 hogsheads of tobacco" (Johnson 1911: II:514–516; Dahlgren and Norman 1988:183–87). Allerton received partial payment and extended credit for the rest until the next year. The Örnen [Eagle] returned to Sweden, where its captain sold the tobacco to merchants and customers. (Johnson, 1911, II: 514–515)

EB Pipes at Fort Wilhelmus, Burlington Island, New Jersey

A small log redoubt called Fort Wilhelmus was built on what is now Burlington Island, in the narrows of the Delaware, in 1624. Historian Henry Bisbee (1972:11) described it as "a palisaded fort . . . built on the down river end of the island." A Dutch trading post remained on the island, and in the late 1650s, Alexander d'Hinijossa, a veteran of the West India Company's Brazilian campaigns and the vice director of New Netherland, moved to the island and "made it a pleasure garden, built good houses upon it, and sowed and planted it" (James and Jameson 1959:98; Veit 2002:25–27). Sir Robert Carr, one of the leaders of the English conquest of New Netherland in 1664, seized the island from d'Hinijossa, and sold the property to English settlers.

Charles Conrad Abbott (1899:314) described how he stumbled upon seventeenth-century Dutch pipe stems and other artifacts on the island: "During a recent ramble I found a yellow brick upon the sand; and looking farther, another, and curious old red bricks and bits of roofing tiles, and pipe-stems; scattered everywhere odds and ends that could only have come from some old house nearby. . . . A hundred questions plagued me at once and I took refuge in the book stack." Abbott also detailed his excavation of "beer mugs, and schnapps bottles and wineglasses . . . and then the pipes and pipe stems! I have a pile of over five hundred." Of those 500, at least 15 bore the telltale "EB" (Abbott 1899:321; Veit 2002:29).

One of those curved red roof tiles remained at the University of Pennsylvania, where it later prompted Richard Veit and Charles Bello to search out 194 surviving artifacts of the "Dutch Traders' House" on Burlington Island (Veit 2002:28). The average bore diameter of the white clay kaolin pipe stems suggests that they were manufactured around 1660, leading Veit (2002:29–30) to conclude that the "Dutch Trader's House" might have been one house New Netherland Vice Director Alexander d'Hinijossa built and Sir Robert Carr later seized.

EXCAVATIONS AT MINISINK ISLAND REVEALED EB PIPE FRAGMENTS IN A NATIVE GRAVE

Some of northern New Jersey's Native people considered Edward Bird's tobacco pipes important enough to take with them into the hereafter. An excavation report from 1915 documented the discovery of at least 22 Native graves dating back to the middle of the seventeenth century at Minisink Island (Heye and Pepper 1915; Mounier 2003:184–85; Veit and Bello 2001:47–64). It is unknown how many individuals were buried in this aboriginal graveyard, which had been looted on many occasions between the 1860s and the second decade of the twentieth century.

Excavators George Heye and George Pepper noted the presence of many artifacts reflecting widespread trade with Europeans, including pewter and ceramics, pipes, brass kettles, metal bells, pewter spoons, items of flint and steel, hundreds of beads (made from glass, shell, and catlinite), and inscribed shell ornaments. The presence of three EB pipes indicates that Natives in northeastern New Jersey were in close contact with Dutch merchants.

The pipe stems probably date from the late seventeenth century, since the pewter pipes found in close association with them are believed to date to circa 1650 to 1700 and since the site was abandoned by 1712 (Heye and Pepper 1915:53–54; Mounier 2003:184–85).

EB PIPES AT NEW SWEDEN'S CAPITOL, THE PRINTZHOF

On February 15, 1643, New Sweden's third governor, Johann Printz, reached the Delaware River (Sickler 1937:12). Item 12 of his orders required him to encourage the cultivation of tobacco for export back to Sweden and the world market: "Next to this, he shall pay good and close attention to the cultivation of tobacco and appoint thereto a certain number of laborers, pressing the matter so that that cultivation may increase and more and more continued and extended, so that he can send over a good quantity of tobacco on all ships coming hither" (Johnson 1930:84–85). By June 11, 1644, Printz could report that "the tobacco which is now sent over makes altogether 20,467 lbs" (Johnson 1930:107).

Printz found Fort Christina to be inadequate for his court. He moved his center of administration north to Tinicum Island and called his new settlement Nya Göteborg, or Fort New Gothenberg (Dahlgren and Norman 1988:65; Becker 2008:3 and herein). On November 6, 1643, Queen Christina

Figure 14.2. "EB" marks on pipes
from Becker's excavations at the
Printzhof, ca. 1645–1655. Collec-
tions of the Pennsylvania State
Museum, Harrisburg. Photo by
David A. Furlow.

and Swedish Council formally granted Governor Printz ownership of the
Printzhof, German for "Printz's Court" (Linn and Egle 1880:808–809). The
Printzhof consisted of a main residence, a blockhouse fort, a warehouse,
a barn, a brewhouse, a palisade, and, in all probability, a bathhouse sauna
(Johnson 1911: I:347–49; Dahlgren and Norman 1988:65–66).

In 1937 Donald Cadzow led a team of Works Project Administration
excavators to Tinicum Island in search of Governor Printz's stronghold.
While seventeenth-century artifacts were recovered, the identity of the site
was in doubt until Marshal Becker's excavation in 1976 and follow-up investigations in the mid-1980s (Becker 2008, and herein).

Becker's excavations produced a number of EB pipe stems that subsequently found their way to the Pennsylvania State Museum in Harrisburg,
where Delaware archaeologists Craig Lukezic, Alice Guerrant, and I examined them on May 12, 2011. Dr. Kurt Carr and David Burke devoted several
hours to letting our group examine and photograph, inter alia, two excellent funnel-angle EB pipe stems and several bulbous EB pipe artifacts (Figures 14.2 and 14.3). Governor Printz may have smoked one of the pipes in
the state museum's collection as part of a ceremony ratifying a fur-trading
agreement with the Lenape or Susquehannock Indians.

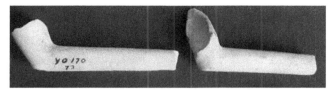

Figure 14.3. Funnel-angle EB pipes from Becker's excavations at the Printzhof. Collections of the Pennsylvania State Museum, Harrisburg. Photo by David A. Furlow.

SUSQUEHANNOCK SITES IN LANCASTER COUNTY, PENNSYLVANIA

The Susquehannock nation traded frequently with the Swedes, Dutch, and English and also made war against the English in Maryland and the Dutch in New Netherland. Archaeologists who excavated, reexcavated, interpreted, and reinterpreted the Strickler Site, the location of a large Susquehannock village in Lancaster County, Pennsylvania (occupied circa 1645 to 1660), found seven pipes with the EB mark in raised letters on a flattened, very diminutive heel (Kent 2001:266, 348–67). Those EB pipes, once a part of the social life of a prominent Indian town, are now on display in the Pennsylvania State Museum in Harrisburg.

Archaeologists have also found EB pipes while excavating the smaller, later, nearby Oscar Leibhart and Byrd Leibhart Susquehannock village sites (Kent 2001:267, 367–71, 372–379). Susquehannocks occupied the Oscar Leibhart village from roughly 1665 to 1674, during a period of rapid and sustained depopulation and crisis. The two EB pipes found at the Byrd Leibhart village, occupied from circa 1676 to circa 1680, were far smaller than those found on the nearby Strickler and Oscar Leibhart sites.

EDWARD BIRD PIPE STEMS AND THE CHRONOLOGY OF EARLY AMERICAN TRADE

Archaeologists and historians should expect to see a wide variety of EB pipes emerge from the ground, often at the same site, tailored to a wide variety of consumer tastes. Albany archaeologist Paul Huey and nautical archaeologist Jerome Hall have produced the most scholarly studies of the many kinds of Edward Bird pipes, including many pipes, stems, and bowls that they attribute to Edward Bird, yet that do not do not bear the ubiquitous EB mark. Their rich work merits sustained study, especially as to the many funnel-angle pipes Edward made specifically for export to the

Natives of New Netherland, who traditionally made, used, and traded similarly funnel-angled pipes carved in stone (Van Laer 1932a:102).

Edward Bird followed, on a massive scale, the precedent of English colonial pipe makers, who manufactured Native-friendly clay tobacco pipes in the Chesapeake and sold them in the early seventeenth century. "Robert Cotton tobacco pipe maker," the first English pipe maker at Jamestown, produced Native-friendly funnel-angle pipes in 1608 (Luckenbach and Kiser 2006:164). The as-yet-unidentified "Bookbinder" pipe maker who worked at the Chesopean Site in Virginia Beach continued Robert Cotton's innovation by producing and selling red clay elbow (funnel-angle) pipes that have been found throughout early colonial sites in Virginia and Maryland and as far afield as the Renews Site in Newfoundland (Luckenbach and Kiser 2006:165–67).

Edward Bird may have begun manufacturing Native-friendly funnel-angle pipes on a massive scale after seeing these Virginia colonial pipes during the 1640s, when New Netherland merchants Augustine Herrman and Isaac Allerton opened a thriving tobacco trade with Virginia, or Bird may have done so in response to a specific request from Arent van Curler, later Van Corlaer, a Dutch merchant plying the New Netherland trade (Huey 2008:43).

As excavations continue, many more fragments of Edward Bird's pipes will emerge from the ground and the sea, on both sides of the Atlantic and probably in the Mediterranean as well. Many will not feature the well-known EB mark on the heel. Close attention to the style and condition of a pipe may enable its origin and age to be determined. Photographs, line drawings, and detailed descriptions of Bird's pipes should be published by those who find them to assist in the long-term assembly of a comprehensive list of EB pipe artifacts. Such attention to detail can contribute to the development of a long-term chronology.

A comprehensive Edward Bird pipe chronology can help set reasonably clear date ranges for these pipes and other artifacts buried in association with them. And that, in turn, can measure the seventeenth-century trade flows that shaped the course of Atlantic history.

Conclusion

A New World Made by Trade

CRAIG LUKEZIC AND JOHN P. MCCARTHY

New Netherland was founded perched at the edge of empires and forming a borderland at various times separating English, French, Dutch, and
Swedish imperial interests in North America. Initially, the Europeans primarily sought wealth through trade with the indigenous peoples and only
secondarily did they pursue permanent settlement. Over time, as markets
and imperial fortunes shifted, the French and Dutch traded their holdings in North America for others in the Caribbean and continental South
America. While New Netherland was in a zone of contention among European powers, all these nations were Protestant, and usually allied in the
ongoing Thirty Years' War in Europe. When one imperial interest overcame
another, citizenship was usually offered to the existing colonists, whose
property rights were respected.

The papers collected here use archaeology to illuminate a wide range
of topics. These are frequently mundane matters that escaped the notice
of the literate people of the time and were only revealed through physical
evidence that archaeology provides. This chapter summarizes some key results, drawing some conclusions and suggesting avenues of future research.

New Netherland was a place of trade and commerce and the Dutch
relied on the participation of Native Americans. Violence against them,
such as Kieft's War (1643–1645), substantially hurt fur-trade business interests, ultimately threatening the future of the colony (Jacobs 2009:76).
Native people became professional hunters, and the economy was based on
their contributions of faunal resources: foodstuffs as well as furs. As Pipes

showed, their services provided deer and bear meat for the colonists' tables, along with the beaver pelts that filled their coffers.

The trading station or "factory" was the building block of the Dutch mercantile empire. As mentioned in De Cunzo, 23 stations, or blockhouses, were constructed along a 35-mi stretch of the Delaware River. Most of these small forts were fortified warehouses and not built to sustain serious military assault. Dutch traders jockeyed for the best access to Native trade routes, while blocking or flanking the competing Swedish stations and English ones in the Connecticut River.

Luscier and Kirk present a rare glimpse into one of these factories. Quamhemesicos was the actual ground of the cultural and material interchange between the Europeans and Mahicans. The remains of architecture of both peoples were positioned side by side, with Dutch brick and pantiles in contact to a ring of wooden post molds. They encountered evidence of trade goods including tobacco pipes, a cloth bale seal, and the remains of wampum/sewant production.

Yet, as Rothschild (2006:104) observed, there is no real confusion as to who resided where in New Netherland; Native goods were rare in Dutch homes, while the Dutch inundated Natives with European goods meant to stimulate production of beaver. As Rothschild (2006:73) also observed, the degree to which trade partners adopts the material culture of the other is an important indicator of the power relationships affecting identity.

The importance of sustaining peaceful trade with both Algonquian and Iroquoian peoples was the rationale of many Dutch West India Company regulations. Officials proscribed trade zones in Beverwijck, or Fort Orange, and at Fort Casimir (Huey 1988a; De Cunzo herein). Paternalistic policies were perhaps aimed at protecting Native people from "sharp practices" resulting from alcohol abuse but also sought to protect traders from being robbed along the trail, thus protecting company profits. At Fort Casimir, the trade zone was near the fort, and a hut was available for the traveling Native traders. At Beverwijck, some Dutch agents invited Natives into their homes or provided temporary housing in outbuildings (Venema 2003:178). As we have seen in De Cunzo's chapter, the regulations at Fort Casimir were inconsistently enforced, and Native and European free agents could roam seeking trade advantages. Court records suggest zones of strong control near the fort structure and a zone of weak official control of the far edge the settlement. It is possible that Native people delineated trading areas in a similar fashion. In southern Delaware, the Nanticoke defined such an area near the fork of Broad Creek and Nanticoke River as the exclusive trading zone where John Smith and other outsiders were permitted to land (Griffith and Busby 2011).

Cantwell and Wall suggest that trade was more complex than simply an exchange of material goods, with Native women acting as their own agents and having their own motives for trade activities. Material gain through exchange may have been secondary to developing intimate relationships with European men. As there was shortage of European women, this situation was enjoyed or at least tolerated by the Dutch leadership until the Dutch Reform church gained influence over the daily lives of the colonists.

A major theme in Shorto's (2005) *The Island at the Center of the World* is that the industrious nature of the Dutch predetermined that New Netherland would become the core of American industrial development. Such being true, most of the physical remains of New Netherland and New Sweden were subsequently obliterated. Unlike Jamestown in Virginia and St. Mary's City in Maryland, most of the archaeological footprint of New Amsterdam and surrounding communities was destroyed or buried by modern development of the Lower Hudson and Delaware River Valleys.

Ian Burrow provided an excellent gazetteer of the New Netherland sites in New Jersey. He charts, with an experienced eye, site locations and provides a sober assessment of what might still remain. One site, Achter Col, may be intact in rare green space, and elements of the original town of Bergen may survive in modern house yards. In addition, he presents the distinct artifacts that archaeologists should look for to identify Dutch components. This chapter is essentially an action plan for finding and preserving New Netherland in New Jersey. According to Burrow, "The richness of Dutch material culture and the restrictive trading practices of the seventeenth century combine to make the archaeological signature of the colonial Dutch into an almost textbook case of pattern recognition." Burrow goes on to mention roemer glasses, Dutch majolica, EB tobacco pipes, and *sith* and *mathook* iron reaping tools as artifacts distinctive to Dutch occupations.

The Dutch made particular effort to re-create their sense of Europe in the non-European world, with buildings, furnishings, tableware, and food prepared in Dutch ways (Orser 2012:749; Maika et al. 2014:471). There are few objects that seem to be more quintessentially Dutch than kookpotten or what was termed *grapen*. However, does their presence testify to the presence of a Dutch site, the pervasiveness of Dutch trade, or do they indicate the practice of Dutch foodways? Truly, the kookpot was an ordinary object, used to make humble dishes as stews and porridges. It was an earthen pot, while many people of the middle and upper classes could afford one of metal. One may have had to use care when heating and cooling these by a fire, as the pot might crack.

Janowitz and Schaefer noted that the lack of any evidence of wear seen on many sherds suggests these pots were fragile and had a short working life. They established that many earthenware were imported from Bergen op Zoom, but it is unknown whether any were made in New Netherland. Such vessels were widely traded, though, as their fragments are noted to have been found at English and Native American sites in the Chesapeake.

However, kookpotten were not as widely distributed as white ball clay tobacco pipes. Furlow presented the life and works of Edward Bird and family who were English pipe makers in Amsterdam. Their products can be found in Europe, Africa, and the Americas. The biography of Edward Bird is a stellar example of industry in Amsterdam during the Golden Age. Due to their religious convictions, the Bird family relocated to tolerant Amsterdam. They established a pipe-making company, a niche that was not always profitable, and marketed to the world. It appears the Birds adopted the funnel shape bowl to appeal to the Native people in the North America. This global perspective is a critical feature of the Dutch trade success. Pipe fragments with the initial "EB" embossed in them, can be found in most archaeological labs in the eastern seaboard.

Huey's work on marbles is truly intriguing. This chapter, which focuses on their presence in New Netherland, is the part of a larger monograph documenting known marbles found in on the East Coast in contexts dating before 1800. Play with small spheres began in ancient time, using cherry pits. By the late Middle Ages, these spheres were being manufactured in ceramic or stone for a game we call marbles. Throughout northern Europe, games of cards, dice, and marbles were considered to be idle wastes of time and banned in favor of martial exercises or more productive activities. As the Dutch were more tolerant and less strict with these decrees, marbles appear in higher frequency in Dutch sites.

Through careful measurement, Huey has observed that many of these were made with care to produce a uniform size, and the store ones were made using specialized milling machinery. It is possible the latter may have been employed as ammunition for stone bows, a device used to fell birds with valuable plumage.

The above artifact types, kookpotten, white clay tobacco pipes, and marbles seem to be strongly associated with Dutch ethnicity. Can they individually or collectively be used as "index fossils" for a Dutch domestic presence? Perhaps, but only with an abundance of caution as Dutch trade items appear in Native and European sites all across eastern North America.

The results of the excavation at the Pritzhof and New Gothenburg demonstrate the interaction and blending of the material cultural of the Swedes, Dutch, and the native Lenape. Becker's excavations revealed a palisade line of stakes that is similar to those found at Fort Casimir, and some English settlements. As with the trading station at Quamhemesicos Island on the Hudson River, a Native hut was located immediately adjacent to the European compound. Knapped and worked shards of green bottle glass attest to the interactions of the Lenape and Swedes at this location. Becker also found a Dutch roemer with prunts, Dutch brick, and tobacco pipes, with notable similarities to those found at Dutch sites. Colonists from both counties were connected to what might be thought of as a North Atlantic world of material goods where ethnicity or nationality may not have factored very strongly in consumer choices, so long as the goods were European.

Some previous studies of the material aspects of the Dutch New World have argued that the Dutch maintained their identity through their material choices as they adapted to new physical and social environments (e.g., Cantwell and Wall 2008; Maika et al. 2014) and yet at the same time, in attempting to make Dutch something that was not, they were not immune to the influences of a new landscape and new people, creating something new: New Netherland (Maika et al. 2014:471).

Modern notions of national identity, however, may not have existed in the minds of the colonists, or at least not have been so significant as to have had much effect on behavior in the New World. Many museums and popular history books portray the early modern or colonial period as a story describing the predestined rise of the modern state, and the contemporary public views our heritage through the lens of modern national identities. However, during the seventeenth century, the homelands of Europe were not yet nation-states as they later became to be understood, and the identities of most people were more complicated that can be summarized by any notion of national identity. Provincial and village identities were likely more powerful in the minds of most colonists, and regardless would have had little effect on the material that made its way into the archaeological record. Markets and the goods available, do not necessary equate to identity as it resided in the minds of Dutch, Swedes, Finns, and other colonists. Perhaps the one realm of discernable distinction between the Dutch and Swedes was architecture. While most the standing architecture from the period of New Netherland and New Sweden has been lost, archaeological footprints remain. Swedes and Finns are assumed to have constructed log cabins with a corner fireplace, as documented in the earlier excavation of the Printzhof. Such construction would have left little beneath the plowzone for an archaeologist to observe. The Dutch may have constructed longhouses at this time, as recorded in Achter Col for bowery in a rural settings, and gable-fronted structures for urban setting as documented by Huey (1988a) at Fort Orange and in Venema's (2003:64–79) *Beverwijck*.

Drinking Houses were the stage and setting for public and private conversations in the colony. People of varied backgrounds, of wealth or poverty, interacted with the regular aid of alcohol and tobacco. They were spaced as waypoints along the main road in Beverwijck, or at the entrance to a community. While the planters of the Chesapeake had to settle for rum and cider, the breweries of New Netherland produced beer for regular consumption.

Archaeology provides a different perspective than that which documents provide. The staff of de Vrouw Maria provided clientele with hearty meals of venison and pork, which may not have been expected for a drinking house. While little evidence of tobacco consumption appeared, the clientele enjoyed beer from fine glassware.

A major flashpoint for civil conflict was selling alcohol to Native people. Court documents record cases at Beverwijck and Fort Casimir. Much of the violence and uncontrolled behavior involved in these events resulted from the selling of distilled spirits. While these infractions were adjudicated, one wonders what was happening day to day and how it may have affected the acculturation process.

One notable but important topic that deserves more study is the lifeways of the forcefully imported Africans. Some of the enslaved were shipped from Portuguese colonies in Africa, and others were brought from Brazil or the Caribbean. In these Catholic countries, the enslaved were organized into "brotherhoods" or mutual aid societies within a hierarchical framework. When the West India Company captured Brazil, they adopted this existing slave system, and transplanted it into New Netherland. Jeroen Dewulf (2017) found Portuguese names and other clues in the documentary record that indicate the first Africans participated in the Iberian culture. He goes on to suggest this first generation, or "charter generation," melded and became the foundation for African American culture in New York, and possibly mid-Atlantic area. Therefore, archaeological evidence of the early generations of Africans in New Netherland would be extremely valuable in exploring this social system, as their presence usually stays in the peripheral of the documentary record, not noticed by the literate people of the time. Cantwell and Wall (2015) suggest one feature containing marbles, which is presented by Huey in this volume, may be associated with African rituals.

Over time, the various centers of Dutch settlement began to express regional differences. New Amsterdam and the Hudson River were the commercial and administrative center of the colony. Hence, most of the existing documentary evidence is focused on that area. The settlements along the Delaware and Connecticut Rivers were more in border zones, providing a buffer against English and Swedish powers. The people of the Delaware River were ethnically mixed from the beginning, and the material culture reflects this. As noted, Dutch, Swedes, Finns, Germans, French, Africans, and Lenape founded the settlements along the Delaware. Jasper Danckaerts (1913), founder of a settlement of Friesland pietists on the Bohemia River in what is now the Eastern Shore of Maryland interacted with many of these differing types of people during his travel across New Netherland in 1679–1680. His journal documented their subtle but clearly present spirit of tolerance and cooperation. Today, while we drive through the footprint of New Netherland on congested turnpikes, instead of following a poorly blazed trail through the woods, that spirit lives on in us.

We are struck by the wide range of types and styles of the artifacts the authors report. The variety of luxury ware range from Italian inspired majolica, Chinese inspired faience, stemware from Venice, stoneware from the German cities, along with kitchen earthenware from small towns in the Low Countries. Yet these global trading networks that define the early modern period were composed from family units. From Renaissance Italy, merchants develop their networks from the marriage bond with other merchant families, in the same community, or in foreign countries to minimize risk by building familial bonds of trust (Prajda 2012). Throughout cities in Europe, mercantile networks transcended ethnic and political boundaries. In Sweden, Christina Dalhede (2018) found German, Scottish, Dutch, and Walloon mercantile families were interconnected and developed a fluid cultural identity she termed "Misch-Europaer." In New Netherland, the large mercantile families of Verbrugge, Momma, Van Resselaer, and Van Twillers controlled much of the trade (Jacobs 2009). Yet the networks of these families reached from various ports in the western hemisphere, from

Moscow to Manhattan. The mixed global identity that had flourished in the cosmopolitan cities of Europe had spread to New Netherland before the existence of the modern nation state.

Perhaps the sources of our data shape our conceptions of the realities of life in the colony. By reading the official correspondence and documents for the colonial elite to the royal authorities, we find a realm of desperate inter-imperial conflict following global strategies. In this view, we have the Dutch, Swedes, and English contesting the Delaware Valley and the Puritans, Native peoples, and Dutch fighting for the regions around the Connecticut River.

The other realm is that presented by the scholars in this volume. It is a world of trade, interaction, and exploration. All or most parties interacted with others to meet their even most basic needs. The archaeology reveals the small things of everyday life: the remains of cooking pots, dinnerware, deer bones, pipes, drinking glasses, and so on. Traffic in these mundane items seemingly altered the course of empires. For example, colonists from Sweden and England, poorly supplied by their mother countries, were effectively cut off during the social and political conflicts of the 1640s to 1650s (McMillian 2015). They came to rely on each other and on Dutch traders who made their rounds to the plantations, providing the colonists with needed supplies, thus enabling them to survive during this period and thrive into the following decades.

Such realities intersect with the embassy of Augustine Herrman to Maryland. In 1659, the colonies of Maryland and New Amstel were in conflict and on a course to possible war. Herrman acted as an envoy on representing New Netherland to negotiate a stable border with Governor Philip Calvert and the Maryland Council. While this official diplomacy was a failure, from private meetings an unofficial trading relationship between the two colonies emerged, with both colonies prospering (Koot 2018:120). Additionally, when imperial negotiations failed in Europe, Lord Baltimore sent instructions to Governor Calvert to plan an invasion to subjugate New Amstel. In July of 1661, the council heard the plan, but it declined to act, instead choosing to continue peaceful commercial relationships (Koot 2018:113). This decision briefly saved the colony of New Amstel, preserving New Netherland until the invasion of the Duke of York. For a moment in time, the interest and need for these artifacts, the objects that we study, by local people living on the frontier changed the fate of empires.

REFERENCES CITED

Abbott, Charles Conrad. 1989. *Recent Rambles; or, In Touch with Nature.* Philadelphia and London: J. B. Lippincott.

Acrelius, Israel. 1874. *A History of New Sweden.* Translated by William M. Reynolds. Philadelphia: Historical Societies of Pennsylvania and Delaware.

AKRF, URS, and Linda Stone. 2012. *Final Report: South Ferry Terminal Project, Volume 1, Text and Figures.* Report prepared for the Metropolitan Transit Authority, New York, NY, on file at the New York City Landmarks Commission.

Alderney Maritime Trust. 2016. Key Artifacts, Large Shot. *Alderney Elizabethan Wreck.* http://www.alderneymaritimetrust.org/alderney-elizabethan-wreck/chronology-nationality-identity-key-artefacts/, accessed July 15, 2016.

Anderson, Karen. 1991. *Chain Her by One Foot: The Subjugation of Native Women in Seventeenth-Century New France.* New York: Routledge.

Anonymous. 1718. *Extract uyt de Generale Keure en Ordonnantie der Stad Rotterdam.* Stad, Rotterdam: Gedrukt bij Hendrik van Waesberge, Ordinaris Drukker der voorsz.

———. 1728. *La plus nouvelle academie universelle des jeux, ou divertissemens innocens.* Volume I. Amsterdam: Chez J. Covens & C. Mortier.

———. 1753. "Copenhagen, Oct. 16." *London Gazette,* October 27–30, p. 1.

———. 1771. "The Dutch Method of Making Marbles." *The Gentleman's Magazine* 41:347–348.

———. 1785. *Beschrijving van de merkwaardigste voortbrengselen der natuur, met aanwijzing van der zelver nut, bijzonder voor den mensch.* Volume I. Uitgegeven door de Bataafsche Maatschappij: tot nut van 't algemeen. Amsterdam: Cornelis de Vries, Hendk van Munster, en Johannes van der Hey.

———. 1894. *The Colonial Laws of New York from the Year 1664 to the Revolution.* Vol. 1. Albany: James B. Lyon.

———. 1905a. *Minutes of the Common Council of the City of New York.* Vol. 1. New York: Dodd, Mead.

———. 1905b. *Minutes of the Common Council of the City of New York.* Vol. 3. New York: Dodd, Mead.

———. 1905c. *Minutes of the Common Council of the City of New York.* Vol. 4. New York: Dodd, Mead.

Antczak, Andrzej, Konrad A. Antczak, and Ma Magdalena Antczak. 2015. Risky Business: Historical Archaeology of the Dutch Salt Enterprise on La Tortuga Island, Venezuela (1624–38). *Post Medieval Archaeology* 49(2):189–219.

Armstrong, Edward. 1856. *The History and Location of Fort Nassau upon the Delaware.* Newark, NJ: Daily Advertiser Print.

Atkin, Malcom, and Russell Howes. 1993. The Use of Archeology and Documentary Sources in Identifying the Civil War Defenses of Gloucester. *Post-medieval Archeology* 27:15–42.

Baart, Jan. 1977. Opgravingen in Amsterdam: 20 jaar stadskernonderzoek, Dienst der Publieke Werken (Amsterdam) / Afdeling Archeologie, Amsterdams Historisch Museum, Fibula–Van Dishoek–Haarlem.

———. 1987. Portugese Faience, 1600–1660: Een studie van bodemvondsten en museumcollecties. In *Exodo: Portugezen in Amsterdam, 1600–1680,* edited by R. Kistemaker and T. Levie, p. 18–24. Amsterdam: Amsterdams Historisch Museum, De Bataafse Leeuw.

———. 1989. Archeologische Dienst Amsterdam DEEL 1: Publicaties 1972–1989, Dienst Openbare Werken Amsterdam, Afdeling Archeologie, Gemeente Amsterdam.

———. 2001. Nieuwe inzichten in oude huishoudens. *Jaarboek Amstelodamum* 93: 195–209.

———. 2005. Cloth Seals at Iroquois Sites. *Northeast Historical Archaeology* 34:77–88.

Baart, J. M., W. Krook, and A. C. Lagerweij. 1986. "Opgravingen aan de Oostenburgermiddenstaat." In *Van VOC tot Werkspoor: het Amsterdamse industrieterrein Oostenburg,* edited by P. C. Jansen, J. B. Kist, A. J. Bonke, pp. 83–151. Utrecht: Stichting Matrijs.

Baart, Jan, Wiard Krook, Ab Lagerweij, Nina Ockers, Hans van Regteren Altena, Tuuk Stam, Henk Stoepker, Gerard Stouthart, and Monika van der Zwan. 1977. *Opgravingen in Amsterdam: 20 jaar stadskernonderzoek.* Amsterdam: Bussem.

Balassa, Ian, and Gyula Ortutay. 1979. *Hungarian Ethnography and Folklore.* Translated by Maria and Kenneth Bales. *Digital Library of Hungarian Studies.* http://mek.oszk. hu/02700/02790/html/67.html, accessed August 10, 2017.

Barnes, Donna R., and Peter G. Rose. 2012. *Childhood Pleasures: Dutch Children in the Seventeenth Century.* Syracuse: Syracuse University Press.

Bartels, Michiel. 1999a. *Cities in Sherds 1: Finds from Cesspits in Deventer, Dordrecht, Nijmegen and Tiel (1250–1900).* Amerfoot: Stichting Promotie Archeologie and Rijksdienst voor Cultureel Erfgoed.

———. 1999b. *Cities in Sherds 2 Catalogue: Finds from Cesspits in Deventer, Dordrecht, Nijmegen and Tiel (1250–1900).* Amerfoot: Stichting Promotie Archeologie and Rijksdienst voor Cultureel Erfgoed.

Baum, Gerald R. 1973a. The New Netherland Tavern: I. *de Halve Maen* 48(3):9–15.

———. 1973b. The New Netherland Tavern: II. *de Halve Maen* 48(4):11–15.

Beaudry, Mary, Janet Long, Henry M. Miller, Fraser D. Neiman, and Garry Wheeler Stone. 1983. A Vessel Typology for Early Chesapeake Ceramics: The Potomac Typological System. *Historical Archaeology* 17(1):18–43.

Becker, Marshall Joseph. 1977. "Swedish" Colonial Yellow Bricks: Notes on Their Uses and Possible Origins in Seventeenth Century America. *Historical Archaeology* 11:112–118.

———. 1979. Ethnohistory and Archaeology in Search of the Printzhof: The Seventeenth-Century Residence of Swedish Colonial Governor Johan Printz. *Ethnohistory* 26(1):15–44.

———. 1980. Lenape Archaeology: Archaeological and Ethnohistoric Considerations in Light of Recent Excavations. *Pennsylvania Archaeologist* 50(4):19–30.

———. 1984. Lenape Land Sales, Treaties, and Wampum Belts. *Pennsylvania Magazine of History and Biography* 108(3):351–356.

———. 1987. *A Report on the 1986 Excavations at the Printzhof Site (36 DE 3): Operation 13.* Manuscript on file, West Chester University of Pennsylvania.

———. 1988. A Summary of Lenape Socio-Political Organization and Settlement Pattern at the Time of European Contact: The Evidence for Collecting Bands. *Journal of Middle Atlantic Archaeology* 4:79–83.

———. 1990a. A Wolf's Head Pouch: Lenape Material Culture in the Collections of the Skokloster Museum, Sweden. *Archeomaterials* 4(1):77–95.

———. 1990b. Two Seventeenth-century Clubs in the Collections of the Skokloster Museum, Sweden. *European Review of Native American Studies* 4(1):19–28.

———. 1993. Lenape Shelters: Possible Examples from the Contact Period. *Pennsylvania Archaeologist* 63(2):64–76.

———. 1997. The Palisade at the Printzhof: A Swedish Fort of 1643 on the Delaware River. Paper presented at the annual meeting of the Council for Northeast Historic Archaeology, Altoona, PA.

———. 1999. Archaeology at the Printzhof (36DE3): The Only Documented Early Seventeenth Century Swedish Site in the Delaware Valley. *Journal of Middle Atlantic Archaeology* 15:77–94.

———. 2000. European Trade and Colonization in the Territory of the Lenape during the Seventeenth Century: A Modern Historical Model for Greek Colonization in Italy and Elsewhere in Magna Graecia. *Bulletin of the Archaeological Society of New Jersey* 55:33–43.

———. 2006. The Prinzhof (36DE3): A Swedish Colonial Site that was the First European Center of Government in Present Pennsylvania. *Bulletin of the Archaeological Society of Delaware* 43 (Fall 2006): 1–34.

———. 2008. *The Printzhof: The Swedish Outpost that Served as the First European Center of Government in Present Pennsylvania.* Manuscript on file, Philadelphia: University of Pennsylvania Museum.

———. 2011. Lenape Culture History: The Transition of 1660 and Its Implications for the Archaeology of the Final Phase of the Late Woodland Period. *Journal of Middle Atlantic Archaeology* 27:53–72.

Benson, Barbara E. 2002. Courthouses of New Castle County. *Delaware Lawyer* 20:20–26.

Bielinski, Stefan. 1991. How a City Worked: Occupations in Colonial Albany. In *A Beautiful and Fruitful Place: Selected Resselaerswijck Seminar Papers,* edited by Nancy Anne McClure Zeller, pp. 119–136. New York: New Netherland Publishing.

Bisbee, Henry. 1972. *Burlington Island: The Best and Largest on the South River, 1624–1972.* Burlington, NJ: Heidelberg Press.

Bitter, P., S. Ostkamp, and R. Roedema. 2002. *De beerput als bron: Archeologische vondsten van het dagelijks leven in het oude Alkmaar, i.s.m. Afdeling Monumentenzorg en Archeologie.* Gemeente Alkmaar, Uitgever: Historische Vereniging Alkmaar.

Blackburn, Roderic H., and Nancy A. Kelley (editors). 1987. *New World Dutch Studies: Dutch Arts and Culture in Colonial America, 1609–1776.* Albany: Albany Institute of History and Culture.

Blackburn, Roderic H., and Ruth Piwonka. 1988. *Remembrance of Patria: Dutch Arts and Culture in Colonial America, 1609–1776.* Albany: Albany Institute of History and Art.

Bodian, M. 1997. *Hebrews of the Portuguese Nation: Conversos and Community in Early Modern Amsterdam.* Bloomington: Indiana University Press.

Bonine, C. A. 1956. Archeological Investigation of the Dutch "Swanendael" Settlement under DeVries, 1631–1632. *The Archeolog* 8(3):1–17.

———. 1964. The South Bastion of the Devries Palisade of 1631 (7S-D11) Lewes, Delaware. *The Archeolog* 16(2):13–19.

Bottoms, Edward, and Cynthia Hanson. 2006. *Pots, Pipes, and Trash Pits: Volume I of the Jamestown Trilogy Series.* Chesapeake: Archaeological Society of Virginia.

Bradley, Charles S. 2000. Smoking Pipes for the Archaeologist. In *Studies in Material Culture Research*, edited by Karlis Karklins, pp. 104–133. Tucson: Society for Historical Archaeology.

Bradley, James W. 2007. *Before Albany: An Archaeology of Native-Dutch Relations in the Capital Region, 1600–1664.* Albany: New York State Museum.

Bradley, James W., and Gordon De Angelo. 1981. European Clay Pipe Marks from Seventeenth Century Onondaga Iroquois Sites. *Archaeology of Eastern North America* 9:109–133.

Bragdon, Kathleen. 1981. Occupational Differences Reflected in Material Culture. In *Documentary Archaeology in the New World*, edited by Mary C. Beaudry, pp. 83–91. Cambridge: Cambridge University Press.

———. 1996a. Gender as a Social Category in Native Southern New England. *Ethnohistory* 43(4):573–592.

———. 1996b. *Native Peoples of Southern New England, 1500–1650.* Norman: University of Oklahoma Press.

Brasser, Ted J. 1978. Mahican. In *Handbook of North American Indians, Volume 15: Northeast*, edited by Bruce G. Trigger, pp. 198–212. Washington: Smithsonian Institution.

Brongers, J. A., and H. F. Wijnman. 1968. Chronological Classification of Roemers with the Help of Seventeenth Century Paintings in the Low Countries. In *Rotterdam Papers: A Contribution to Medieval Archaeology*, edited by J. G. N. Renaud, pp. 15–21. Rotterdam: Coordinatie Commissie van Advies inzake Archeologisch Onderzoek binnen het Ressort Rotterdam.

Broos, Ben. 1989. Improving and Finishing Old Master Drawings: An Art in Itself. *Hoogster-Naumann Mercury* 8:34–55.

Brown, Janice. n.d. Fort Nassau. Gloucester County, New Jersey, History and Genealogy http://www.nj.searchroots.com/Gloucesterco/fortnassau.htm#Location, accessed November 12, 2017.

Brown, William (editor). 1885. *Archives of Maryland.* Baltimore: Maryland Historical Society.

Brumble, H. David, III (translator). 1982. *G. A. Bredero, The Spanish Brabanter: A Seventeenth-Century Dutch Social Satire in Five Acts.* Binghamton, NY: Center for Medieval & Early Renaissance Studies.

Burema, Lambertus. 1953. *De Voeding in Nederland van de Middeleeuwen tot de Twintigste Eeuw.* Assen: Van Gorcum.

Burrow, Ian. 2011. On the Brink (Dorp): The Archaeology and Landscape of the Fortified New Netherland Village of Bergen, Jersey City, New Jersey. *Bulletin of the Archaeological Society of New Jersey* 66:65–73.

Burrows, Edwin, and Mike Wallace. 1999. *Gotham: A History of New York City to 1898.* New Haven: Oxford University Press.

Butts, Edward. 2009. *Henry Hudson: New World Voyager.* Toronto: Dundurn.

Cadzow, Donald A. 1936. *Archaeological Studies of the Susquehannock Indians of Pennsylvania—Safe Harbor Report No. 2.* Harrisburg: Pennsylvania Historical Commission.

Camp, Helen. 1993. *Archaeological Excavations at Pemaquid, Maine, 1965–1974.* Augusta: Maine State Museum.

Cantwell, Anne-Marie, and Diana diZerega Wall. 2001. *Unearthing Gotham: The Archaeology of New York City.* New Haven: Yale University Press.

———. 2008. Landscapes and Other Objects: Creating Dutch New Netherland. *New York History* 89(4):315–346.

———. 2011. Engendering New Netherland: Implications for Archaeological and Historical Interpretations for Early Colonial Societies. *Archaeologies: Journal of the World Archaeological Congress* 7(1):121–153.

———. 2015. Looking for Africans in Seventeenth-Century New Amsterdam. In *The Archaeology of Race in the Northeast*, edited by Christopher N. Matthews and Allison Manfra McGovern, pp. 29–55. Gainesville: University Press of Florida.

Card, Jeb J. (editor). 2013. *The Archaeology of Hybrid Material Culture.* Southern Illinois University Center for Archaeological Investigations Occasional Paper No. 39. Carbondale: Southern Illinois University Press.

Carmiggelt, A., H. van Gangelen, G. Kortekaas, and W. van Zeist. 1987. *Uitgeput Huisraad: Twee Groninger beerputten in historisch-archaeologisch perspectief.* Groningen: Stichting Monument en Materiaal.

Cats, Jacob. 1655. *Invallende gedachten, op voorvallende gelegentheden.* Amsterdam: Jan Jacobsz Schipper.

Catts, Wade P. 2013. "Equaling the Celebrated Rivers of the Amazon": An Historical Archaeological Perspective of the Colonial Settlements of the Delaware River Valley. Keynote speech presented at the annual meeting of the Council for Northeast Historical Archaeology, Wilmington, Delaware.

Catts, Wade P., Jay F. Custer, JoAnn Jamison, Michael D. Scholl and Karen Iplenski. 1995. *Final Archaeological Investigations at the William Strickland Plantation Site (7K-A-117), A Mid-Eighteenth Century Farmstead, State Route 1 Corridor, Kent County, Delaware.* DelDOT Archaeology Series No. 119. Prepared for the Delaware Department of Transportation. Newark: University of Delaware Department of Anthropology, Center for Archaeological Research.

———. 2006. *Thomas Robinson House (7NC-C-11), Brandywine Hundred, New Castle County, Delaware: Archaeological Investigations at the Summer Kitchen, Smokehouse, and East Yard*. Prepared for the Delaware Division of Historical and Cultural Affairs. West Chester, PA: John Milner Associates.

Catts, Wade P., and Timothy Mancl. 2013. "To Keep the Banks, Dams, and Sluices in Repair": An Historical Context for Delaware River Dikes, New Castle County, Delaware. Prepared for New Castle Conservation District and Delaware Department of Natural Resources and Environmental Control. West Chester, PA: John Milner Associates.

Catts, Wade P., and Mark Tobias. 2006. *Report of the Archeological Investigations of the New Castle Court House Plaza (7NC-E-105A), New Castle, Delaware*. Prepared for the Delaware Division of Historical and Cultural Affairs. West Chester, PA: John Milner Associates.

Cavallo, Katherine D. 2004. An Analysis of Marked and Decorated White Clay Tobacco Pipes from the Lower Patuxent Drainage. Manuscript on file, Department of Research, Historic St. Mary's City.

Cederlund, Carl Olof. 2006. *Vasa I: The Archaeology of a Swedish Warship of 1628*. Stockholm: Statens Maritima Museer.

Cheever, Susan. 2015. *Drinking in America: Our Secret History*. New York: Twelve.

Chapman, H. Perry, and Wouter Th Kloek Jr. 1996. *Jan Steen: Painter and Storyteller*. Washington and Amsterdam: National Gallery of Art and Rijksmuseum.

Chenoweth, John M. 2006. "What'll Thou Have": Quakers and the Characterization of Tavern Sites in Colonial Philadelphia. *Northeast Historical Archaeology* 35:77–92.

Christie's. 1996. *Dutch, Flemish and German Old Master Drawings Including Property Sold in Aid of the Museum "Het Rembrandthuis," Amsterdam*. Amsterdam: Christie's.

Clark, Peter. 1983. *The English Alehouse: A Social History, 1200–1830*. London: Longman.

Clevis, Hemmy, and Jaap Kottman (editors). 1989. *Weggegoid en Teruggevonden: Aardewerk en Glas uit Deventer vondstcomplexen, 1375–1750*. Kampen: Stichting Archaeologie Ijssel/Vechtstreek.

Clevis, H., and H. van Gangelen (editors). 2009. Werra Keramiek uit Enkhuizen opnieuw bekeken—*Studies aangeboden aan Jan Thijssen, SPA*. Uitgevers, Zwolle.

Coe, Michael D. 2006. *The Line of Forts: Historical Archaeology on the Colonial Frontier of Massachusetts*. Hanover, NH: University Press of New England.

Cofield, Rod. 2009. Where Did All the Taverns Go? Exploring English Adaptation to the Chesapeake through Drinking Establishments. Paper presented at The Early Chesapeake: Reflections and Projections, Omohundro Institute of Early American History and Culture, Solomons, MD.

Cofield, Rod, and Lisa Holly-Robbins. 2009. Tavern Assemblage? What Tavern Assemblage? Paper presented at the Middle Atlantic Archaeology Conference, Ocean City, MD.

Cohen, David Steven. 1987. Dutch-American Farming: Crops, Livestock and Equipment, 1623–1900. In *New World Dutch Studies: Dutch Arts and Culture in Colonial America*,

1609–1776, edited by Roderic Blackburn and Nancy Kelley, pp. 185–200. Albany: Albany Institute of History and Art.

———. 1992. *The Dutch-American Farm*. New York University Press.

Cohen, Paul. 2008. Was There an Amerindian Atlantic? *Reflections on the Limits of a Historiographical Concept. History of European Ideas* 34(4):388–410.

Coleman, Jon T. 2003. Terms of Dismemberment, Part I of III. *Common-Place: The Interactive Journal of Early American Life*. https://www.common-place-archives.org/vol-04/no-01/coleman/coleman-2.shtml, accessed April 22, 2017.

Commelin, Caspar. 1726. *Beschryvinge van Amsterdam: zynde een naukeurige verhandelinge van desselfs eerste oorspronk uyt den huyse der heeren van Amstel, en Amstellant, haar vergrooting, rykdom, en wyze van regeeringe, tot den jare 1691*. Volume II. Amsterdam: Andries Van Damme, Johannes Ratelband, De Weduwe A. Van Aaltwyk, em Hermanus Uytwerf.

Conroy, David W. 1991. Puritans in Taverns: Law and Popular Culture in Colonial Massachusetts, 1630–1720. In *Drinking: Behavior and Belief in Modern History*, edited by Susanna Barrows and Robin Room, pp. 29–60. Berkeley: University of California Press.

———. 1995. *In Public Houses: Drink and the Revolution of Authority in Colonial Massachusetts*. Institute of Early American History and Culture, Williamsburg. Chapel Hill: University of North Carolina Press.

Cooper, Alexander B. 1905. *Fort Casimir: The Starting Point in the History of New Castle in the State of Delaware, its Location and History, 1651–1671*. Wilmington: Historical Society of Delaware.

Cotter, John. 2002. Losing Your Marbles: Post-medieval Gaming Marbles of Pottery and Stone from Canterbury Excavations. In *Canterbury's Archaeology, 1997–1998*, edited by John Wilson and Jane Elder, pp. 43–48. Canterbury: Canterbury Archaeological Trust.

Courtney, Paul, and Yolanda Courtney. 1992. A Siege Examined: The Civil War Archeology of Leicester. *Post-medieval Archeology* 26:47–90.

Cox, C. Jane. 2002. Shipworth's Addition (1664–1682): Tobacco-Pipes from an Early Quaker Homelot. In *The Clay Tobacco-Pipe in Anne Arundel County, Maryland (1650–1730)*, edited by Al Luckenbach, C. Jane Cox, and John Kille, pp. 66–71. Annapolis: Anne Arundel County Trust for Preservation.

———. 2008. Excavations at Leavy Neck, Providence, Maryland: A Solitary, Poor, Nasty, Brutish, and Short Life. In *Anne Arundel County's Lost Towns Project, Draft Summary*. Report on file, Maryland Historical Trust, Crownsville. Annapolis: Anne Arundel County Trust for Preservation.

Craig, Peter S. 1992. The Search for the Printzhof Governor Printz's Mansion. *Swedish Colonial News* 1(5):2–3.

———. 1999. *1671 Census of the Delaware*. Monograph Series No. 4. Philadelphia: Genealogical Society of Pennsylvania.

Crass, David C. 1988. The Clay Pipes from Green Spring Plantation (44JC9), Virginia. *Historical Archaeology* 22(1):83–97.

Curtenius, Peter T. 1765. Advertisement. *New-York Mercury*, September 30, p. 1.

Custer, Jay F., Keith R. Doms, Adrienne Allegratti, and Kristen Walker. 1998. Preliminary

Report on Excavations at 7NC-E-60, New Castle County, Delaware. *Bulletin of the Archaeological Society of Delaware* 35:3–27.

Dalhede, Christina. 2018. Foreign Merchant in Early Modern Sweden: A Case of Intermarriage, Trade and Migration. In *Facing Otherness in Early Modern Sweden: Travel, Migrations and Material Transformations, 1500–1800*, edited by Magdalena Naum and Frederik Ekengren. Woodbridge, UK: Boydell.

Dallal, Diane. 1996. Van Tienhoven's Basket: Treasure or Trash? In *One Man's Trash Is Another Man's Treasure*, edited by A. G. A. van Dongen, pp. 214–224. Museum Boymans van Beuningen, Rotterdam.

Danckaerts, Jasper. 1913. *Journal of Jasper Danckaerts, 1679–1680*. Edited by Bartlett Burleigh James and J. Franklin Jameson. New York: Charles Scribner's Sons.

Davey, Peter. 1980. *The Archaeology of the Clay Tobacco Pipe, III: Britain, the North and West*. British Archaeological Reports International Series 78. Oxford: BAR Publishing.

———. 1983. *The Archaeology of the Clay Tobacco Pipe VIII: América*. British Archaeological Reports International Series 175. Oxford: BAR Publishing.

Davey, Peter, and Dennis J. Pogue. 1991. *The Archaeology of the Clay Tobacco Pipe XII: Chesapeake Bay*. British Archaeological Reports International Series 566. Oxford: BAR Publishing.

Davis, Natalie Zemon. 1994. Iroquois Women, European Women. In *Women, "Race," and Writing in the Early Modern Period*, edited by Margo Hendricks and Patricia Parker, pp. 243–258. New York: Routledge.

Deagan, Kathleen. 2013. Hybridity, Identity, and Archaeological Practice. In *The Archaeology of Hybrid Material Culture,* Southern Illinois University Center for Archaeological Investigations Occasional Paper No. 39, edited by Jeb B. Card, pp. 260–277. Carbondale: Southern Illinois University Press.

De Cunzo, Lu Ann. 2013. Borderland in the Middle: The Delaware Colony on the Atlantic Coast. In *Scandinavian Colonialism and the Rise of Modernity: Small Time Agents in a Global Arena*, edited by Magdalena Naum and Jonas M. Nordin, pp. 189–208. New York: Springer.

De Cunzo, Lu Ann (editor). 2018. *Unearthing New Castle's Past: Archaeology in the Garden at the Read House and Gardens, New Castle, Delaware*. Draft report on file, Department of Anthropology, University of Delaware, Newark.

Deetz, James F., and Patricia Scott Deetz. 2000. *The Times of Their Lives: Life, Love, and Death in Plymouth Colony*. New York: W. H. Freeman.

DeMello, Ulysses Pernambucano. 1983. Clay Pipes from North-East Brazil. Translated by Elizabeth Weeks. In *The Archaeology of the Clay Tobacco Pipe VIII: America*. British Archaeological Reports International Series 175, edited by Peter Davey, pp. 259–275. Oxford: BAR Publishing.

De Roever, Margriet. 1987. The Fort Orange "EB" Pipe Bowls: An Investigation of the Origin of American Objects in Dutch Seventeenth-Century Documents. In *New World Dutch Studies: Dutch Arts and Culture in Colonial America, 1609–1776*, edited by R. H. Blackburn and N. A. Kelley, pp. 51–61. Albany: Albany Institute of History and Art.

de Sousa, Gabiel Soares. 1587. *Noticia de Brazil* (Sao Paolo). Vol. 2:26.

De Vries, D. 1909 [1655]. Korte Historiael Ended Journaels Aenteyckninge. In *Narratives of New Netherland 1609–1664*, edited by J. Franklin Jameson, pp. 181–234. New York: Charles Scribner's Sons.

de Wit, Abraham de Jonge. 1700. *De Ingebeelde Edelman, Blyspel*. Amsterdam: J. Lescailje, op den Middeldam.

de Wit, M. J. M. 2009. *Hernieuwd onderzoek in vestingstad Oudeschans: Een archeologische begeleiding aan de Tweede Kwartierstraat 4 te Oudeschans, gemeente Bellingwedde (Gr.)*. ARC-Publicaties 184. Groningen: Uitgegeven door ARC bv. http://www.arcbv.nl/publicaties/publicaties/.

Dewulf, Jeroen. 2017. *The Pinkster King and the King of Kongo: The Forgotten History of America's Dutch-Owned Slaves*. Jackson: University Press of Mississippi.

Diamond, Joseph. 2004. *Archaeological Excavations at the Matthewis Person House, Kingston, New York*. Report on file, Department of Buildings and Grounds, County of Ulster, Kingston, NY.

Dillian, Carolyn, Charles Bello, Richard Veit, and Sean McHugh. 2014. Charles Conrad Abbot's Archaeological Investigations at a Seventeenth Century House on Burlington Island, New Jersey. In *Historical Archaeology of the Delaware Valley, 1600–1850*, edited by Richard Viet and David Orr, 49–74. Knoxville: University of Tennessee Press.

DiPaolo Loren, Diana. 2008. *In Contact: Bodies and Spaces in the Sixteenth- and Seventeenth-Century Eastern Woodlands*. Lanham, MD: Altamira.

———. 2012. Fear, Desire, and Material Strategies in Colonial Louisiana. In *The Archaeology of Colonialism. Intimate Encounters and Sexual Effects*, edited by Barbara Voss and Eleanor Casella, pp. 105–121. Cambridge: Cambridge University Press.

———. 2014. Casting Identity: Sumptuous Action and Colonized Bodies in Seventeenth-century New England. In *Rethinking Colonial Pasts through Archaeology*, edited by Neal Ferris, Rodney Harrison, and Michael V. Wilcox, pp. 251–266. Oxford: Oxford University Press.

Doherty, Joan F. 1986. *Hudson County: The Left Bank*. Chatsworth, CA: Windsor.

Donnan, Hastings, and Thomas Wilson. 1999. *Borders: Frontiers of Identity, Nation and State*. Oxford: Berg.

Douglass, L. F. 1841. *Topographical Map of Jersey City, Hoboken, and the Adjacent Country*. Jersey City: L. F. Douglass.

Duco, Don. 2002 [1981]. The Amsterdam pipe maker Eduard Bird, A Review of His Life and Work. *Amsterdam Pipe Museum, Pijpenkabinet Foundation and Amsterdam Pipe Shop*. http://www.pijpenkabinet.nl/Artikelen/Bird/art-E-Bird.html, accessed April 25, 2017.

Dunn, Shirley W. 1992. Interpreting the Little-Known Minuit Maps of c. 1630. *The Hudson Valley Regional Review* 9(2):26–38.

———. 1994. *The Mohicans and Their Land, 1609–1710*. New York: Purple Mountain Press, Fleischmanns.

———. 2009. *The River Indians: Mohicans Making History*. New York: Purple Mountain Press, Fleischmanns.

DuVal, Kathleen. 2006. *The Native Ground: Indians and Colonists in the Heart of the Continent*. Philadelphia: University of Pennsylvania Press.

Eckman, Jeannette. 1951. Life among the Early Dutch at New Castle. *Delaware History* 6(3):246–302.

Egan, Geoff. 1999 [1985]. FRG3: Leaden Cloth Seals. *Datasheet Volume I*. Hereford: The Finds Research Group, 700–1700.

Elzinga, G., and D. Korf. 1978. *Vondsten uit eigen bodem*. Fries Museum Facetten 9. Leeuwarden: Fries Museum.

Emmer, Pieter C. 2014. The Rise and Decline of the Dutch Atlantic, 1600–1800. In *Dutch Atlantic Connections, 1680–1800: Linking Empires, Bridging Borders*, edited by Gert Oostindie and Jessica V. Roitman, pp. 339–356. Leiden: Brill.

Emmer, Pieter C., and Wim Klooster. 1999. The Dutch Atlantic, 1600–1800: Expansion without Empire. *Itinerario* 23(2):48–69.

Endrei, Walter, and Geoff Egan. 1982. The Sealing of Cloth in Europe, with Special Reference to the English Evidence. *Textile History* 13(1):47–75.

Engelbrecht, William. 2003. *Iroquoia: The Development of a Native World*. Syracuse: Syracuse University Press.

Erftemeyer, J., A. P. E. Ruempol, and C. E. M. Woestenburg. 1987. Gebruiksvoorwerpen en citaten. In *Huisraad van een Molenaarsweduwe*, edited by J. R. ter Molen, A. P. E. Ruempol, and A. G. A. van Dongen, pp. 33–51. Rotterdam: Museum Boijmans van Beuningen.

Evans, Thomas Grier (editor). 1901. *Records of the Reformed Dutch Church in New Amsterdam and New York: Baptisms, 1639–1730*. New York: New York Genealogical and Biographical Society.

Everitt, Alan. 1973. The English Urban Inn, 1560–1760. In *Perspectives in English Urban History*, edited by Alan Everitt, pp. 91–137. London: Macmillan.

Fabend, Firth Haring. 2003. Sex and the City: Relations between Men and Women in New Netherland. In *Revisiting New Netherland: Perspectives on Early Dutch America*, edited by Joyce D. Goodfriend, pp. 263–283. Leiden: Brill.

Faulkner, Alaric. 1980. Identifying Clay Pipes from Maine: Some Rules of Thumb. *Bulletin of the Maine Archaeological Society* 20(1):17–49.

———. 1985. Archaeology of the Cod Fishery, Damariscove Island. *Historical Archaeology* 19:57–86.

———. 1989. Gentility on the Frontiers of Acadia, 1635–1674: An Archaeological Perspective. In *New England/New France, 1600–1850*, Dublin Seminar for New England Folklife Proceedings, edited by Peter Benes, pp. 82–100. Boston: Boston University Press.

Faulkner, Alaric, and Gretchen Faulkner. 1987. *The French at Pentagoet, 1634–1674: An Archaeological Portrait of the Acadian Frontier*. Spec. Publications of New Brunswick Museum and Occasional Publications in Maine Archaeology, no. 5. Augusta: Maine Historic Preservation Commission.

Fayden, Meta P. 1993. *Indian Corn and Dutch Pots: Seventeenth Century Foodways in New Amsterdam/New York City*. Doctoral dissertation, Department of Anthropology City University of New York, New York. Ann Arbor: University Microfilms International.

Federal Writers Project. 1938. *The Swedes and Finns in New Jersey*.

Feister, Lois M. 1985. Archaeology in Rensselaerswyck: Dutch Seventeenth Century Domestic Sites. *New Netherlands Studies* 84(2–3):80–88.

Feister, Lois M., and Paul R. Huey. 2012. *The History and Archeology, 1974–1994, of Crailo State Historic Site, Rensselaer, New York*. Division for Historic Preservation, New York State Office of Parks, Recreation and Historic Preservation, Waterford.

Feister, Lois M., and Joseph S. Sopko. 2003. *Archeology at Senate House State Historic Site, Kingston, Ulster County, New York, 1970–1997*. Bureau of Historic Sites, New York State Office of Parks, Recreation and Historic Preservation, Waterford.

Fenton, William N. 1998. *The Great Law and the Longhouse: A Political History of the Iroquois Confederacy*. Norman: University of Oklahoma Press.

Ferguson, Alice L. L. 1941. The Susquehannock Fort on Piscataway Creek. *Maryland Historical Magazine* 36:1–9.

Fernow, Berthold. 1877. *Documents relating to the History of the Dutch and Swedish Settlements on the Delaware River*. Albany: Argus.

Fischer, David Hackett. 2008. *Champlain's Dream: The European Founding of North America* New York: Simon & Schuster.

Fisher, Charles L. 2008. Archaeological Collections from New Netherland at the New York State Museum. In *From De Halve Maen to KLM: 400 Years of Dutch-American Exchange*, edited by Margriet Bruijn Lacy, Charles Gehring, and Jenneke Oosterhoff, pp. 11–23. Munster: Nodus Publikationen.

Fleming, James. 1741. *A Collection of All the Irish and English Statutes Now in Force and Use, Relating to His Majesty's Revenue of Ireland*. Dublin: Philip Crampton.

Foard, Glenn. 2012. *Battlefield Archeology of the English Civil War*. British Archaeological Reports British Series 570. Oxford: BAR Publishing.

Folkerts, Jan. 1991. Kiliaen van Rensselaer and Agricultural Productivity in His Domain: A New Look at the First Patroon and Rensselaerswijck before 1664. In *A Beautiful and Fruitful Place: Selected Rensselaerwijck Seminar Papers*, edited by Nancy Zeller, pp. 295–308. Albany: New Netherland.

Foote, Thelma, 2004. *Black and White Manhattan: The History of Racial Formation in Colonial New York City*. New York: Oxford University Press.

Forster, William A., and Kenneth B. Higgs. 1973. The Kennemerland, 1971: An Interim Report. *International Journal of Nautical Archaeology and Underwater Exploration*. 2(2): 291–300.

Fox, Georgia L. 1999. The Kaolin Clay Tobacco Pipe Collection from Port Royal, Jamaica. In *The Archaeology of the Clay Tobacco Pipe: XV*, British Archaeological Reports International Series 809, edited by Peter Davey. Oxford: BAR Publishing.

Funk, Elisabeth Paling, and Martha Dickinson Shattuck (editors). 2011. *A Beautiful and Fruitful Place. Selected Rensselaerwijck Seminar Papers, Volume 2*. Albany: State University of New York Press.

Funk, R. E., and R. D. Kuhn. 2003. *Three Sixteenth-Century Mohawk Iroquois Village Sites*. New York State Museum Bulletin 503. Albany: New York State Education Department.

Fur, Gunlög. 2006. *Colonialism in the Margins: Cultural Encounters in New Sweden and Lapland*. Leiden: Brill.

———. 2009. *A Nation of Women: Gender and Colonial Encounters among the Delaware Indians*. Philadelphia: University of Pennsylvania Press.

Furlow, David A. 2010. Edward Bird, Jamestown, and the Mid-Seventeenth Century Dutch Tobacco Pipe Trade. Paper presented at the Jamestown Archaeology Conference, Williamsburg, VA.

Ganeau, Étienne, and François Plaignard (editors). 1707. *Memoires pour L'Histoire des Sciences & des Beaux Arts*. Trevoux: De l'Imprimerie de S. A. S.

Gardner, William M., and R. Michael Stewart. 1978. *A Cultural Resources Reconnaissance of Portions of the Middletown-Odessa Regional Sewage System, New Castle County, Delaware*. Report prepared by Thunderbird Research Corporation Front Royal, VA, on file at the Delaware Division of Historical and Cultural Affairs, State Historic Preservation Office, Dover.

Gawronski, Jerzy, and Ranjith Jayasena. 2008 [2003]. *Serviesgoed uit een 18de-eeuwse beerput: archeologische opgraving Derde Weteringdwarsstraat*. Amsterdamse Archeologische Rapporten 28. Bureau Monumenten & Archeologie, Gemeente Amsterdam, Amsterdam.

———. 2011 [2008]. *Wonen achter de Oudezijds Voorburgwal: archeologische opgraving Oudezijds Armsteeg, Amsterdam*. Amsterdamse Archeologische Rapporten 60. Bureau Monumenten & Archeologie, Gemeente Amsterdam, Amsterdam.

———. 2013 [2006]. *Een beerput van welgestelden in de Amsterdamse grachtengordel, 1675–1750: Archeologische Opgraving Herengracht 12, Amsterdam*. Amsterdamse Archeologische Rapporten 71. Amsterdam: Bureau Monumenten and Archeologie.

Gawronski, Jerzy, Ranjith Jayasena, and S. IJzerman. 2016. De Gelaagde Stad Onder het Waterlooplein. *Jaarboek Amstelodamum* 103(1):38–47.

Gawronski, Jerzy, Ranjith Jayasena, and Jørgen Veerkamp. 2010 [2005]. *Van Amstelbocht tot Binnengasthuis: Archeologische Opgraving Oude Turfmarkt, Amsterdam*. Amsterdamse Archeologische Rapporten 31. Amsterdam: Bureau Monumenten and Archeologie, Gemeente Amsterdam.

———. 2012 [2010]. *"Ons Genoegen": archeologische opgraving, Elandsstraat 101, Amsterdam*. Amsterdamse Archeologische Rapporten 67. Amsterdam: Bureau Monumenten and Archeologie, Gemeente Amsterdam.

Gawronski, Jerzy (editor). 2012. *Amsterdam Ceramics: A City's History and an Archaeological Ceramics Catalogue, 1175–2011*. Amsterdam: Uitgeverij Bas Lubberhuizen/Bureau Monumenten and Archeologie.

Gehring, Charles T. 1992. De Suyt Rivier: New Netherland's Delaware Frontier. In *de Halve Maen* 65(2):21–25.

Gehring, Charles T. (editor). 1977. *Delaware Papers (English Period): A Collection of Documents Pertaining to the Regulation of Affairs on the Delaware, 1664–1682*. New York Historical Manuscripts Series. Baltimore: Genealogical Publishing Company.

Gehring, Charles T. (editor and translator). 1980. *Land Papers, 1630–1664*. New York Historical Manuscripts Series. Baltimore: Genealogical Publishing Company.

———. 1981. *Delaware Papers (Dutch Period): A Collection of Documents Pertaining to the Regulation of Affairs on the South River of New Netherland, 1648–1664*. New York Historical Manuscripts Series. Baltimore: Genealogical Publishing Company.

———. 1983. *Council Minutes, 1652–1654*. New York Historical Manuscripts Series. Baltimore: Genealogical Publishing Company.

———. 1991. *Laws and Writs of Appeal, 1647–1663*. New Netherland Documents Series. Syracuse: Syracuse University Press.

———. 1995. *Council Minutes, 1655–1656*. New Netherland Documents Series. Syracuse: Syracuse University Press.

———. 2000. *Correspondence, 1647–1653*. New Netherland Documents Series. Syracuse: Syracuse University Press.

———. 2003. *Correspondence, 1654–1658*. New Netherland Documents Series. Syracuse: Syracuse University Press.

Gehring, Charles T., and William A. Starna (editors). 2008. *A Description of New Netherland. Adriaen van der Donck 1655*. Translated by Willem Goedhuys. Lincoln: University of Nebraska Press.

———. 2013. A Journey into Mohawk and Oneida Country, 1634–1635: The Journal of Harmen Meyndertsz van den Bogaert. Revised ed. Syracuse: Syracuse University Press.

Geismar, Joan. 1983. *The Archaeological Investigation of the 175 Water Street Block, New York City*. Report prepared for HRO International, New York, prepared by Professional Services Industries, Soil Systems Division, Marietta, GA, on file, New York City Landmarks Preservation Commission.

George, Diane F., Bernice Kurshin, and Kelly M. Britt. 2019. O Brave New World: A Look at Identity and Dissonance. In *Archaeology of Identity and Dissonance: Contexts for a Brave New World*, edited by Diane F. George and Bernice Kurshin, pp. 1–18.Gainesville: University Press of Florida.

Gerritsen, Anne, and Giorgio Riello. 2015. Introduction: The Global Lives of Things, Material Culture in the First Global Age. In *The Global Live of Things: The Material Culture of Connections in the Early Modern World*, edited by Anne Gerritsen and Giorgio Riello, pp. 1–28. London: Routledge.

Gilbert, Allan, and Meta F. Janowitz. 1990. Chemical Analysis of New World and Old World Redware Pastes. Paper presented at the annual meeting of the Council for Northeast Historical Archaeology, Kingston, ON.

Goddard, Ives. 1978. Delaware. In *Handbook of North American Indians: Vol. 15, Northeast*, edited by Bruce Trigger, pp. 213–239. Washington: Smithsonian Institution.

Greenfield, Haskell J. 1989. From Pork to Mutton: A Zooarchaeological Perspective on Colonial New Amsterdam and Early New York City. *Northeast Historical Archaeology* 18:85–110.

Grinnell, George Bird. 1892. *Blackfoot Lodge Tales the Story of a Prairie People*. New York: Charles Scribner's Sons.

Groeneweg, Gerrit C. 1982. *Opgravingen in Steenbergen: Verslag van het Archaeologisch onderzoek naar het voormalige Gasthuis van Steenbergen*. Bijdragen tot der Studie van het Brabantse Heem, 21. Eindhoven, the Netherlands.

Gosden, Chris. 2004. *Archaeology and Colonialism: Cultural Contact from 5000 B.C. to the Present*. Cambridge: Cambridge University Press.

Greene, Jack P. 2007. Colonial History and National History: Reflections on a Continuing Problem. *William and Mary Quarterly* 64(2): 235–250.

Grossman, Joel. 1985. *The Excavation of Augustine Heerman's Warehouse and Associated Seventeenth Century Dutch West India Company Deposits.* Report prepared for Fox & Fowle P.C., HRO International, and New York City Landmarks Preservation Commission, on file, New York City Landmarks Preservation Commission.

———. 2009. *Dutch Ethnobotany and Medicinal Plants in Seventeenth Century New Amsterdam.* Paper presented at the New York Botanical Garden.

———. 2011. Archaeological Indices of Environmental Change and Colonial Ethnobotany in Seventeenth-Century Dutch New Amsterdam. In *Environmental History of the Hudson River: Human Uses that Changed the Ecology, Ecology that Changed Human Uses*, edited by Robert E. Henshaw, pp. 77–122. Albany: State University of New York Press.

Grumet, Robert. 1980. Sunksquaws, Shamans, and Tradeswomen: Middle Atlantic Women during the Seventeenth and Eighteenth Centuries. In *Women and Colonization: Anthropological Perspectives*, edited by Mona Eienne and Eleanor Leacock, pp. 43–62. New York: Praeger.

———. 1995. *Historic Contact: Indian People and Colonists in Today's Northeastern United States in the Sixteenth through Eighteenth Centuries.* Norman: University of Oklahoma Press.

———. 2014. *The Munsee Indians: A History.* Norman: University of Oklahoma Press.

Guilday, J. E. 1971. *Biological and Archaeological Analysis of Bones from a Seventeenth Century Indian Village (46-Pu-31) West Virginia.* Report of Archaeological Investigations, No. 4. Morgantown: West Virginia Geological and Economic Survey.

Hacquebord, Louwrens, and Wim Vroom (editors). 1988. *Walvisvaart in de Gouden Eeuw: Opgravingen op Spitsbergen.* Amsterdam: De Bataafsche Leeuw.

Haefeli, Evan. 2007. On First Contact and Apotheosis: Manitou and Men in North America. In *Ethnohistory* 54(3):407–443.

Hall, Jerome Lynn. 1996. A Seventeenth Century Northern European Shipwreck in Monte Christi Bay, Dominican Republic. Ph.D. Dissertation, Texas A & M University. https://nautarch.tamu.edu/Theses/pdf- files/Hall-PhD199 6.pdf, accessed April 10, 2021.

Hamaker, H. G. (editor). 1873. *De Middeneeuwsche Keurboekken van de Stad Leiden.* Leiden: S.C. van Doesburgh.

Harrington, J. C. 2006a. Tobacco Pipes from Jamestown. In *Pots, Pipes, and Trash Pits: Volume I of the Jamestown Trilogy Series*, edited by Edward Bottoms and Cynthia S. Hansen, pp. 29–35. Chesapeake, VA: Archaeological Society of Virginia.

———. 2006b. Dating Stem Fragments of Seventeenth and Eighteenth Century Clay Tobacco Pipes. In *Pots, Pipes, and Trash Pits: Volume I of the Jamestown Trilogy Series*, edited by Edward Bottoms and Cynthia S. Hansen, pp. 36–40. Chesapeake, VA: Archaeological Society of Virginia.

Harrington, Peter. 2004. *English Civil War Archeology.* London: BT Batsford.

Hartgen Archeological Associates, Inc. 2002. *At the River's Edge: Two-Hundred-Fifty*

Years of Albany History. Volume II, Data Retrieval, SUCF Parking Structure, Maiden Lane, Albany, New York. Hartgen Archeological Associates, Inc., Rensselaer, NY.

———. 2005. *Beyond the North Gate, Archeology on the Outskirts of Colonial Albany.* Report prepared for the Albany Parking Authority. On file, New York State Historic Preservation Office, Albany.

Hatfield, April Lee. 2004. *Atlantic Virginia: Intercolonial Relations in the Seventeenth Century.* Philadelphia: University of Pennsylvania Press.

Havard, Gilles. 2003. *Empire et Metissages: Indiens et Francais dans le Pays d'en Haut, 1660–1715.* Quebec: Septentrion and Paris: Presses de l'Universite de Paris-Sorbonne.

Haynes, E. Barrington. 1964. *Glass through the Ages.* Baltimore: Penguin.

Heckewelder, John. 1819. *An Account of the History, Manners, and Customs of the Indian Nations who Once Inhabited Pennsylvania and the Neighboring States.* Philadelphia: Historical Society of Pennsylvania.

Hefting, Oscar F. 2010. High versus Low: Portuguese and Dutch Fortification Traditions meet in Colonial Brazil (1500–1654). In *First Forts. Essays on the Archaeology of Proto-Colonial Fortifications*, edited by Eric Klingelhofer, pp. 189–208. Leiden: Brill.

Heidtke, K. P. 1992. *Jamaican Red-Clay Tobacco Pipes.* Doctoral dissertation, Anthropology Department, Texas A&M University. Ann Arbor: University Microfilms International.

Heite, Edward F. 2006. American-Made Pipes from the Camden Site. In *Pots, Pipes, and Trash: Volume I of the Jamestown Trilogy Series*, edited by Edward Bottoms and Cynthia S. Hansen, pp. 53–60. Chesapeake: Archaeological Society of Virginia.

Heite, Edward F., and Louise B. Heite. 1986. *Fort Elfsborg, 1643: A Background Study of the Fort Elsinboro Point or Fort Elfsborg, Elsinboro Township, Salem County, New Jersey and New Castle County, Delaware.* Report prepared for Philadelphia District, Corps of Engineers, on file at the Delaware Division of Historical and Cultural Affairs, State Historic Preservation Office, Dover.

———. 1989. Report of the Phase I Archaeological and Historical Investigations at the Site of Fort Casimir, New Castle, Delaware. *Bulletin of the Archaeological Society of Delaware* 25:1–54.

Heite, Louise. 1972. *Appoquinimink: A Delaware Frontier Village.* Manuscript on file at Winterthur Library, Winterthur, Delaware.

———. 1978. *New Castle under the Duke of York: A Stable Community.* Master's thesis, History Department, University of Delaware.

Hertzberg, Hazel. 1966. *The Great Tree and the Longhouse: The Culture of the Longhouse.* New York: Macmillan.

Heye, George G., and George H. Pepper. 1915. *Exploration of a Munsee Cemetery near Montague, New Jersey.* New York: Museum of the American Indian.

Hinderaker, Eric, and Rebecca Horn. 2010. Territorial Crossings: Histories and Historiographies of the Early Americas. *William and Mary Quarterly* 67(3):395–432.

Hochstrasser, Julie Berger. 2007. *Still Life and Trade in the Dutch Golden Age.* New Haven: Yale University Press.

Hodges, Graham Russell. 1999. *Root & Branch: African Americans in New York & East Jersey.* Chapel Hill: University of North Carolina Press.

Hoff, Henry B. 2010. The First Settlers of New York. *American Ancestors* 11(1):28–29, 39.

Hoffecker, Carol E., Richard Waldron, Lorraine E. Williams, and Barbara E. Benson. (editors). 1995. *New Sweden in America*. Newark: University of Delaware Press.

Holm, Thomas Campanius. 1834. *A Short Description of the Province of New Sweden. Now called by the English Pennsylvania in America, 1702*. Translated by Peter S. Du Ponceau. Philadelphia: Historical Society of Pennsylvania.

Hopkins, Griffith Morgan, Jr. 1861. *Map of the Counties of Bergen and Passaic, New Jersey: From Actual Surveys*. Philadelphia: G. H. Corey.

Hordon, Robert M. 2004. Minisink Valley. In *Encyclopedia of New Jersey*, edited by Maxine Lurie and Marc Mappen, p. 525. New Brunswick: Rutgers University Press.

Horsmanden, Daniel. 1971. *The New York Conspiracy*. Edited by Thomas J. Davis. Boston: Beacon Press.

Houghton, John. 1727. *Husbandry and Trade Improv'd: Being a Collection of Many Valuable Materials Relating to Corn, Cattle, Coals, Hops, Wool, &c. Volume II*. London: Printed for Woodman and Lyon.

Huey, Lois Miner. 2010. *American Archaeology Uncovers the Dutch Colonies*. New York: Marshall Cavendish.

Huey, Paul R. 1974. *Archeology at the Schuyler Flatts: 1971–1974*. Report prepared for the Town of Colonie, NY, on file at the New York State Historic Preservation Office, Albany.

———. 1984. Dutch Sites of the Seventeenth Century in Rensselaerswyck. In *The Scope of Historical Archaeology: Essays in Honor of John L. Cotter*, edited by David G. Orr and Daniel G. Crozier, pp. 63–85. Philadelphia: Laboratory of Anthropology, Temple University.

———. 1987. Archaeological Evidence of Dutch Wooden Cellars and Perishable Wooden Structures at Seventeenth and Eighteenth Century Sites in the Upper Hudson Valley. In *New World Dutch Studies: Dutch Arts and Culture in Colonial America, 1609–1776*, edited by Roderic H. Blackburn and Nancy A. Kelly, pp. 185–200. Albany: Albany Institute of History & Art.

———. 1988a. *Aspects of Continuity and Change in Colonial Dutch Material Culture at Fort Orange, 1624–1664*. Doctoral dissertation, Department of American Civilization, University of Pennsylvania, Philadelphia. University Microfilms International, Ann Arbor.

———. 1988b. The Archaeology of Colonial New Netherland. In *Colonial Dutch Studies: An Interdisciplinary Approach*, edited by Eric Nooter and Patricia Bunomi, pp. 52–77. New York: New York University Press.

———. 1991. The Archeology of Fort Orange and Beverwijck. In *A Beautiful and Fruitful Place: Selected Rensselaerwijck Seminar Papers*, edited by Nancy Anne McClure Zeller, pp. 327–49. Albany: New Netherlands.

———. 2003. Thirty Years of Historical Archaeological in the City of Albany. In *People, Places and Material Things: Historical Archaeology of Albany*, pp. 11–22. Albany: New York State Museum and University of State of New York.

———. 2005. The Archaeology of 17th-Century New Netherland Since 1985: An Update. *Northeast Historical Archaeology* 34:95–118.

———. 2008. From Bird to Tippett: The Archaeology of Continuity and Change in Colonial Dutch Material Culture after 1664. In *From De Halve Maen to KLM: 400 Years of Dutch-American Exchange*, edited by Margriet Bruijn Lacy, Charles Gehring, and Jenneke Oosterhoff, pp. 41–56. American Association of Netherlandish Studies. Munster: Nodus Publikationen.

———. 2010. Dutch Colonial Forts in New Netherland. In *First Forts: Essays on the Archaeology of Proto-Colonial Fortifications*, edited by Eric Klinghofer. Brill: Boston.

Hunter, Douglas. 2009. *Half Moon: Henry Hudson and the Voyage that Redrew the Map of the World*. New York: Bloomsbury.

Hunter, Richard, and Ian Burrow. 2014. Historical Archaeology in Trenton: A Thirty-Year Retrospective. In *Historical Archaeology of the Delaware Valley, 1600–1850*, edited by Richard Viet and David Orr, pp. 323–73. Knoxville: University of Tennessee Press.

Hunter, Robert. 2006. *Ceramics in America*. Hanover, NH: University Press of New England.

Hunter Research, Inc. 2004. *Preliminary Archaeological Investigations at the Apple Tree House/Van Wagenen House, Academy Street, Jersey City, New Jersey*. Report on file, New Jersey Historic Preservation Office, Trenton.

———. 2011. *Delaware Department of Transportation U.S. Route 301, Section 1 (Purple) St. Georges Hundred, New Castle County, Delaware. Reedy Island Cart Road Site 4 (7NC-F-153, N14533) and a Portion of Adjacent Survey Area A&HC 5, Management Summary*. Report prepared for the Delaware Department of Transportation, on file, Delaware Division of Historical and Cultural Affairs, State Historic Preservation Office, Dover.

———. 2012. *The Apple Tree/Van Wagenen House, 298 Academy Street, Bergen Square, City of Jersey City, Hudson County, New Jersey: Archaeological Investigations (2006–2010), ADA Ramp, Porch Construction, and Interior and Exterior Restoration*. Report on file, New Jersey Historic Preservation Office, Trenton.

———. 2013a. *Delaware Department of Transportation U.S. Route 301, Section 2 (Yellow) St. Georges Hundred, New Castle County, Delaware. Elkins A and B (7NC-G-174) End of Fieldwork Summary Phase III Data Recovery*. Report prepared for the Delaware Department of Transportation, on file, Delaware Division of Historical and Cultural Affairs, State Historic Preservation Office, Dover.

———. 2013b. *Historical Background Research Report for Paulus Hook Park Renovation Project, Washington and Grand Streets, Jersey City, Hudson County, New Jersey*. Report prepared for Historic Paulus Hook Association Jersey City, New Jersey and Clarke Caton and Hintz, Trenton, New Jersey, on file, New Jersey Historic Preservation Office, Trenton.

———. 2015. *End-of-Fieldwork Letter Report, Archaeological Monitoring and Phase I Archaeological Testing, Proposed Site Plan Improvements, Van Wagenen/Apple Tree House, 298 Academy Street, Jersey City, New Jersey*. Report on file, New Jersey Historic Preservation Office, Trenton.

———. 2017. *Archaeological Investigations 2015–16: Van Wagenen/Apple Tree House, City of Jersey City, Hudson County, New Jersey*. Report on file, New Jersey Historic Preservation Office, Trenton.

Hurry, Silas D., and Robert W. Keeler. 1991. A Descriptive Analysis of the White Clay Tobacco Pipes from the St. John's Site in St. Mary's City, Maryland. In *The Archaeology of the Clay Tobacco Pipe XII: Chesapeake Bay,* British Archaeological Reports International Series 566, edited by Peter Davey and Dennis J. Pogue, pp. 37–71. Oxford: BAR Publishing.

Hurst, John G., David S. Neal, and H. J. E. van Beuningen. 1986. *Pottery Produced and Traded in North-West Europe 1350–1650.* Rotterdam Papers VI. Rotterdam: Museum Boymans van Beuningen, Stichting Het Nederlands Gerbruiksvoorwerp.

Israel, Jonathan I. 1989. *Dutch Primacy in World Trade, 1585–1740.* Oxford: Clarendon Press.

Jacobs, Jaap. 2005. *New Netherland: A Dutch Colony in Seventeenth-Century America.* Leiden: Brill.

———. 2009. *The Colony of New Netherland: A Dutch Settlement in Seventeenth-Century America.* Ithaca: Cornell University Press.

———. 2015. *Atlas of Dutch North America, Dutch Colonial Fortifications in North America, 1614–1676.* New Holland Foundation, Amsterdam. http://www.newholland-foundation.nl/wp-content/uploads/2015/11/PDF-Dutch-Colonial-Fortifications-in-North-America.pdf, accessed September 24, 2017.

Jameson, J. Franklin (editor). 1909. *Narratives of New Netherland, 1609–1664.* New York: Charles Scribner's Sons.

Janowitz, Meta F. 1993. Indian Corn and Dutch Pots: Seventeenth-Century Foodways in New Amsterdam/New York. *Historical Archaeology* 27(2):6–24.

———. 2013. Decline in the Use and Production of Red-Earthenware Cooking Vessels in the Northeast, 1780–1880. *Northeast Historical Archaeology* 42:92–110.

Janowitz, Meta, Kate T. Morgan, and Nan A. Rothschild. 1985. Cultural Pluralism and Pots in New Amsterdam–New York City. In *Domestic Pottery of the Northeastern United States 1625–1850,* edited by Sarah P. Turnbaugh, pp. 29–48. New York: Academic Press.

Jayasena, Ranjith M. 2011. "Revolutionary War and an Amsterdam Privy: The Remarkable Background of a Rhode Island Ship Token." *Northeast Historical Archaeology* 30:123–130.

———. 2017. Email, Bureau Monumenten and Archeologie, Amsterdam, September 19.

Jefferson Patterson Park and Museum. 2018. Compton 18CV279. *Archaeological Collections in Maryland.* https://www.jefpat.org/NEHWeb/18CV279-%20Compton%20Final%20Finding%20Aid.aspx, accessed June 12, 2018.

Jennings, Paul. 2007. *The Local: A History of the English Pub.* Stroud: Tempus.

Jockin-la Bastide, J. A., and G. van Kooten. 1980. *Cassell's Dutch Dictionary: English-Dutch Dutch-English Dictionary.* New York: Macmillan.

Jogues, Isaac. 1909. Letter and Narrative of Father Isaac Jogues, 1643, 1645. In *Narratives of New Netherland 1609–1664,* edited by J. Franklin Jameson, pp. 235–54. New York: Charles Scribner's Sons.

Johnson, Amandus. 1911. *The Swedish Settlements on the Delaware, 1638–1664.* Philadelphia: Swedish Colonial Society.

———. 1930. *The Instruction for Johan Printz, Governor of New Sweden.* Philadelphia: Swedish Colonial Society.

Johnson, Laura E. 2005. *"This Area Has Always Been a Trading Place": The South River in the Dutch Atlantic World, 1626–1644.* Manuscript on file, Department of Anthropology, University of Delaware, Newark.

Jordan, Kurt. 2016. Categories in Motion: Emerging Perspectives in the Archaeology of Postcolumbian Indigenous Communities. *Historical Archaeology* 50(3):62–80.

Kaijser, Ingrid, Ernst Nathorst-Böös, and Inga-Lill Persson. 1982. *Ur sjömannens kista och tunna: Personliga tillhörigheter på Wasa.* Stockholm: Sjöhistoriska Museet/Maritime History Museum.

Kalb, K. R., J. Kopleck, D. Fimbel, and I. J. Sypko. 1982. An Urban Ferry Tale. *Bulletin of the Archaeological Society of New Jersey* 38:119.

Kent, Barry C. 2001. *Susquehanna's Indians.* Revised ed. Harrisburg: Pennsylvania Historical and Museum Commission.

Ketchum, William C. 1987. *Potters and Pottery of New York State, 1650–1900.* Syracuse: Syracuse University Press.

Kicken, D., A. M. Koldeweij, J. R. ter Molen (editors). 2000. *Gevonden voorwerpen: Opstellen over middeleeuwse archeologie voor H.J.E. van Beuningen.* Commissie van Advies inzake Archeologisch Onderzoek binnen het Ressort Rotterdam, Rotterdam Papers 11. Rotterdam, the Netherlands.

King, Julia. 1988. A Comparative Midden Analysis of a Household and Inn in St. Mary's City, Maryland. *Historical Archaeology* 22(2):17–39.

King, Robert E., and Mary Hancock. 1970. *A Feasibility Study for Possible Future Excavations in Search of Governor Johan Printz's Settlement on Tinicum Island.* Report on file, the University Museum of Archaeology and Anthropology, University of Pennsylvania.

Kleyn, Jan de. 1965. *Volksaardewerk in Nederland 1600–1900.* W. de Haan N. V., Zeist, the Netherlands.

Klooster, Wim. 2016. *The Dutch Moment: War, Trade, and Settlement in the Seventeenth-Century Atlantic World.* Ithaca: Cornell University Press.

Koot, Christian, J. 2018. *A Biography of a Map in Motion: Augustine Herrman's Chesapeake.* New York University Press, New York.

Kraft, Herbert C. 1996. *The Dutch, the Indians & the Quest for Copper: Pahaquarry & the Old Mine Road.* West Orange, NJ: Seton Hall University Museum.

———. 2001. *The Lenape-Delaware Indian Heritage, 10,000 BC to AD 2000.* Union, NJ: Lenape Books.

Kross, Jessica. 1997. "If You Will Not Drink with Me, You Must Fight with Me": The Sociology of Drinking in the Middle Colonies. *Pennsylvania History* 64(1):28–55.

Kuhn, Charles L. 1965. *German and Netherlandish Sculpture, 1280–1800: The Harvard Collections.* Cambridge: Harvard University Press.

Kuijpers, E. 2005. *Migrantenstad: Immigratie en sociale verhoudingen in 17e-eeuws Amsterdam.* Uitgeverij Verloren, Hilversum.

Kukk, Inge. 2006. The Painting Collection. In *Dorpat–Yuryev–Tartu and Voronezh: the*

Fate of the University Collection, edited by Urmas Tönisson, pp. 264–363. Tartu, Estonia: Ilmamaa.

Kümin, Beat. 2002. Public Houses and Their Patrons in Early Modern Europe. In *The World of the Tavern: Public Houses in Early Modern Europe*, edited by Beat Kümin and B. Ann Tlusty editors, pp. 44–62. Burlington: Ashgate.

Kümin, Beat, and B. Ann Tlusty. 2002. The World of the Tavern: An Introduction. In *The World of the Tavern: Public Houses in Early Modern Europe*, edited by Beat Kümin and B. Ann Tlusty, pp. 1–11. London: Routledge.

Kuznetsov, Yury, and Irene Linnk. 1982. *Dutch Paintings in Soviet Museums*. New York: Harry N. Abrams.

Lacy, Margriet (editor). 2013. *A Beautiful and Fruitful Place: Selected Rensselaerwijck Seminar Papers, Volume 3*. Albany: New Netherlands Institute.

Largy, T. B., L. Lavin, M. E. Mozzi, and K. Furgerson. 1999. Corncobs and Buttercups: Plant Remains from the Goldkrest Site. In *Current Northeast Paleoethnobotany*, New York State Museum Bulletin 494, edited by J. P. Hart, pp. 69–84. Albany: University of the State of New York Press.

Lavin, Lucianne. 2004. Mohican/Algonquian Settlement Patterns: An Archaeological Perspective. In *Mohican Seminar 1: The Continuance—An Algonquian Peoples Seminar, Selected Research Papers, 2000*, edited by S. W. Dunn, pp. 19–28. New York State Museum Bulletin 501. Albany: University of the State of New York.

Leach, Peter, Wade P. Catts, and Craig Lukezic. 2014. *"The Starting Point in the Historic of New Castle": Geophysics and the Exploratory Archaeology at the site of Fort Casimir (7NC-E-105E), City of New Castle, Delaware*. Report prepared for and on file at the Delaware Division of Historical and Cultural Affairs, State Historic Preservation Office, Dover.

Leiby, Adrian C. 1964. *The Early Dutch and Swedish Settlers of New Jersey*. New Jersey Historical Series 10. Trenton: New Jersey Historical Commission.

Levie T. 1987. Marranen in de zeventiende eeuw. In *Exodo–Portugezen in Amsterdam 1600–1680*, edited by R. Kistemaker and T. Levie, pp. 7–17. Amsterdam: Amsterdams Historische Museum / Bataafse Leeuw, Amsterdam.

Li, Xiaoxiong. 1992. *Liquor and Ordinaries in Seventeenth Century Maryland*. Doctoral dissertation, History Department, Johns Hopkins University. Ann Arbor: University Microfilms International.

Liebmann, Matthew. 2013. Parsing Hybridity: Archaeologist of Amalgamation in Seventeenth-Century New Mexico. In *The Archaeology of Hybrid Material Culture*, Southern Illinois University Center for Archaeological Investigations Occasional Paper No. 39, edited by Jeb B. Card, pp. 25–49. Carbondale: Southern Illinois University Press.

Lightfoot, Kent G. 2004. The Archaeology of Colonization: California in Cross-Cultural Perspective. In *The Archaeology of Colonial Encounters*, edited by Gil Stein, pp. 207–236. Santa Fe: School of American Research.

Lindeström, Peter. 1925. *Geographia Americae with an Account of the Delaware Indians*. Edited and translated by Amandus Johnson. Philadelphia: Swedish Colonial Society.

Linn, John B., and William H. Egle. 1880. *Papers Relating to the Colonies on the Dela-*

ware, 1614–1682. Harrisburg, PA: Penn. Archives, 2nd Ser., E. K. Meyers. Volume 5:808–809.

Linnet, Jakob. 2009. Denmark. In *Problem Gambling in Europe: Challenges, Prevention, and Interventions,* edited by Gerhard Meyer, Tobias Hayer, and Mark Griffiths, pp. 17–35. New York: Springer Science + Business Media.

Lionel Pincus and Princess Firyal Map Division, New York Public Library. 1844. Map of New-York Bay and Harbor and the Environs. New York Public Library Digital Collections. http://digitalcollections.nypl.org/items/510d47da-efca-a3d9-e040-e00a18064a99, accessed December 31, 2019.

Lipman, Andrew. 2015. *The Saltwater Frontier: Indians and Contest for the American Coast.* New Haven: Yale University Press.

Llorens Planella, M. T. (Teresa Paneca). 2015. *Silk, Porcelain and Lacquer: China and Japan and Their Trade with Western Europe and the New World, 1500–1644, A Survey of Documentary and Material Evidence.* Doctoral thesis, Centre for the Arts in Society, Faculty of Humanities, Leiden University.

Louis Berger and Associates. 1987. *Druggists, Craftsmen, and Merchants of Pearl and Water Streets, New York: The Barclays Bank Site.* Report prepared for London and Leeds Corporation and Barclays Bank PLC, New York, on file, New York City Landmarks Preservation Commission.

———. 1989. *The Compton Site, circa 1651–1684, Calvert County, Maryland, 18CV279.* Report prepared for CRJ Associates, Inc., Camp Springs, MD, on file, Jefferson Patterson Park and Museum.

———. 1990. *The Assay Site: Historical and Archaeological Investigations of the New York City Waterfront.* Report prepared for HRO International, Ltd., New York, NY, on file, New York City Landmarks Preservation Commission.

Lucas, Michael T. 2016. "To Our Inn We March'd Away": Public Contexts for Consuming Alcohol and Tobacco in a Small Chesapeake Town, 1690–1720. *Journal of Middle Atlantic Archaeology* 32:93–115.

Luckenbach, Al, C. Jane Cox, and John Kille. 2002. *The Clay Tobacco-Pipe in Anne Arundel County, Maryland (1650–1730).* Annapolis: Anne Arundel County Trust for Preservation.

Luckenbach, Al, and Taft Kiser. 2006. Seventeenth Century Tobacco Pipe Manufacturing in the Chesapeake Region: A Preliminary Delineation of Makers and Their Styles. *Ceramics in America,* edited by Robert Hunter. http://www.chipstone.org/article.php/294/Ceramics-in-America-2006/Seventeenth-Century-Tobacco-Pipe-Manufacturing-in-the-Chesapeake-Region:-A-Preliminary-Delineation-of-Makers-and-Their-Styles, accessed December 12, 2019.

Lugones, Maria. 2010. Toward a Decolonial Feminism. *Hypatia* 25(4):742–759.

Lukezic, Craig. 2017. Archaeological Investigation at Fort Casimir in New Castle. *De Halve Maen* 90:55–62.

Lukezic, Craig, Wade P. Catts, and Peter Leach. 2016. Update of Fort Casimir/Trinity. Paper presented at the annual New Netherland Institute Conference, New Brunswick, NJ.

MAAR Associates. 1991. *Historical Documentation & Archaeological Investigations Con-*

ducted at Governor Printz Park Essington, Delaware County, Pennsylvania. Report prepared for and on file at the American Swedish Historical Museum, Philadelphia, and the Pennsylvania Historical and Museum Commission, Harrisburg.

McCarthy, Michael R., and Catherine M. Brooks. 1988. *Medieval Pottery in Britain AD 900–1600*. Leicester: Leicester University Press.

McCashion, John H. 1979. A Preliminary Chronology and Discussion of Seventeenth and Early Eighteenth Century Clay Tobacco Pipes from New York State Sites. In *The Archaeology of the Clay Tobacco Pipe, II: The United States of America*, British Archaeological Reports International Series 60, edited by Peter Davey, pp. 63–149. Oxford: BAR Publishing.

McCashion, John H., and T. Robinson. 1977. The Clay Tobacco Pipes of New York under the Sidewalks of New York: Archaeological Investigations near the U.S. Customs House on Manhattan Island, New York. *Bulletin of New York State Archaeological Association* 71:2–19.

McDaid, Christopher L. 2013. *"The Best Accustomed House in Town": Taverns as a Reflection of Elite Consumer Behavior in Eighteenth Century Hampton and Elizabeth City County, Virginia*. Doctoral dissertation, Archaeology Department, University of Leicester.

McKinley, Albert E. 1900. The English and Dutch Towns of New Netherland. *American Historical Review* 6(1):1–18.

McMahon, Reginald. 1969. Vriessendael: A Note. *New Jersey History* 87(3):173–180.

———. 1971. The Achter Col Colony on the Hackensack. *New Jersey History* 89(4):221–240.

McMillian, Lauren K. 2015. *Community Formation and the Development of a British-Atlantic Identity in the Chesapeake: An Archaeological and Historical Study of the Tobacco Pipe Trade in the Potomac River Valley ca. 1630–1730*. Doctoral dissertation, University of Tennessee, 2015.

McNulty, Robert H. 1971. Common Beverage Bottles: Their Production, Use, and Forms in Seventeenth and Eighteenth-Century Netherlands: Part I. *Journal of Glass Studies* 13:91–119.

———. 2004. *Dutch Glass Bottles of the Seventeenth and Eighteenth Centuries: A Collectors Guide*. Bethesda, MD: Medici Workshop.

Maghrak, Theodore M. 2013. *The Huguenot Home: Consumption Practices and Identity in Early Eighteenth-Century New York City*. Master's thesis, Anthropology Department, University of Massachusetts, Boston.

Magnusson, Brian B. 2003. Classical Elements in Early Scandinavian-American Architecture. Some Initial Impressions. In *The Problem of Classical Idea in the Art and Architecture of the Countries around the Baltic Sea*, edited by Krista Kodres, Piret Lindpere, and Eva Näripea, pp. 222–248. Tallin, Estonia: Eesta Kunstiakadeemia.

Maika, Dennis J., Mark Meuwese, Anfra C. Mosterman, Susanah Rommy, D. L. Noorlander, Anne-Marie Cantwell, and Diana d-Zerega Wall. 2014. Roundtable: The Past, Present, and Future of New Netherland Studies. *New York History* 95(3):446–490.

Mancl, Timothy, Elizabeth LaVigne, Peter Leach, William Chadwick, and Wade P. Catts. 2014. *Phase I Archaeological Survey of the Broad Marsh Dike, New Castle County,*

Delaware. Report on file, Delaware Division of Historical and Cultural Affairs, State Historic Preservation Office, Dover.

Mann, Barbara Alice. 2000. *Iroquoian Women*. New York: Peter Lang.

Marsden, Peter. 1975. *The Wreck of the Amsterdam*. New York: Stein and Day.

Masten, Arthur H. 1877. *The History of Cohoes, New York: From Its Earliest Settlement to the Present Time*. Albany: Joel Munsell.

Meacham, Sarah Hand. 2009. *Every Home a Distillery: Alcohol, Gender, and Technology in the Colonial Chesapeake*. Baltimore: Johns Hopkins University Press.

Meeske, Harrison F. 1998. *The Hudson Valley Dutch and Their Houses*. Fleischmanns, NY: Purple Mountain Press.

Meussdoerffer, Franz G. 2009. A Comprehensive History of Beer Brewing. In *Handbook of Brewing: Processes, Technology, Markets*, edited by Hans Michael Esslinger, pp. 1–42. Weinheim, Germany: Wiley-VCH Verlag GmbH & Co. KGaA.

Middleton, Simon. 2010. Order and Authority in New Netherland: The 1653 Remonstrance and Early Settler Politics. *William and Mary Quarterly* 63(1):31–68.

Miller, Henry M. 1983. The History of Nominy Plantation with Emphasis on the Clay Tobacco Pipes. *Historic Clay Tobacco Pipe Studies* 2:1–38.

———. 1983. *A Search for the "Citty of Saint Maries."* St. Mary City Archaeological Series No. 1. St. Mary's City, MD: Historic St. Mary's City.

———. 1986. *Killed by Wolves: Analysis of Two Seventeenth Century Sheep Burials at the St. John's Site and a Comment on Sheep Husbandry in the Early Chesapeake*. St. Mary's City Research Series No. 1. St. Mary's City, MD: Historic St. Mary's City.

———. 1991. Tobacco Pipes from Pope's Fort, St. Mary's City, Maryland: an English Civil War Site on the American Frontier. In *The Archaeology of the Clay Tobacco Pipe XII: Chesapeake Bay*, British Archaeological Reports International Series 566, edited by Peter Davey and Dennis J. Pogue, pp. 73–88. Oxford: BAR Publishing.

———. 2007. Swedes and Dutch in Early Maryland. *Swedish Colonial News* 3(6):14–17.

Mitchell, Vivienne. 1976. Decorated Brown Clay Pipebowls from Nominy Plantation: Progress Report. *Quarterly Bulletin of the Archaeological Society of Virginia* 31:2.

Moody, Kevin L. 2005. Quackenbush Square House. In *Beyond the North Gate: Archeology on the Outskirts of Colonial Albany*, Hartgen Archeological Associates, Inc., pp. 89–160. Report prepared for the Albany Parking Authority, on file, New York State Historic Preservation Office.

Moogk, Peter. 2000. *La Nouvelle France: The Making of French Canada—A Cultural History*. East Lansing: Michigan State University Press.

Monroe, J. Cameron, and Seth Mallios. 2004. A Seventeenth-Century Colonial Cottage Industry: New Evidence and a Dating Formula for Colono Tobacco Pipes in the Chesapeake. *Historical Archaeology* 38(2):68–82.

Mounier, R. Alan. 2003. *Looking beneath the Surface: The Story of Archaeology in New Jersey*. New Brunswick: Rutgers University Press.

Municipal Archives of Amsterdam (Stadsarchief Gemeente Amsterdam). Index Burgher Books, 1531–1652.

Murray, David. 2000. *Indian Giving: Economies of Power in Indian-White Exchange*. Amherst: University of Massachusetts Press.

Murphy, Peter G., and Alice T. Murphy. 2011. Stone Spheroids of the Carolina Piedmont. *Central States Archaeological Journal* 58(3):153–154.

Museum Boijmans van Beuningen. 2018. D. G. van Beuningen Collection. *Museum Boijmans van Beuningen.* http://collectie.boijmans.nl/en/selection/van-beuningen-de-vriese-2, accessed June 12, 2018.

Nash, J. M. 1972. *The Age of Rembrandt and Vermeer.* New York: Holt, Rinehart and Winston.

Nassaney, Michael. S. 2000. Archaeology and Oral History in Tandem: Interpreting Native American Ritual, Ideology, and Gender Relations in Contact-Period Southeastern New England. In *Interpretations of Native American Life: Material Contributions to Ethnohistory,* edited by Michael Nassaney and Eric Johnson, pp. 412–431. Gainesville: University Press of Florida.

———. 2004. Native American Gender Politics and Material Culture in Seventeenth-Century Southeastern New England. *Social Archaeology* 4(3):334–367.

———. 2015. *The Archaeology of the North American Fur Trade.* Gainesville: University Press of Florida.

Naum, Magdelena. 2010. Re-emerging Frontiers: Postcolonial Theory and Historical Archaeology of the Borderlands. *Journal of Archaeological Method and Theory* 17(2):101–131.

Newman, Margaret. 2005. *Van Wagenen House, Jersey City.* National Register of Historic Places Nomination Form. On file, New Jersey Historic Preservation Office.

Noël Hume, Ivor. 1988. *Martin's Hundred.* New York: Alfred A. Knopf.

O'Callaghan, Edmund B. 1845. *History of New Netherland: Or, New York under the Dutch.* New York: D. Appleton.

O'Callaghan, E. B. (editor). 1868. *Laws and Ordinances of New Netherland, 1638–1674.* Albany: Weed, Parsons.

O'Callaghan, E. B., and John Romeyn Brodhead (editors). 1856. *Documents Relative to the Colonial History of New-York: Procured in Holland, England, and France.* Albany: Argus.

Omwake, H. G. 1958. Kaolin Pipes from the Schurz Site. *Bulletin of the Archaeological Society of Connecticut* 29:2–13.

Oosten, van R. 2014. *De stad, het vuil en de beerput: Een archeologisch-historische studie naar de opkomst, verbreiding en neergang van de beerput in stedelijke context (13de tot 18de eeuw).* Dissertation, Leiden: Sidestone Press.

Orser, Charles E., Jr. 2012. An Archaeology of Eurocentrism. *American Antiquity* 77(4):737–55.

Ostkamp, S. 2014. Hollants Porceleyn en Straetwerck: De voorgeschiedenis van Delft als centrum van de Nederlandse productie van faience en het ontstaan van Delfst wit. In *Vormen uit Vuur* 223/224, 2014/1, *Nederlandse Vereniging van vrienden van ceramiek en glas,* pp. 3–45.

———. 2017. Beerput in't Catgen: Keramiek. In *Ons'Lieve Heer op Solder: Archeologisch onderzoek Oudezijds Voorburgwal 38–40, Amsterdam (2013–2014),* edited by J. Gawronski and R. Jayasena. Amsterdamse Archeologische Rapporten 100, Gemeente Amsterdam.

Ostkamp, S., R. Roedema, and R. van Wilgen. 2001. Gebruikt en Gebroken: vijf eeuwen bewoning op drie lokaties in het oostelijk stadsdeel. Rapporten over de Alkmaarse Monumentenzorg en Archeologie nummer 10. Gemeente Alkmaar.

Parker, Geoffrey. 1977. *The Dutch Revolt*. Ithaca: Cornell University Press.

———. 2013. *Global Crisis: War, Climate Change and Catastrophe in the Seventeenth Century*. New Haven: Yale University Press.

Pavonia. 2018. Wikipedia. https://en.wikipedia.org/wiki/Pavonia, accessed January 24, 2018.

Pearson, Jonathan (translator). 1869. *Early Records of the City and County of Albany and Colony of Rensselaerswyck (1656–1675)*. Albany: J. Munsell.

———. 1916. *Early Records of the City and County of Albany, and Colony of Rensselaerswyck: Volume 2* (Deeds 3 and 4, 1678–1704). New York State Library, History Bulletin 9. Albany: University of the State of New York.

Pena, Elizabeth. 1990. *Wampum Production in New Netherland and Colonial New York: The Historical and Archaeological Context*. Doctoral dissertation, Archaeology Department, Boston University. Ann Arbor: University Microfilms International.

Pennington, Janet. 2002. Inns and Taverns of Western Sussex, England, 1550–1700: A Documentary and Architectural Investigation. In *The World of the Tavern: Public Houses in Early Modern Europe*, edited by Beat Kümin and B. Ann Tlusty, pp. 116–135. London: Routledge.

Pickman, Arnold, and Nan A. Rothschild. 1981. *64 Pearl Street: An Archaeological Excavation in 17th Century Landfill*. Report on file, New York Landmarks Conservancy, New York.

Platt, J. 1771. Curious Enquiry into the Formation of Marbles. *The Gentlemen's Magazine* 41:153–154.

———. 1773. Method of Making Marbles, Explained. *The Gentlemen's Magazine* 43:18.

Pipes, M. L. 2002. Appendix J, Faunal Report Illegal Dutch Trader's House. In *On the Outside Looking In: Four Centuries of Change at 625 Broadway*. Hartgen Archeological Associates, Inc. Report prepared for the Picotte Companies, Albany, on file, New York State Historic Preservation Office.

———. 2005. Faunal Analysis. In *Beyond the North Gate: Archeology on the Outskirts of Colonial Albany*, Hartgen Archeological Associates, Inc., pp. 89–160. Report prepared for the Albany Parking Authority, on file, New York State Historic Preservation Office.

———. 2006. Food Remains from the Schuyler Flatts, Mid-seventeenth Century Dutch Diet on the Colonial Frontier. Paper presented at the annual conference of the New Netherlands Institute, Albany, NY.

Platt, J. 1771. "Curious Enquiry into the Formation of Marbles." *The Gentlemen's Magazine* 41:153–154.

———. 1773. "Method of Making Marbles, explained." *The Gentlemen's Magazine* 41:18.

Pluis, Jan. 1979. *Kinderspelen op tegels*. Assen: Van Gorcum.

Plumley, Lisa E. 2002. Larrimore's Point (1684–1730): Tobacco Pipes from an Early Urban Site at London Town. In *The Clay Tobacco-Pipe in Anne Arundel County, Mary-*

land (1650–1730), edited by Al Luckenbach, C. Jane Cox, and John Kille, pp. 86–91. Annapolis: Anne Arundel County Trust for Preservation.

———. 2004. *Fish into Wine: The Newfoundland Plantation in the Seventeenth Century.* Chapel Hill: University of North Carolina Press.

Ponte, M. 2019. Al de swarten die hier ter stede comen' Een Afro-Atlantische gemeenschap in zeventiende-eeuws Amsterdam. *TSEG: The Low Countries Journal of Social and Economic History* 15(4):33–62.

Prajda, Katalin. 2012. Unions of Interest: Florentine Marriage Ties and Business Networks in the Kingdom of Hungary during the Reign of Sigismund of Luxemburg. In *Marriage in Premodern Europe: Italy and Beyond*, edited by Jacqueline Murray, pp. 147–166. Toronto: CRRS.

Prak, M. 2004. *Gouden Eeuw: Het raadsel van de Republiek, Uitgeverij SUN.* Amsterdam: Nijmegen.

Price, Richard, and Keith Muckleroy. 1974. The Second Season of Work on the Kennemerland Site, 1973: An Interim Report. *International Journal of Nautical and Underwater Exploration* 3(2):257–268.

Purple, Samuel S. (editor). 1890. *Records of the Reformed Dutch Church in New Amsterdam and New York: Marriages, from 11 December 1639, to 26 August 1801.* New York: New York Genealogical and Biographical Society.

Radisson, P. E. 1858. *Voyages of Peter Esprit Radisson.* London: Gideon D. Scull.

Ranger, Robin. 1866. *Wolves and Foxes.* New York: Sunday-School Union, 200 Mulberry-Street.

Renaud, J. G. N. 1948. *Oud Gebruiksaardewerk.* Amsterdam: Allert de Lange.

Rice, Kym S. 1983. *Early American Taverns: For the Entertainment of Friends and Strangers.* Chicago: Regnery Gateway.

Richter, Daniel K. 1992. *The Ordeal of the Longhouse: The Peoples of the Iroquois League in the Era of European Colonization.* Chapel Hill: University of North Carolina Press.

———. 2001. *Facing East from Indian Country: A Narrative History of Early America.* Cambridge: Harvard University Press.

———. 2015. Mid-Atlantic Colonies, R.I.P. *Pennsylvania History* 82(3):260–281.

Ring, Edgar. 2012. Kinder und Jugendliche in Lüneburg—eine Darstellung anhand archäologischer Quellen. In *Lübecker Kolloquium zur Stadtarchäologie im Hanseraum VIII: Kindheit und Jugend, Ausbildung und Freizeit*, edited by Manfred Gläser, pp. 273–283. Lübeck: Verlag Schmidt-Römhild.

Rink, Oliver A. 1986. *Holland on the Hudson: An Economic and Social History of Dutch New York.* Ithaca: Cornell University Press.

Roberts, Daniel G. 1987. The History and Archaeology of Immanuel Episcopal Church, New Castle, Delaware. *Pennsylvania Archaeologist* 57:1–33.

Rockman [Wall], Diana, and Nan A. Rothschild. 1984. City Tavern, Country Tavern: An Analysis of Four Colonial Sites. *Historical Archaeology* 18(2):112–121.

Romney, Susannah Shaw. 2014. *New Netherland Connections: Intimate Networks and Atlantic Ties in Seventeenth-Century America.* Chapel Hill: University of North Carolina Press.

———. 2016. "With & alongside His Housewife": Claiming Ground in New Netherland and the Early Modern Dutch Empire. *William and Mary Quarterly* 73(2):187–224.

Roodenburg, Marie-Cornélie. 1993. *De Delftse Pottenbakkersnering in de Gouden Eeuw (1575–1675): De Produktie van Rood Pottengoed.* Hilversum: Verloren.

Rose, Peter. 1989. *The Sensible Cook: Dutch Foodways in the Old and the New World.* Syracuse: Syracuse University Press.

Rothschild, Nan A. 1995. Social Distance between Dutch Settlers and Native Americans. In *One Man's Trash Is Another Man's Treasure,* edited by Alexandra Van Dongan, pp. 189–202. Rotterdam: Museum Bomanns-Van Beunignen.

———. 2003. *Colonial Encounters in a Native American Landscape: The Spanish and the Dutch in North America.* Washington: Smithsonian.

———. 2006. Colonialism, Material Culture, and Identity in the Rio Grans and Hudson River Valleys. *International Journal of Historical Archaeology* 10(1):73–108.

Rothschild, Nan A., and Arnold Pickman. 1990. *The 7 Hanover Square Excavation Report: A Final Report.* Report on file, New York City Landmarks Preservation Commission, New York.

Rothschild, Nan A., Diana Rockman Wall, and Eugene Boesch. 1987. *The Archaeological Excavations of the Stadt Huys Block: A Final Report, CEQR 79–04.* Report on file, New York City Landmarks Preservation Commission, New York.

Rouxel, C., and F. Halma. 1686. *Dictionnaire nouveau, François & Flamand, . . . Nieuw woorden-boek der Fransche en Nederlandtsche Tale.* Amsterdam: Chez Abraham Wolfgang.

Salinger, Sharon V. 2002. *Taverns and Drinking in Early America.* Baltimore: Johns Hopkins University Press.

Schaefer, Richard Gerhard. 1994. *A Typology of Seventeenth-Century Dutch Ceramics and its Implications for American Historical Archaeology.* Doctoral dissertation, American Civilization Department, University of Pennsylvania. Ann Arbor: University Microfilms International.

———. 1998. *A Typology of Seventeenth-Century Dutch Ceramics and Its Implications for American Historical Archaeology.* British Archaeological Reports International Series 702. Oxford: BAR Publishing.

———. 2012. This Old House I: Flushing's Bowne House. Paper presented at the annual meeting of the Council for Northeast Historical Archaeology, St. John's, NL.

———. 2015. A Dutch Pot from the Cradle of Religious Liberty. Paper presented at the 48th Annual Conference on Historical and Underwater Archaeology, Seattle.

Schama, Simon. 1987. *The Embarrassment of Riches: An Interpretation of Dutch Culture in the Golden Age.* New York: Alfred A. Knopf.

Scharf, J. Thomas. 1888. *A History of Delaware, 1609 to 1888.* Philadelphia: L. J. Richard.

Schlenker, Björn. 2007. Archäologie am Elternhaus Martin Luthers. In *Luther in Mansfeld: Forschungen am Elternhaus des Reformators,* Archäologie in Sachsen-Anhalt, Sonderband 6, edited by Harald Meller, pp. 17–112. Halle: Landesmuseum für Vorgeschichte.

Schwartz, Stuart B. 1987. The Formation of a Colonial Identity in Brazil. In *Colonial Iden-*

tity in the Atlantic World, 1500–1800, edited by Nicholas Canny and Anthony Pagden, pp. 15–50. Princeton: Princeton University Press.

Sharpe, Shawn, Al Luckenbach, and John Kille. 2002. Burle's Town Land (ca. 1649–1676): A Marked Abundance of Pipes. In *The Clay Tobacco-Pipe in Anne Arundel County, Maryland (1650–1730),* edited by Al Luckenbach, C. Jane Cox, and John Kille, pp. 28–39. Annapolis: Anne Arundel County Trust for Preservation.

Shattuck, Martha. 1994. Women and Trade in New Netherland. *Itinerario* 18(2):28–44.

Shorto, Russell. 2005. *The Island at the Center of the World: The Epic Story of Dutch Manhattan and the Forgotten Colony That Shaped America.* New York: Vintage.

———. 2012. A Tour of New Netherland: A Lost World. New Amstel. New Netherland Institute. https://www.newnetherlandinstitute.org/history-and-heritage/digital-exhibitions/a-tour-of-new-netherland/delaware/new-amstel/, accessed July 1, 2018.

Sickler, Joseph S. 1937. *The History of Salem County New Jersey: Being the Story of John Fenwick's Colony, the Oldest English Speaking Settlement on the Delaware River.* Salem, NJ: Sunbeam.

Silliman, Stephen W. 2013. What, Where, and When Is Hybridity. In *The Archaeology of Hybrid Material Culture,* Southern Illinois University Center for Archaeological Investigations Occasional Paper No. 3, edited by Jeb B. Card, pp. 486–499. Carbondale: Southern Illinois University Press.

Simpson, Audra. 2014. *Mohawk Interruptus: Political Life Across the Borders of Settler States.* Durham: Duke University Press.

Sipe, C. Hale. 1929. *The Indian Wars of Pennsylvania.* Harrisburg: Telegraph.

Slootmans, C. J. F. 1970. *Tussen Hete Vuren,* Part 1. Tilburg: Stichting Zuidelijk Historisch.

Smith, George. 1862. *History of Delaware County, Pennsylvania.* Philadelphia: Henry B. Ashmead.

Snow, Dean R. 1994. *The Iroquois.* Cambridge: Blackwell.

Snow, Dean R., Charles T. Gehring, and William A. Starna (editors). 1996. *In Mohawk Country: Early Narratives about a Native People.* Syracuse: Syracuse University Press.

Soderlund, Jean. 2015. *Lenape Country: Delaware Valley Society before William Penn.* Philadelphia: University of Pennsylvania Press.

Solecki, R. 1950. The Archaeological Position of Historic Fort Corchaug, Long Island, and Its Relation to Contemporary Forts. *Bulletin of the Archaeological Society of Connecticut* 24:5–40.

Sorenson, Marie Louise Stig. 2000. *Gender Archaeology.* Cambridge: Polity.

Spencer-Wood, Suzanne M., and Laurajane Smith. 2011. *The Impact of Feminist Theories on Archaeology.* Special issue, *Archaeologies: Journal of the World Archaeological Congress* 7.

Stanhope, Philip Dormer, 4th Earl of Chesterfield. 1853. *The Works of Lord Chesterfield, Including His Letters to His Son, &c., to Which Is Prefixed an Original Life of the Author.* New York: Harper & Brothers.

Starna, William A. 2013. *From Homeland to New Land: A History of the Mahican Indians, 1600–1830.* Lincoln: University of Nebraska Press.

Stasiulis, Daiva, and Nira Yuval-Davis. 1995. Introduction: Beyond Dichotomies—Gender, Race, Ethnicity and Class in Settler Societies. In *Unsettling Settler Societies: Ar-*

ticulations of Gender, Race, Ethnicity and Class, edited by Daiva Stasiulis and Nira Yuval-Davis, pp. 1–37. London: Sage.

Stoler, Ann Laura. 1989. Rethinking Colonial Categories: European Communities and the Boundaries of Rule. *Comparative Studies in Society and History* 31(1):134–161.

Stolk, Marijn. 2018. Exploring Immigrant Identities: The Link between Portuguese Ceramics and Sephardic Immigrants in Seventeenth Century Amsterdam. *EX NOVO Journal of Archaeology* 3:101–120. http://archaeologiaexnovo.org/2016/wp-content/uploads/2019/01/7_Stolk_DEF5.pdf, accessed December 31, 2019.

Sutton, Peter C. 1992. *Dutch & Flemish Seventeenth-Century Paintings: The Harold Samuel Collection*. Cambridge: Cambridge University Press.

Symonds, James. 2019. Diaspora and Identity: An Integrated Archaeological and Historical Investigation into Material Life, Ethnicity, and Diet in the District of Vlooienburg, Amsterdam (AD 1600–1800). Universiteit van Amsterdam. https://www.uva.nl/discipline/archeologie/onderzoek/diaspora-and-identity/diaspora-and-identity.html?1577795039122, accessed December 30, 2019.

Tantillo, L. F. 2011. *The Edge of New Netherland*. Nassau, NY: Tantillo Fine Art for the New Netherland Institute.

Theuerkauff-Liederwald, Anna-Elisabeth. 1968. Der Romer, Studien zu einer Glasform. *Journal of Glass Studies* 10:114–155.

———. 1969. Der Romer, Studien zu einer Glasform, II. *Journal of Glass Studies* 11:43–69.

Thompson, Mark L. 2013. *The Contest for the Delaware Valley: Allegiance, Identity, and Empire in the Seventeenth Century*. Baton Rouge: Louisiana State University Press.

Thompson, Peter. 1999. *Rum Punch and Revolution: Taverngoing and Public Life in Eighteenth-Century Philadelphia*. Philadelphia: University of Pennsylvania Press.

Tooker, Elizabeth. 1984. Women in Iroquois Society. In *Extending the Rafters: Interdisciplinary Approaches to Iroquoian Studies*, edited by Michael K. Foster, Jack Campisi, and Marianne Mithun, pp. 109–123. Albany: State University of New York Press.

Trelease, Allen W. 1960. *Indian Affairs in Colonial New York: The Seventeenth Century*. Ithaca: Cornell University Press.

Tremblay, Katherine, and Louise Renaud. 1999. *Les jeux et les jouets de Place-Royale*. Quebec: Ministère de la Culture et des Communications.

Trigger, Bruce R. 1984. Indian and White History: Two Worlds or One. In *Extending the Rafters: Interdisciplinary Approaches to Iroquoian Studies*, edited by Michael K. Foster, Jack Campisi, and Marianne Mithun, pp. 17–33. Albany: State University of New York Press.

Trocolli, Ruth. 1999. Women Leaders in Native North America. In *Manifesting Power: Gender and the Interpretation of Power in Archaeology*, edited by Tracy L. Sweely, pp. 49–61. London: Routledge.

Tuchman, Barbara W. 1988. *The First Salute: A View of the American Revolution*. New York: Alfred A. Knopf.

Underhill, Lora A. W. 1934. *Descendants of Edward Small of New England and the Allied Families, with Tracings of English Ancestry*. 3 vols. Boston: Houghton Mifflin.

U.S. Coast and Geodetic Survey. 1843. *Delaware River from Forresdale to Burlington and Bristol*. http://www.westjerseyhistory.org/surveys/NJ-coastal-surveys/T-0167Dela-

ware%20River%20from%20Forresdale%20to%20Burlington%20and%20Bristol%20
-%201843.jpg, accessed October 12, 2018.

van Bellingen, Stephan. 2013. *Archeologische sporen van sport en spel: verloren speel-goed in Brussel. Erfgoed Brussel* 8:76–86.

van der Chijs, J. A. 1886. *Nederlandisch-Indisch plakaatboek, 1602–1811.* Volume 2. The Hague: Batavia Landscrukkerij, M. Nijhoff.

van der Sleen, W. G. N. 1973. *A Handbook on Beads.* Liege: Librairie Halbart.

van Haaster, H. 2002. Botanisch onderzoek naar de voedingsgewoonten in de herberg "de Kleine Karthuizer" te Amsterdam (1600–1750), BIAXiaal 128, BIAX Consult, Zaandam.

van Houtte, J.A., 1979. *Economische geschiedenis van de Lage Landen, 800–1800, Unieboek b.v. Bussum.* Bussum, the Netherlands: Fibula-van Dishoeck.

van Laer, A. J. F. (editor). 1908. *Being the Letters of Kiliaen Van Rensselaer, 1630–1643, and Other Documents Relating to the Colony of Rensselaerswyck.* Albany: University of the State of New York.

———. 1918. *Early Records of the City and County of Albany and the Colony of Rensselaer-swyck.* Vol. 3. Albany: University of the State of New York.

———. 1920. *Minutes of the Court of Fort Orange and Beverwyck, 1652–1656.* Vol. 1. Albany: University of the State of New York.

———. 1922. *Minutes of the Court of Rensselaerswyck, 1648–1652.* Albany: University of the State of New York.

———. 1928. *Minutes of the Court of Albany, Rensselaerswyck and Schenectady, 1675–1680.* Vol. 2. Albany: University of the State of New York.

———. 1932a. *Minutes of the Court of Albany, Rensselaerswyck and Schenectady, 1680–1685.* Vol. 3. Albany: University of the State of New York.

———. 1932b. *Correspondence of Jeremias van Rensselaer: 1651–1674.* Albany: University of New York.

———. 1974a. *New York Historical Manuscripts: Dutch.* Vol. 1, Register of the Provincial Secretary, 1638–1642. Edited by Kenneth Scott and Kenn Stryker-Rodda. Baltimore: Genealogical Publishing.

———. 1974b. *Council Minutes of the Director General and the Council of New Nether-land, 1638–1649.* Baltimore: Genealogical Publishing.

van Rensselaer, Kiliaen, Arnold J. F. van Laer, Nicholas de Roever, and Alan H. Strong. 1908. *Van Rensselaer Bowier Manuscripts: Being the Letters of Kiliaen Van Rensselaer, 1630–1643, and Other Documents Relating to the Colony of Rensselaerswyck.* New York State Library. Albany: University of the State of New York.

van Rensselaer, Maria. 1935. *Correspondence of Maria van Rensselaer, 1669–1689.* Albany: University of the State of New York.

van Rijn, G. 1901. *Atlas van Stolk: Katalogus der historie-, spot- en zinneprenten betrek-kelijk de geschiedenis van Nederland verzameld door A. van Stolk Cz.* Vol. 5. Amsterdam: Frederik Muller.

van Westing, Hans. 2012. *Drie Drentse Schansen; Zwartendijksterschans, Emmerschans, Katshaarschans.* Groningen: Institute of Archaeology, University of Groningen.

van Zandt, Cynthia. 1998. *Negotiating Settlement: Colonialism, Cultural Exchange, and*

Conflict in Early Colonial America, 1580–1660. Doctoral dissertation, History Department, University of Connecticut, Storrs. Ann Arbor: University Microfilm International.

———. 2008. *Brothers among Nations: The Pursuit of Intercultural Alliances in Early America, 1560–1660.* Oxford: Oxford University Press.

Veit, Richard. 2000. Following the Yellow Brick Road: Dutch Bricks in New Jersey, Fact and Folklore. *Bulletin of the Archeological Society of New Jersey* 55:70–76.

———. 2002. *Digging New Jersey's Past: Historical Archaeology in the Garden State.* New Brunswick: Rutgers University Press.

Veit, Richard, and Charles A. Bello. 2001. Tokens of Their Love: Interpreting Native American Grave Goods from Pennsylvania, New Jersey, and New York. *Archaeology of Eastern North America* 29:47–64.

Venema, Janny. 2003. *Beverwijck, a Dutch Village on the American Frontier 1652–1664.* Albany: State University of New York Press.

———. 2010. *Kiliaen van Rensselaer (1586–1643): Designing a New World.* Albany: State University of New York Press.

Victor, Megan. 2019. Under the Tavern Table: Excavations at the Tavern on Smuttynose Island, Maine and Implications for Commensal Politics and Informal Economy. *International Journal of Historical Archaeology* 23(1):34–56.

Vitelli, Giovanna. 2011. Change and Continuity, Practice and Memory: A Response to Stephen Silliman. *American Antiquity* 76(1):177–189.

Voss, Barbara L. 2008. Domesticating Imperialism: Sexual Politics and the Archaeology of Empire. *American Anthropologist* 110(2):191–203.

Voss, Barbara L., and Eleanor Conlin Casella (editors). 2011. *The Archaeology of Colonialism: Intimate Encounters and Sexual Effects.* Cambridge: Cambridge University Press.

Wacker, Peter O. 1974. *Land and People: A Cultural Geography of Pre-industrial New Jersey.* New Brunswick: Rutgers University Press.

Walker, A. H. 1876. *Atlas of Bergen County.* Reading, PA: C. C. Pease.

Walker, Iain C. 1977. Clay Tobacco Pipes, with Particular Reference to the Bristol Industry. *History and Archaeology,* Nos. 11A-11D. Ottawa: Parks Canada.

Wall, Diana diZerega, and Anne-Marie Cantwell. 2008. Engendering New Netherland: Implications for Interpreting Early Colonial Societies. Paper presented at the Sixth World Archaeological Congress, Dublin, Ireland.

Wallace, Anthony F. C. 1972. *Rise and Rebirth of the Seneca.* New York: Vintage.

Wallet, B. 2007. Amsterdam: Ashkenazim until 1795. In *Encyclopedia Judaica,* 2nd ed. vol. 1, edited by Fred Skolnik and Michael Berenbaum, pp. 106–107. Detroit and Jerusalem: Macmillian Reference/Thomson Gale and Keter.

Waterman, Kees-Jan. 2008. Parameters of the Fur Trade in New Netherland: Eighteenth-Century Evidence. In *From De Halve Maen to KLM: 400 Years of Dutch-American Exchange*, edited by Margriet Bruijn Lacy, Charles Gehring, and Jenneke Oosterhoff, pp. 135–148. Munster: Nodus Publikationen.

Weslager, Clinton, A. 1967. *The English on the Delaware: 1610–1682.* New Brunswick: Rutgers University Press.

———. 1982. The City of Amsterdam's Colony on the Delaware, 1656–1664, with Unpublished Dutch Notarial Abstracts. *Delaware History* 20:1–26.

———. 1987. *The Swedes and Dutch at New Castle, with High-Lights in the History of the Delaware Valley, 1638–1664.* Wilmington, DE: Middle Atlantic Press.

———. 1995. Summary, Criticism, and Comments on Future Directions in the Study of New Sweden, In *New Sweden in America*, edited by Carol E. Hoffecker, Richard Waldron, Lorraine E. Williams, and Barbara E. Benson, pp. 350–357. Newark: University of Delaware Press.

———. 2001. The City of Amsterdam's Colony on the Delaware, 1656–1664. In *350 Years of New Castle, Delaware: Chapters in a Town's History*, edited by Constance J. Cooper. Wilmington, DE: Cedar Tree Books for the New Castle Historical Society.

———. 2003. *The Delaware Indians: A History*. Revised reprint. New Brunswick: Rutgers University Press.

Weslager, C. A., and A. R. Dunlap. 1961. *Dutch Explorers, Traders and Settlers in the Delaware Valley, 1609–1664.* Philadelphia: University of Pennsylvania Press.

White, Bruce M. 1999. The Woman who Married a Beaver: Trade Patterns and Gender Roles in the Ojibwa Fur Trade. *Ethnohistory* 46(1):109–147.

Whitehead, William A. 1881. *Documents relating to the Colonial History of the State of New Jersey.* Archives of the State of New Jersey, First Series, Vol. 3: 1703–1709. Newark, NJ: Daily Advertiser.

Wholey, Heather A. 2006. The Socioeconomic Landscape of Northern Delaware's Taverns and Innkeepers: The Blue Ball Tavern and Vicinity. *Northeast Historical Archaeology* 35:63–76.

Wilcoxen, Charlotte. 1979. Arent van Curler's Children. *New York Genealogical and Biographical Record* 110(2):82–84.

———. 1985. Household Artifacts of New Netherland, from Its Archaeological and Documentary Records. *New Netherland Studies, Bulletin Koninklijke Nederlandse Oudheidkundige Bond* 84(2/3):120–129.

———. 1987. *Dutch Trade and Ceramics in America in the Seventeenth Century.* Albany: Albany Institute of Art and History.

Willemsen, Annemarieke. 2003. *Die kinderen van Torenstad: Middeleeuws speelgoed.* Lelystad: Uitgeverij AO (Actuele Onderwerpen).

———. 2008. Looking through Classroom Windows: Daily Life at a Latin School in the Netherlands around 1500. In *Manuscript Studies in the Low Countries: Proceedings of the Groninger Codicologendagen in Friesland, 2002*, edited by Anne M. As-Vijvers, Jos M.M. Hermans, and Gerda C. Huisman, pp. 2–20. Groningen and Leeuwarden: Egbert Forsten and Fryske Akademy.

Williams, James Homer. 2001. Coerced Sex and Gendered Violence in New Netherland. In *Sex without Consent: Rape and Sexual Coercion in America*, edited by Merril D. Smith, pp. 61–80. New York: New York University Press.

Williams, Kim-Eric. 2007. In Memoriam. *Swedish Colonial News* 3(7):19.

Willmott, Hugh. 2002. *Early Post-medieval Vessel Glass in England, c. 1500–1670.* CBA Research Report 132. York: Council for British Archeology.

Wilson, James Grant (editor). 1903. *Memoirs of an American Lady by Mrs. Anne Grant*. New York: Dodd, Mead.

Winter, Johanna Maria van. 1976. *Van Soeter Cokene, recepten uit de oudheid en middeleeuwen*. Haarlem: Fibula-Van Dishoeck.

Wise (Blume), Cara L. 1975. *Report of the 1972 and 1974 Excavations at Robinson House, New Castle County, Delaware*. Report on file, Delaware Division of Historical and Cultural Affairs, State Historic Preservation Office, Dover.

Wolfert, Paula. 2009. *Mediterranean Clay Pot Cooking*. Hoboken: John Wiley & Sons.

Wood, W. H. 1855. *Map of Jersey City, Hoboken and Hudson Cities*. Jersey City: R. B. Kashow.

Wulf, Jacobus Philippus. 1766. *Generalen Index ofte substantieel kort-bondig begryp der materien, begrepen in de vyf placcaert-boecken van Vlaenderen, behelsende alle de Placcaerten, Edicten, Decreten, Reglementen, Ordonnantien. Instructien ende Tractaeten, geëmaneert voor de Provincie van Vlaenderen, beginnende van den Jaere 1152. tot ende met 1763*. Volume 2. Ghent: Petrus De Goesin, Drucker.

Yakota, Kariann 2007. Post Colonialism and Material Culture in the Early United States. *William and Mary Quarterly* 64(2):263–270.

Young, Stanley P., and Edward A Goldman. 1944. *The Wolves of North America, Part I, Their History, Life Habits, Economic Status, and Control*. American Wildlife Institute. New York: Dover .

Zabriskie, George O. 1972. The Rapalje-Rapelje Family. *De Halve Maen* 46(4):7–16.

Zeller, Nancy Anne McClure (editor). 1991. *A Beautiful and Fruitful Place: Selected Rensselaerwijck Seminar Papers*. Albany: New Netherlands.

Zink, Clifford. 1985. *Dutch Framed Houses in New York and New Jersey*. Master's thesis, Graduate School of Architecture, Planning, and Preservation, Columbia University.

———. 1987. *Dutch Framed Houses in New York and New Jersey*. Winterthur Portfolio 22(4):265–294.

CONTRIBUTORS

Marshall Joseph Becker has published two books, a number of book chapters, and nearly 200 articles on the Lenape, Colonists, and other peoples of the Americas in scholarly journals as well as popular magazines.

Ian Burrow is an archaeologist and historian based in New Jersey and is the principal and owner of BurrowIntoHistory, LLC.

Anne-Marie Cantwell is professor emerita at Rutgers University-Newark.

Wade P. Catts is president and principal of South River Heritage Consulting, based in Newark, Delaware.

Lu Ann De Cunzo is professor and chair in the Department of Anthropology at the University of Delaware.

David A. Furlow is an attorney and historian. David and his wife Lisa H. Pennington are recipients of a 2020 National Society Daughters of the American Revolution Historic Preservation Medal for their preservation of the Captain Isaac Doten House (1747) in Plymouth.

Charles T. Gehring is director of the New Netherland Research Center in New York State's Office of Cultural Education.

Paul R. Huey developed and directed the historical archaeological resource management and research program for the New York State Historic Sites.

Meta F. Janowitz is senior material culture specialist at AECOM in Burlington, New Jersey, and a member of the faculty of the School of Visual Arts in New York City.

Matthew Kirk is a historical archeologist and a registered-professional-archeologist (RPA) employed with Hartgen Archeological Associates, Inc.

William B. Liebeknecht is an archaeological principal investigator employed by Dovetail Cultural Resource Group in Wilmington, Delaware.

Michael T. Lucas is curator of historical archaeology at the New York State Museum.

Craig Lukezic is the cultural resource manager for the Navy at the PAX River Base.

Adam Luscier works as a project director in archaeology with Hartgen Archeological Associates.

John P. McCarthy is currently retired from cultural resource management and is the author or coauthor of over twenty-five book chapters and journal articles.

Marie-Lorraine Pipes is a consulting zooarchaeologist and is adjunct professor at SUNY Geneseo.

Richard G. Schaefer is research director and senior historian for Historical Perspectives, Inc.

Marijn Stolk earned her PhD from the University of Amsterdam, as a member of the Diaspora and Identity project.

Kristina S. Traudt is currently at the University of Massachusetts-Boston.

Diana diZerega Wall is professor emerita at the City College of New York and the CUNY Graduate Center.

INDEX

CPSIA information can be obtained
at www.ICGtesting.com
Printed in the USA
JSHW020354240821
18102JS00001B/135

THE ARCHAEOLOGY OF NEW NETHERLAND

UNIVERSITY PRESS OF FLORIDA

Florida A&M University, Tallahassee
Florida Atlantic University, Boca Raton
Florida Gulf Coast University, Ft. Myers
Florida International University, Miami
Florida State University, Tallahassee
New College of Florida, Sarasota
University of Central Florida, Orlando
University of Florida, Gainesville
University of North Florida, Jacksonville
University of South Florida, Tampa
University of West Florida, Pensacola